'This book is the bridge between the ideas of early Buc [...]
psychological counseling. It is an excellent introducti [...]
them as the theoretical backbone into a contemporary [...]

**Liang Tien**, *Psy.D., ABPP, Professor, Illumination of Mindfulness Institute,*
*Alliant International University*

'*The Guide to Buddhist Counseling* is an excellent guide for therapists and caregivers, contextualizing contemporary psychological practices with Buddhist principles. It provides real-world insights and case studies for anyone seeking to understand the workings of the mind and emotions through a Buddhist lens.'

**Elaine J. Yuen**, *Educator and Chaplain, USA, Past Chair, Department of Wisdom Traditions,*
*Naropa University*

# The Guide to Buddhist Counseling

Buddhist concepts and practices have become increasingly popular and integrated into professional psychology. This book is the first to propose a theoretical orientation for counseling based on Early Buddhist teaching, and introduce it to counseling professionals for use in mental health treatment and practice.

Lee begins his book by outlining the essential concepts required to understand the Buddhist view of human nature and the world. He presents the Buddhist counseling model and suggests practices for the spiritual advancement of counselors, including self-cultivation plans, contemplative exercises, and different types of meditation. Lastly, he discusses how to apply the model in assessment, conceptualization, and intervention, and uses several case examples to illustrate the actual process.

As a go-to book in Buddhist counseling, this book is a valuable resource for Buddhist chaplains, counselors, and mental health professionals interested in using Buddhism in their clinical practice, as well as graduate students in religious studies and counseling.

**Kin Cheung (George) Lee** is a Lecturer in the Centre of Buddhist Studies at the University of Hong Kong and a Licensed Psychologist in the State of California (PSY28022). He was previously the Director of Clinical Training at California School of Professional Psychology, Hong Kong campus, and the Assistant Chair of the Department of Psychology, University of the West.

# The Guide to Buddhist Counseling

Kin Cheung Lee

Routledge
Taylor & Francis Group

LONDON AND NEW YORK

Designed cover image: Karen Lau

First published 2023
by Routledge
4 Park Square, Milton Park, Abingdon, Oxon OX14 4RN

and by Routledge
605 Third Avenue, New York, NY 10158

*Routledge is an imprint of the Taylor & Francis Group, an informa business*

*British Library Cataloguing-in-Publication Data*
A catalogue record for this book is available from the British Library

ISBN: 9780367458041 (hbk)
ISBN: 9780367458058 (pbk)
ISBN: 9781003025450 (ebk)

DOI: 10.4324/9781003025450

Typeset in Bembo Std
by KnowledgeWorks Global Ltd.

# Contents

# List of Figures

# List of Tables

# Preface

## BACKGROUND OF THIS BOOK

The past two decades have been an exciting time for Buddhism and the field of mental health. Since the emergence of mindfulness, all fields of psychology and counseling seem to have found a new panacea to all sorts of problems, thereby improving existing treatment modalities. This evolution of the field has also sparked a strong interest in Buddhism, resulting in a popularization of Buddhist concepts and practices in counseling across the globe. In other words, many mental health professionals want to go beyond mindfulness and learn Buddhism to benefit their counseling practice. At the same time, many Buddhist spiritual care providers, including monastic members and Buddhist chaplains, hope to learn more about how Buddhism can support their professional counseling practices and services. In the last few years, many voices have suggested promising approaches for applying Buddhism to counseling. Several remarkable approaches, based on major concepts of Buddhist teaching, integrated significant portions of Buddhist teaching into a counseling model. In this regard, this book raises one overriding question: Can we boldly develop a primary counseling approach using Buddhism as the theoretical orientation?

I believe Buddhism offers a comprehensive understanding of human psychology, possessing sufficient theoretical and pragmatic components to formulate a complete theoretical orientation for counseling. In particular, the foundational teaching provided by the historical Buddha posits a clear worldview, a comprehensive account of human nature, a well-defined list and explanation of the causes of suffering, and practical ways to eliminate such suffering. Even further, I am confident that this theoretical backbone can integrate well with a contemporary framework of professional counseling. Like a tried and tested recipe, all the best ingredients are there, so all we need to do is to cook them skillfully and present them accordingly to the customer. This is why I bring to you this book, the first guidebook that uses Buddhism as a theoretical orientation to formulate a counseling model, *The Guide to Buddhist Counseling*.

## PURPOSE OF THIS BOOK

In introducing a complete model of Buddhist counseling, three components will be offered and explained to the reader: (1) The essential Buddhist knowledge required to understand the Buddhist view of human nature and the world, (2) Buddhist practices for the spiritual advancement of counselors, and (3) A treatment model with assessment, conceptualization, and intervention. This book was written for a broad audience of mental health professionals, ranging from graduate students who have never been exposed to Buddhism or Buddhist counseling, to practitioners of Buddhist-informed treatments who hope to learn a new interpretation of Buddhist counseling. The language is straightforward, and case examples support the techniques to ensure the model is as practical as possible. Hopefully, this book can serve as a clear and solid first step into the world of Buddhist counseling.

## BRIEF SUMMARY OF CHAPTERS

You may use the following summary as a "roadmap" to get an overarching sense of this book and select materials that resonate with you.

### Chapter 1: Brief History of Buddhism as an Indigenous Psychology

The first chapter starts off with a brief discussion of the history and development of Buddhism in order to build a foundation to introduce Buddhism as a form of psychology. The chapter also begins to introduce some overarching concepts in Buddhism, such as Non-self and The Middle Path, to help readers step into the Buddhist worldview.

### Chapter 2: Buddhism and Science: Implications to Buddhist Counseling

Chapter 2 shifts the focus to address a hot topic in the field of psychology in the last two decades: the intersections and interactions between Buddhism and science. Special attention was paid to the emergence of Buddhist counseling as an up and coming field as well as existing models of treatment.

### Chapter 3: Major Theoretical Assumptions in Buddhist Counseling

The third chapter returns to the worldview of Buddhism by introducing some of the most important theoretical assumptions in Buddhist teaching, such as the Three Marks of Existence, the Five Aggregates, and the Four Noble Truth. This chapter provides the key theoretical framework to the model of Buddhist counseling.

### Chapter 4: Overview of the Note, Know, Choose Intervention Model

Chapter 4 takes a further step to introduce the Buddhist counseling model for this book, *Note, Know, Choose*. It gives an overview of the process of Buddhist counseling as well as the theoretical rationale of *Note, Know, Choose* to portray a picture of practically applied Buddhism in counseling.

## Chapter 5: Buddhist Spiritual Formation as a Counselor

To start the process of Buddhist counseling, Chapter 5 emphasizes the need for counselors to begin the healing journey from oneself. The chapter includes a number of methods on mind cultivation for mental health professionals.

## Chapter 6: Assessment in Buddhist Counseling

As a first step of Buddhist counseling, this chapter explains the theory and practice of assessment in Buddhist counseling. There are a number of examples and sample dialogue between counselors and clients to illustrate potential applications. Starting from this chapter, the book will consistently use the case example of Cindy to demonstrate the application of concepts in each chapter.

## Chapter 7: Buddhist Counseling Case Conceptualization

Chapter 7 addresses a critical topic in any intervention model, case conceptualization, and illustrates how to apply Buddhist teaching to comprehend and analyze the suffering of clients. The chapter introduces a specific model of conceptualization of *Note*, *Know*, *Choose* and uses case examples for illustration.

## Chapter 8: Intervention and Techniques: Note

Chapter 8 introduces the first intervention phase, Note, to foster stability of mind. The key is to help the client develop a mindful haven and heightened awareness of their body and mind.

## Chapter 9: Intervention and Techniques: Know

As a core phase of the model, Chapter 9 introduces the theory and technique of Know to foster insights into the client. Applying awareness fostered in Note, readers can see how a counselor can guide the client to see and discern their clinging and craving as well as the potentials of letting go.

## Chapter 10: Intervention and Techniques: Choose

This chapter introduces the Choose interventions to help the client make a variety of skillful choices ranging from internal mind acts to daily life decisions. In particular, Chapter 10 discusses a core intervention based on the Early Buddhist model of cognition, Mind Moment Analysis.

## Chapter 11: Termination

Chapter 11 explains the last stage of Buddhist counseling, the process of termination. This chapter applies the Buddhist concept of life and death to discuss the ending and continuation of Buddhist counseling beyond the termination of the counselor-client relationship.

## Chapter 12: Ethical Considerations in Buddhist Counseling

The last chapter briefly introduces four ethical principles of Buddhist counseling including Beneficence, Interconnectedness, Compassion, and Competency. The chapter also discusses several ethical considerations for the practice of Buddhist counseling.

## CONSIDERATIONS IN USING THIS BOOK

As a newly developed treatment model, some limitations are inevitable, so several provisos in using this book must be considered:

First, I have tried integrating several case examples to illustrate the actual process of Buddhist counseling, including a hypothetical case in several chapters based on authentic counseling materials. However, the cases are straightforward, such as depression and anxiety, instead of severe psychological disorders such as psychotic symptoms and bipolar disorders. Moreover, most of the case examples are taken from Asian cultures, which makes cultural adaptation essential when applying counseling concepts and techniques in different cultures.

Second, you **DO NOT** have to be a Buddhist to practice Buddhist counseling. The approach is non-faith-based, meaning that practitioners do not have to have faith in the religious aspects of Buddhism, such as praying to the Bodhisattvas or chanting the Heart Sutra. However, you **DO** need to have confidence in the presented Buddhist theory, much as you believe in the theory behind Cognitive Behavioral Therapy, Psychoanalysis, Client-Centered Therapy, Emotionally-Focused Therapy, Dialectical Behavioral Therapy, or any other counseling orientation.

Third, as a theoretical orientation based on Buddhism instead of prominent and traditional counseling approaches, there will be some different theoretical assumptions. Specifically, one distinction of Buddhism is the assumption of non-self (*anatta*), which is also the overarching goal of the Buddhist counseling intervention model presented in this book. As some readers may be new to Buddhism, I suggest they have an open attitude to the Buddhist concepts by temporarily putting down any existing assumptions about the world, life, and human nature, and reflexively apply these concepts and practices to themselves. This attitude was helpful to my own learning of Buddhism as a clinical psychologist.

## APPROPRIATE COURSES

Finally, this book can serve as a reference for courses related to spiritual care and Buddhist studies:

- Spiritual Care and Counseling courses in Master of Divinity in Buddhist Chaplaincy programs.
- Theory and practice courses in Masters of Buddhist Counseling programs.
- Buddhist counseling, Buddhist psychology, and Buddhist chaplaincy courses in Masters of Buddhist Studies programs.

- Buddhist counseling, Buddhist psychology, and Buddhist chaplaincy diploma or certificate courses in Buddhist psychology, psychotherapy, counseling, or comparative psychotherapy.
- Mindfulness-related courses in traditional Master of Counseling, Master of Social Work, Masters of Marriage and Family Therapy, graduate programs in clinical counseling, school psychology, and similar programs.

## A STARTING POINT

I am profoundly grateful for your decision to open this book and read my view of Buddhist counseling. I hope that this book becomes one of the starting points of the field of Buddhist counseling and that it can gradually develop into a mainstream treatment model. At the same time, it is important to note that this book is only my interpretation of Buddhist counseling and you may have your own view. Please feel free to extract, integrate, or re-interpret the content of this book or trace back the original Buddhist teaching for the benefit of you and your clients because I trust that your inner wisdom will guide you in adapting Buddhism to your client's needs. I look forward to learning about your view of Buddhist counseling and perhaps collaboratively working to build this field. I hope you enjoy this book.

*Kin Cheung (George) Lee*

# Acknowledgements

I want to express my sincere gratitude to all my family members, mentors, friends, colleagues, and every important person in my life. Without you, I would never be the "George" I am now and would not be able to finish this book. Therefore, I want to take this opportunity to wholeheartedly thank each one of you:

My parents, Dr. Lee Shin and Miss Chung Po Po.
My wife, Ms. Karen Lau.
My sons, Sage Lee and Jake Lee.
My sister, Ms. Venus Lee.

My friend and mentor, Dr. Liang Tien.
My Sifu, Venerable Sik Hin Hung.

My professors and mentors, Dr. Patricia Haynes, Dr. Thierry Devos, Dr. Ruth Chung, Dr. Ginger Clark, Dr. Mary Andres, Dr. Terece Bell, Dr. James Garbanati, Dr. Jane Naomi Iwamura, Dr. William Chu, President Stephen Morgan, President Minh-Hoa Ta, and Dr. G. A. Somaratne.

My supervisors, Ms. Iris Wong, Dr. Glenn Masuda, Dr. Scott Hartman, Dr. Karen Rathburn, and Dr. Hiroshi M. Sasaki.
My friends and colleagues, Dr. Jessica Tang, Dr. Amrita Nanda, Dr. Bonnie Wu, Dr. Guang Xing, Dr. Georgios Halkias, and Dr. Jean Kristeller

I also want to send my special thanks to Dr. Elaine Yuen and Dr. Adrian Davis who have given me highly valuable feedback and suggestions to improve the quality of this book.

Thank you so much to you all for being a valuable part of my life.

CHAPTER 1

# Brief History of Buddhism as an Indigenous Psychology

In the 2,500 years since the time of the historical Buddha, Buddhism has been interpreted and elaborated into many different forms in response to various cultural, political, and historical environments. In most contemporary cultures, Buddhism is regarded as a religion that involves rituals, liturgies, and worship of the Buddha. The symbols of superhuman higher powers are usually Buddhas and bodhisattvas, enlightened beings with immeasurable compassion. In each lineage of Buddhism there is usually a faith-based system for followers to take refuge in the historical Buddha and other Buddhas and bodhisattvas for safety, inner peace, or blessings. Perhaps due to the religious position of Buddhism, when I talk about applying Buddhism to counseling, many individuals assume that Buddhism is a religion and start questioning the efficacy of applying a faith to counseling. My response is simple: If you learn about the early beginnings of Buddhism, you will begin to see Buddhism as a psychology instead of a religion.

Similar to Stoicism, Existentialism, and Confucianism, Buddhism provides a comprehensive analysis of the human mind and behavior and a systematic approach to the elimination of human suffering. Buddhism has only one ultimate goal: to liberate individuals from suffering through the analysis of the mind as well as personal cultivation and growth. Regardless of the diversification of Buddhist teachings into numerous schools and lineages over the last two thousand years, this ultimate goal has never changed. Therefore, this book incorporates mind analysis and cultivation methods (as based upon the five *Pāli Nikāyas*, the earliest collection of the Buddha's discourses) into a professional counseling model for contemporary societies. Its purpose is to provide a viable treatment option for helping professionals, including counselors, therapists, social workers, chaplains, psychologists, psychiatrists, and their clients. In other words, this book aims to redefine Buddhism as a viable theoretical orientation for counseling and to provide practical methods and techniques to facilitate the work of helping professionals. The first step on this journey is to understand the Buddha's philosophy of mind.

## THE BUDDHA BEFORE BUDDHISM

The teachings of the Buddha offer a comprehensive analysis of the human mind and an understanding of how to become completely liberated from suffering. Instead of being a god-like figure who has the mystical power to govern and change human affairs by meting out

DOI: 10.4324/9781003025450-1

rewards and punishments, the Buddha can be regarded as a philosopher, a teacher, a religious leader, and a person capable of addressing psychological problems. In most early accounts of the Buddha's life, the Buddha was depicted as an ordinary person who got sick and hurt but who was also devoted to teaching and sharing his realizations. While acknowledging Early Buddhist scriptures documenting the Buddha's discourses on supernatural powers (such as the *Kevatta Sutta*, which examines psychic power or telepathy), the Buddha's primary intervention method was to use dialogues, questions, didactics, silence, or other skillful teaching methods to alleviate suffering. He was primarily referred to as a teacher, which also involved the role of a counselor in that cultural context.

## LIFE OF THE BUDDHA

During the 5th century B.C., a republic called Shakya was geographically located in what is now the southern border of modern Nepal. According to legend, the leader of Shakya, Śuddhodana Gautama, learned from a prophet that his future son would become either a great king or, through renunciation, a great spiritual leader. In response to the prophecy, Śuddhodana decided to raise his son luxuriously, thereby sheltering him from any reason that might cause him to pursue a spiritual path. When Māyā Gautama, Śuddhodana's wife, died soon after giving birth to the young prince, her sister, Mahāpajāpatī Gautama, became the step-mother of the future Buddha, raising the prince throughout his childhood. From the moment of his birth as the prince of Shakya, Siddhārtha Gautama was immersed in a privileged life of abundant food, elegant clothes, and endless entertainment. He also received a royal education to become the future king, excelling in many branches of knowledge, including the art of warfare. As arranged by his father, Prince Siddhārtha was married at age 16 and lived a fairy tale life until the day his curiosity took him beyond the palace walls.

At age 29, Siddhārtha decided to embark on the first adventure of his life: to see the world outside his palace, the real world that his father had striven so hard to hide from him. Immediately after his departure, he saw a world beyond his imagination: aging people, incurable illnesses, death, poverty, and tears. Astonished and overwhelmed, Siddhārtha gradually realized that he was living in a world with unavoidable miseries and, to compound matters, no one had found a way to escape suffering. Despite the shock to his innocence brought about by this experience, Siddhārtha adamantly sought an answer. Upon encountering an ascetic monk who seemed to be undisturbed by the miseries of life, the young prince started to wonder whether he might find his answer in renunciation. Eventually, Siddhārtha left his palace, his wife, his infant son, and his family to start his life as a religious ascetic.

During that time in ancient India, abstinence from sensual pleasures, self-imposed poverty, and self-mortification exercises to pursue salvation were widespread practices. After undergoing extreme asceticism for six years, Siddhārtha, on the brink of starvation, discovered that severe renunciation only increased suffering. He realized that only the Middle Path—a path of moderation beyond the extremes of sensual indulgence and self-mortification—led to peace of mind. Following this insight, at the age of 35, and after 49 days of meditation under a Bodhi tree, Siddhārtha discovered the law of dependent origination, realized the Four Noble Truths, attained enlightenment, and became known as the Buddha or the "Awakened One."

In his first discourse, the *Dhammacakkappavattana Sutta: Setting the Wheel of Dhamma in Motion*, the Buddha explicated his understanding of the Middle Path leading to nibbāna, the highest and happiest psychological state possible (Dhamma, 1997). One of his foremost realizations is that neither extreme asceticism and self-mortification nor pursuit and indulgence in materialism and sensual pleasures will end suffering. As a prince, the Buddha lived a life of luxurious enjoyment, providing enormous physical and mental satisfaction. However, taking delight in such indulgence will never satiate the mind's desire; instead, they only perpetuate and strengthen desire, lust, and the thirst for more sensual pleasure, resulting in more suffering. As with addictions, individuals become temporarily satisfied by performing an act with a pleasurable reward (e.g., taking cocaine, gambling, sex, etc.) and begin to have cravings for the same level of pleasure. However, tolerance develops, and addicted individuals continuously, and sometimes compulsively, perform the same act with more intensity to experience a similar level of pleasure despite harm to themselves. Therefore, both the Buddha and psychology have regarded this kind of pursuit of sensual pleasure as self-defeating and ultimately unsatisfying.

The other extreme is self-mortification, which is the direct opposite of indulgence in sensual pleasures. For example, in ascetic practices, the Buddha and the fellow practitioners denied themselves food and clothing, immersed themselves in frigid water in cold weather, exposed themselves to the sun in hot weather, or kept standing for days. These self-mortifications are believed to exhaust previously gained bad kamma and help the mind refrain from indulging in sensual pleasures. However, the Buddha found this practice unprofitable because it only results in unnecessary pain and suffering.

The Buddha then emphasized avoiding the two extremes of sensual pleasure and self-mortification. Even when the Buddha was a prince, enjoying the most luxurious and fulfilling life, he could not avoid the inevitable suffering such as sickness and aging. Indeed, it only perpetuates further one's inclination to indulge in sensuality and disturb one's equanimity. On the other hand, practicing self-mortification resulted in painful experiences that produced unnecessary and meaningless suffering. His direct experiences pursuing the two extremes led him to conclude that the pursuit of either did not end suffering. The Buddha then proposed the Middle Path, which involves the teachings of Four Noble Truths, the Noble Eightfold Path, Dependent Origination, and non-self. For the remaining 45 years of his life, he taught these concepts in the regions of contemporary India and Nepal.

## THE UNIQUENESS OF EARLY BUDDHIST TEACHINGS

To understand the uniqueness of Buddhism, it is essential to consider the sociocultural background of the Buddha's life. In 563 B.C.E., religion played a core and definitive role in India. It was a time of diversified religious beliefs, and many advanced practitioners in each religion played the role of sage, offering advice to help with people's suffering. Religious beliefs were divided into two types of teachings: eternalism (sassata-vāda) and annihilationism (uccheda-vāda). The eternalistic religions believed in a metaphysical self, with human existence defined as an eternal soul residing in a temporary body. When the body dies, the soul continues to live and reincarnate to another body based on previous kamma. The soul's ultimate goal is to enter eternal bliss or reunite with a higher power, and the path for doing so was to mortify the flesh in order to overcome such physical bondage. Some traditions, such as Jainism, assert that self-mortification and ascetic practices can cleanse bad kamma and lead one's soul to a state of blissful eternity. Another tradition, Brāhmaṇism, had a basis in this stance. Its ultimate goal is reunification with God, Brahman, who is considered the eternal origin, cause, and foundation of all existence. This type of religion emphasizes self-continuity or soul-continuity, thereby suggesting an eternal agent of existence in each person.

The annihilationists strongly believed in the physical self and regarded the self and the body as one. As such there is no separate entity as a discernible soul, and the death of the physical body means the end of the self, especially as it is also believed that there is no kamma, rebirth, or afterlife. Based on this assumption, annihilationists emphasize immediate sensual pleasures and materialism. Charvaka, for example, is an ancient school of Indian materialism that emphasized direct experience as the most accurate and dependable source of knowledge and critically examining all inferences, questions, conventions, or phenomena. They accept pleasure and pain as part of life and believe in indulgence in pleasure and avoidance of pain. As Charvaka rejects ideas of God or grace, as in other annihilationist schools, they emphasize living in the present moment instead of wasting time postulating on any dubious and unknown matters beyond this life. This type of religion emphasizes self-discontinuity and denies any possibilities outside of self-control.

Driven by his direct experiences in the two pursuits, the Buddha regarded these two systems as two extreme views. Subsequently, the teachings of the Buddha provided an innovative perspective of spiritual practice that was in direct contrast to these popular Indian religious-philosophical systems. The Buddha was the first to propose a middle view underpinned by a non-self. Logically, if a concept does not exist, one will not even mention its existence; for example, "wings of a tiger" would not be a plausible statement. In this sense, when the Buddha used the term "anattā" to describe not-self or non-self (not to be confused with "no self," which is a rejection of the existence of self), he was possibly referring to a provisional existence of self, one that is not ultimate and absolute. One can understand such a self as an ontological existence or a temporary phenomenon experienced by consciousness. In fact, the problem is never whether the self exists; it is about the mental flexibility in seeing multiple perspectives of what constitutes a self and refraining from attaching to any one particular point of view.

This mental flexibility is the Middle Path (majjhimā paṭipadā), a third perspective on the two dualistic extremes. It is a metacognitive view that detaches the mind from the inclination to pursue both extremes. It involves a realization of how the self is a phenomenon instead of an ultimate existent. This third view of personal identity must not be underestimated in contributing to the radical shift in awareness brought about in Indian society. Among all the contemporary religions and spiritual practices in ancient India, including self-continuous and self-discontinuous beliefs, self-existence was regarded as incontrovertible. In other words, it had always been defined as a concrete and indivisible entity regardless of whether it is permanently and continuously existing or temporarily existing for one lifetime. The Buddha challenged these assumptions in a revolutionary way by denying the ultimate existence of self. In this view, the existence of self is merely a concept: one can conceptually label a "self" based on one's experiences, but this "self" is an ontological existence that is divisible into multiple causes and conditions without any permanent existence. Let's consider the following conversation to illustrate this assertion of non-self:

PERSON A: Where is your car?

PERSON B: Here is my Bayerische Motoren Werke (BMW) sports car. I just finished financing it.

PERSON A: What makes it a BMW sport car?

PERSON B: It's got the logo on the front of the car.

PERSON A: So is the logo your car?

PERSON B: No! It has an M88 engine, Michelin Pilot super sports tires, and the finest leather seats!

PERSON A: So you mean the engine is your car? The tires are your car? The seats are your car? Or the windows, the timing belt, and brakes are your car?

PERSON B: No, none of these define my car. The combination of all these make up my car.

PERSON A: Engines are metal, leathers are skin, tires are plastic, so metal, skin, and plastic make up your car?

PERSON B: No! It's a fancy BMW sports car! It's not a bunch of metal, skin, and plastic!

PERSON A: Is there anything else that makes up your car?

PERSON B: No....

PERSON A: So where is your car?

PERSON B: I guess I just label these components as "my car." There is not really a car.

In this example, Person B labels the combination of constituents a "car," but this is nothing more than a construct or logical abstraction based on a reification of the whole. The analogy demonstrates that there is no separate "self" that can be found in any, or in any combination, of the components that make up a self; instead, "self" is a nominal term for the collective experiences of our body, consciousness, and other factors. The gist of the Middle Path is analyzing the self and seeing through its fabricated and conceptual nature of consciousness to let go of the grasping that causes all kinds of suffering.

The Buddha taught that grasping is the root of suffering, and he did so without recourse to any revelation about theology or cosmology; instead, he strongly emphasized a somewhat individualistic approach to spiritual practice and regarded self-cultivation as the most important and immediate pursuit of life. For this reason, Buddhism stands in direct contrast to many religions, which encourage the worshipping of a higher power for salvation.

## DIVERSIFICATION OF BUDDHISM

To understand and apply the teachings of the Buddha adequately, it is crucial to get a sense of how the Buddha's thoughts and ideas have been utilized in numerous articles, books, and presentations in contemporary society. As Early Buddhism was an oral tradition, practitioners used recitation, chanting, and music to help memorize teachings and express their commitment. After the Buddha's passing, his followers congregated to consolidate and authorize his teachings and practices, especially Ānanda and several others who had extraordinary powers of memorization that they used to preserve the Buddha's discourses. This congregation was what we now call the First Buddhist Council, which served as the first officially validated source of the Buddhist scriptures by the monastic community of that time. Since then, as the teachings of the Buddha spread far and wide across Asia, different interpretations of his message developed, as seen in the emergence of many schools of Buddhism. The original teachings of the Buddha are accessible to us only through classical canons of these various schools, but the use of written texts to capture the teachings only began in the early common era, after the proliferation of Buddhist schools had occurred (Bareau, 2005). After years of reformation of the divergence of different Buddhist schools, scholars have identified and categorized types of Buddhism according to their doctrinal similarities, geographical distribution, sociopolitical influences, and other factors. To provide a more simplistic introduction to the essence of Buddhist schools in contemporary society, this book adopts the classification of Buddhism into three main branches: *Theravāda*, *Mahāyāna*, and *Vajrayāna*.

**Theravāda Buddhism**. Theravāda Buddhism is believed to be one of the oldest Buddhist sects (Crosby, 2014). The meaning of Theravāda refers to the "doctrine of the senior monks," signifying the succession of original teachings from the Buddha. Theravāda Buddhism adheres to the recorded discourses of the Buddha in the Pāli Canon known as the five Nikāyas, believed to be the most extensive collection of the Buddha's discourses, as well as the commentaries of the Pāli Canon, such as the Abhidhamma. Theravāda Buddhism emphasizes following in the footsteps of the historical Buddha, which focuses on the liberation of the mind and cessation of suffering. Those who pursue and are successful in such a practice are called arahants, enlightened beings free from suffering and rebirth. Theravāda Buddhism is often referred to as Southern Buddhism due to its transmission from India to South and Southeastern Asia. It remains a dominant form of Buddhism in many Southeastern Asian countries, including Sri Lanka, Burma, Thailand, Cambodia, and Laos. In addition, it has had important influences on Nepal and Indonesia. Well-known teachers of Theravada Buddhism today include the monk Ajahn Brahm.

**Mahāyāna Buddhism**. In the first century C.E., a group of Indian Buddhists led a reform movement seeking to restore the original soteriological intent of the Buddha to enlighten all people (Whelan, 2011). Mahāyāna means the "Great Vehicle." Instead of focusing on the personal attainment of enlightenment, Mahāyāna Buddhists emphasize the collective liberation of all beings by cultivating compassion and wisdom. Uniquely, Mahāyāna Buddhism emphasizes the ideal of becoming a bodhisattva, an enlightened being who has been liberated from suffering but chooses to stay in the realm of cyclical rebirth to aid all beings. Using Early Buddhist scriptures as aids, Mahāyāna Buddhists later developed texts in Sanskrit as part of their sacred scriptures, such as the Lotus Sutra, Diamond Sutra, and Heart Sutra. From a small sect of Buddhist mendicants and householders in Northern India to a global religion, Mahāyāna Buddhism has spread widely in East and Central Asian countries such as Bhutan, Mongolia, China, Taiwan, Korea, and Japan. Due to its geographical distribution across northern India, Mahāyāna Buddhism is sometimes referred to as Northern Buddhism. Some of the notable diversifications of Mahāyāna Buddhism include Chan Buddhism, Pure Land Buddhism, and Zen Buddhism. Thich Nhat Hanh, a global spiritual leader, was a Zen Buddhist.

**Vajrayāna Buddhism**. Vajrayāna Buddhism or Tantric Buddhism is generally regarded as a derivative school of Mahāyāna Buddhism (Wedemeyer, 2012). Vajrayāna, translated as the "diamond vehicle," adopts the core Mahāyāna philosophical doctrines while emphasizing unique practices to actualize the teachings. Driven by some elements of Early Buddhist texts and Mahāyāna sutras, tantras are esoteric traditions based on mystical texts documenting various rituals and rites, including the performance of mudras, the use of mantras such as "Om mani padme hum," meditating on mandalas, visualizations of Buddhas and bodhisattvas, and other esoteric practices, with successors in the lineage receiving empowerment from their masters to realize certain teachings and skills. In about the 7ᵗʰ century C.E., Vajrayāna Buddhism became fully systemized in northern India. Its transmission provided significant support for the development of Tibetan Buddhism, which has become one of the most popular Buddhist schools today and highly influential in North America. Pema Chödrön, a senior teacher in Buddhist compassion, is an American Tibetan Buddhist.

Despite the differences in the theoretical orientations of the Buddhist schools, their primary concern, reflective of the reason for Siddhārtha's renunciation of worldly life, is the same: concern for human well-being and the desire to alleviate the suffering of oneself and others. As demonstrated by the failure of Siddhārtha to find the solution to suffering through renunciation, Buddhism does not consider rejecting worldly phenomena in its entirety as the way of liberation from suffering. Instead, all Buddhism holds that the mind plays an essential role in the experiencing of all types of human suffering; therefore, the transformation of our minds is the most effective antidote. The Buddhist tradition has "concerned itself over the past 2,500 years with cultivating exceptional states of mental well-being as well as identifying and treating problems of the mind" (Smith as cited in Wallace & Shapiro, 2006, p. 690). Emphasizing mental training and the scholarly position that Buddhism is a school of thought open to interpretation, this book provides a contemporary interpretation of Early Buddhist teachings from a professional counseling angle. In that light, all applications of Buddhist teaching described in this book are open for further adaptation, transformation, and interpretation to fit the needs of counselors and clients.

## CONCLUSION

This first chapter has outlined a brief history of Buddhism and its unique teachings of the Middle Path and non-self, constituting core ideas in the counseling model described in this book. To facilitate readers' understanding, I would like to summarize the Buddha's teachings of non-self as follows: "You may say there is a self, but it is not what you think." Provisionally, however, I can label my body and mind as my 'self', an identity I wish could be permanent. Furthermore, I continuously construct my sense of self through my identities, values, social roles, relationships, achievements, and others' evaluations of me.

As an example, I wanted to become a professor since my time at university, and I kept telling myself that I could be a competent, respected, and superior person once I gained this social status. From this perspective, I can convince myself that "I" exist through status and achievements. Things went very well initially, and I became an assistant professor right after completing my first doctoral degree. I did not notice how much I clung to my identity as a "professor" until, several years later, I was rejected for an appointment with harsh comments and labeled as unqualified. I suddenly lost the title of a "professor," damaging my pride and dignity. It was a devastating experience that destroyed a firmly held identity and led me into an episode of depression. It was also a turning point in my life to see the danger in grasping onto an identity to convince myself of my self-worth. With guidance from my teachers, and through spiritual practices, I was able to gradually soften my grip and stop clinging onto being accepted. Such experiences led to the development of a counseling model to benefit others who are hurt by grasping on too tightly to a fabricated self.

Beginning the journey on the Middle Path is not easy because we have formed strong habits of holding on to extreme views of the self. However, personal growth becomes possible when we see this as a process with a clear direction and multiple steps and subgoals. Just like a demanding physical regimen at a gym, it is initially difficult to foster a habit of healthy exercise; there are numerous challenges, failures, and setbacks before one attains a strong and healthy body. Like pushup training, mind training involves devotion to continuous and culminative processes with gradual and subtle gains. Each moment of focusing one's mind on the present moment strengthens the mind's stability, clarity, and concentration. Similarly, then, this book applies the Early Buddhist teaching of mind training to a model of counseling that can help counselors train their own minds and those of their clients. The concept of faith in Early Buddhism is not primarily used to describe a strong belief in the Buddha himself; rather, it refers to confidence in the practice that leads towards liberation from suffering.

## Contemplative Questions for Buddhist Counselors

Buddhism provides practical methods of spiritual cultivation for Buddhist counselors, with such growth being rightly considered as one of the most important ingredients of a successful counseling relationship. For this reason, one feature of this book is to provide a series of contemplative questions to facilitate ongoing Buddhist-inspired practice for readers.

To begin with, please take a moment to step out from your usual thoughts and emotions and come back to the present moment for a contemplative exercise. Let's begin with some meditation and self-reflection. Buddhist practice emphasizes reflection on direct experience so that one can learn better ways to think, speak, act, or live. However, this is a continual process of reflection without any absolute right or wrong answers. There is only an honest moment with yourself, thereby revealing better answers each time we mindfully reflect. So, please don't judge or doubt any of your personal responses.

Sit in an upright position so that your spine can fully support your body while relaxing your shoulders. Take a moment to breathe in and out using a slower pace than your usual rhythm. Try to relax your body and gently focus on the following questions. Read slowly and notice thoughts, comments, and answers that come up:

- "Who am I?"
- "What makes me believe in who I am?"

- "Is it possible that what I have learned about myself in the past wasn't accurate?"
- "What if the nature of who I am is completely different from what I have been told?"
- "What if I am just a concept that I assign to myself?"
- "What if I am susceptible to change, more so than I ever wanted?"
- "What if everything I have, I own, and I love are impermanent?"
- "What if a part of me has always known this but I don't want it and I don't like it?"
- "What if this part of me acknowledges and accepts impermanence?"
- "If everything is impermanent, can I still fully live, love, and laugh during every mindful moment?"
- "How does all this make sense to me?"
- "How does all this not make sense to me?"

Take another moment to notice your bodily sensations, thoughts, images, and other experiences in your body and mind. Take note of any strong thoughts or feelings and try to be curious about what triggered such experiences in you. Again, there are no true and false answers to these questions. Any answers are only important when you contemplate, explore, and digest them. Indeed, each time you come back to these questions, it is likely that you will discover new answers.

For further contemplative questions in this book, please use the same steps for your personal reflections. I believe your answers will continue to evolve each time you read them. To end with, I would like to acknowledge your effort in pondering these questions. It is my pleasure to walk this path with you.

# REFERENCES

Bareau, A. (2005). Buddhism, Schools of: Early Doctrinal Schools of Buddhism. *Encyclopedia of Religion, 2*, 1192–1203.

Crosby, K. (2014). *Theravada Buddhism: Continuity, Diversity and Identity* (Wiley Blackwell guides to Buddhism). Chichester, West Sussex, UK: Malden, MA: Wiley-Blackwell.

Dhamma, R. (1997). *The First Discourse of the Buddha.* Boston: Wisdom Publications.

Hong Kong: Centre of Buddhist Studies, The University of Hong Kong.

Wallace, B. A., & Shapiro, S. L. (2006). Mental Balance and Well-Being: Building Bridges between Buddhism and Western Psychology. *American Psychologist, 61*(7), 690.

Wedemeyer, C. K. (2012). *Making Sense of Tantric Buddhism (South Asia across the disciplines).* New York: Columbia University Press.

Whelan, C. (2011). Mahayana Buddhism. In *Encyclopedia of Global Religions, 2*, 732–737.

# CHAPTER 2

# Buddhism and Science

## *Implications to Buddhist Counseling*

In the last 50 years, Buddhism has received significant scientific attention. Many scholars, including Alan Wallace, Daniel Goleman, Karen Kissel Wegela, Paul Dennison, and Jack Kornfield, have produced a considerable amount of scientific research on meditation and other Buddhist practices. Many of these scientific studies employed MRIs (magnetic resonance imaging) and EEGs (electroencephalographs) to study the neurobiology of meditation practitioners and relate their findings to traditional Buddhist teachings. Some scholars acknowledged these interdisciplinary scholars as "Buddhist scientists" (Barinaga, 2003, p. 44) to signify their substantial contributions to the integrative field of Buddhism and science. In the social sciences, most of the studies that focused on Buddhist-informed therapeutic interventions to improve mental health and wellbeing indicated many positive effects on physical and emotional disturbances. In general, the psychological and neurobiological studies on meditation and Buddhism-related practices are extensive and have led to a dramatic increase in scientific knowledge of the brain and human mind.

Buddhism and science have different approaches to understanding phenomenon, but the Buddha's approach in handling empirical information is rarely discussed in the current literature on Buddhism and science. It is crucial that Buddhist counselors who hope to apply Buddhist teachings to counseling practice understand the Buddha's stance.

## DIFFERENT UNDERLYING ASSUMPTIONS OF BUDDHISM AND SCIENCE

Buddhism and science are two very different approaches to understanding empirical phenomena. The word "science" derives from the Latin word *scire*, "to know." According to the definition given by the Science Council (2009), "Science is the pursuit and application of knowledge and understanding of the natural and social world following a systematic methodology based on evidence." In this definition, science is concerned with knowing the natural and social world by investigating evidence that is observable, measurable, and replicable. Scientific studies generally strive to formulate new theories or test existing theories to find the best explanations for a phenomenon. The field of science provides a systematic enterprise to study many aspects of the universe, such as astronomy, biology, chemistry, ecology, geology, physics, and psychology. This rationale may explain why advanced technologies

DOI: 10.4324/9781003025450-2

like EEGs, MRIs, and fMRIs are used to quantify brain activities and capture objectively observable evidence, thereby explaining the changes brought about by meditation. The first question in discussing the difference between Buddhism and science is: *How important is it to understand the why?*

Instead of pursuing the best explanations for a phenomenon, Early Buddhism only concerned itself with understanding phenomenon related to the liberation from suffering. The Buddha's attitude towards inquiries on worldly phenomena is reflected in his unanswered questions (Karunadasa, 2013). In the face of numerous questions during his 45 years of teaching, the Buddha purposefully rejected answering ten questions regarding four metaphysical and philosophical domains, including the nature of universe, the relationship between soul and body, and the post-mortem survival of the Buddha himself. One of the most plausible reasons the Buddha gave for refusing to answer these questions is that such answers will not help explain or eradicate suffering. On the contrary, answering these questions may actually spawn the pursuit of conceptual and theoretical views and opinions that derail the intent of the Buddhist teachings. Again, liberation from suffering is the only goal in Buddhism.

As Thich Nhat Hanh (1994) explained, the Buddha taught his followers not to waste time and energy in metaphysical speculations but to make a concerted effort in practicing detachment directly. In this sense, Early Buddhism may not be scientific, although it is strongly empirical and goal-oriented. According to the Cambridge English dictionary, the word *empirical* refers to whatever is experienced or seen rather than being explained theoretically. Empirical observation and the examination and contemplation of intrapersonal experiences to generate awareness on causes and ways to cease suffering is the key to Early Buddhism. All other knowledge is inferior to this primary knowledge, suggesting that direct and subjective experience is far more important than an objective evaluation of the process of cultivation.

In contemporary attempts to study Buddhism scientifically, there has been a debate on whether the measures of Buddhist practices, especially meditation, should follow a traditional Western approach by using a neutral "third-person" experimenter to make evaluations, or whether a "first-person" experiential approach should be employed involving participants' reports of their subjective experiences (Davidson & Kaszniak, 2015). Francisco Varela, a renowned expert in human consciousness, has made strong arguments for the first-person approach in order to better understand the benefits of meditation training as well as the fine details of meditative experiences (Varela et al., 1991). Perhaps the Early Buddhist scriptures also resonate this first-person approach.

This debate can be seen in a story in the life of the Buddha himself. The villagers in the *Kalama Sutta: To the Kalamas* (AN 3.65) wished to know whether it is a good practice to expound teachings from ancestors and tradition while also criticizing the teachings of others. Instead of providing a direct answer, the Buddha guided the Kalamas to visualize whether such a practice is beneficial or harmful to oneself. Through the skill-in-means employed in this dialogue, the Kalamas concluded that adhering to one's traditional teaching and rejecting others' teaching without examination is a harmful or unskilful decision. Using this experience, the Buddha introduced the importance of contemplation and explained that spiritual practice should not blindly follow: (1) inherited knowledge through others' reports, legends, traditions, and what is documented in scriptures; (2) logical abstractions through conjecture, inference, analogies, and agreement with options; or (3) random guesses.

In other words, Buddhism is not based on transmitted knowledge, hypothetical explanations, or thoughtless intuitions. Instead, the core foundation of Buddhist practice is to contemplate, analyze, and gain insight into phenomena through direct experience. When the Buddha taught that the notion of self is a delusion, the practitioner did not conceptually or logically debate whether this argument stands. Instead, a true practitioner should concentrate on one's body and mind, carefully observing the arising and ceasing of experiences, and generating knowledge about the nature of body and mind through direct observation to see whether the idea of non-self is empirically verifiable. This is why the fundamental meditation suttas, such as the *Satipaṭṭhāna Sutta*, emphasize observing and analyzing components of the body and mind in fine detail, using personal experience to foster awareness empirically.

But does this mean science has no place in Buddhism? Of course not. As long as empirical observations remain a foundation of Buddhism practice, there are many lessons Buddhism can learn from science. To the benefit of Buddhist counseling, science offers an intriguing perspective to understand body and mind, such as neurological functions and bodily changes during different emotional states, which can supplement Buddhist practices of analysis and contemplation. It also offers a systematic and reliable method to evaluate the efficacy of Buddhist counseling models and collect feedback. Finally, due to contemporary cultural beliefs in science, scientific studies of Buddhist practices bestow a vote of confidence in its followers.

# BUDDHISM AND NEUROSCIENCE: THE NEW UNDERSTANDING OF BRAIN AND MIND

While both Buddhism and neuroscience examine the mind empirically, Buddhism focuses on direct investigation through introspection and contemplation, with neuroscience relying on third-person scientific observation (Zak, 2017). But over the past five decades, neuroscientists have developed a profound interest in studying the psychological and physiological effects of meditation. During that period, Buddhist meditation practice has become a significant topic for neuroscientific studies investigating the brain, the mind, and their relationship. Many scientists, inspired by new neuroimaging technologies and analytical methodologies, have become interested in demystifying meditation. For instance, Hanson and Mendius (2009) have suggested that the advancements in neuroscientific studies on meditation's effects on brain neurobiology have significantly increased scientific understandings of the mind and brain in the past 20 years. After years of studies, one thing that both Buddhism and neuroscience can agree on is: meditation induces significant neurological and behavioral changes.

The next section will discuss two major directions of investigation: anatomical structure and the neural activity of the brain and associated brainwaves.

## Anatomical Structure and Neural Activity of the Brain

To date, more than 20 studies have investigated brain morphometry related to meditation (Tang et al., 2015). One neuroscientific attempt has aimed to locate brain regions of neural activity during meditation practice. Individual studies have reported neutral activity in multiple brain regions such as the cerebral cortex, subcortical grey and white matter, brain stem, and cerebellum. Such results suggest that meditation may involve large-scale neural networks instead of one or two particular regions. Studies show that several areas of the brain seem to be activated when using the different meditative traditions of Buddhism, namely: (1) the frontopolar cortex, the anterior portion of the brain's frontal lobe, which is related to complex and higher-order behaviors and rapid learning (Boschin et al., 2015), which is associated with enhanced metacognitive awareness in meditation (Tang et al., 2015); (2) the sensory cortices and insula, those portions of the cerebral cortex at the outer layer of the brain that are related to body awareness; (3) the hippocampus, a brain structure embedded deep in the temporal lobe related to memory processes and learning; and (4) the anterior cingulate cortex, mid-cingulate cortex, and orbitofrontal cortex, areas related to attention control and emotional regulation (Tang, 2017). The significance is that meditation is likely related to the current scientific understandings of attention control, emotional regulation, bodily awareness, and metacognitive awareness. Studies have also suggested that meditation can induce beneficial effects on attention and emotional regulation (Braboszcz et al., 2017).

## Meditation and Brainwaves

Another common neuroscientific method of investigation of the applications of Buddhist practices involves the study of brainwaves. EEGs are commonly used neuroimaging methods for meditation studies. While there have not been consistent findings on the impact of meditation using EEGs, one reliable finding that does stand out is an increase in gamma brainwaves, usually found in several cortices and subcortical structures associated with cognition and attention (Braboszcz et al., 2017). Several scholars have noticed a higher frequency of gamma activation (>30 Hz) associated explicitly with various meditation practices. For example, Lutz et al. (2004) have conducted a brain imaging study with Tibetan Buddhist practitioners in deep meditation states. They found unusually powerful and pervasive gamma brainwaves of electrical activity compared to the control group, suggesting that meditative training may induce short- and long-term neural changes in attention and awareness. Cahn et al. (2009) also studied practitioners of Vipassanā meditation and found significantly increased gamma (35–45 Hz) power areas. This result suggests that long-term Vipassanā meditation may enhance meditators' sensory awareness and attentional engagement. Furthermore, in their study of Zen meditators, Hauswald et al. (2015) found significantly high gamma (160–170 Hz) power in the cingulate cortex and somatosensory cortices of some participants. This study also asked participants to complete an inventory of meditation and self-reported mindfulness (MAAS) to gauge their level of mindfulness, attention, and awareness in the present moment using a 6-point Likert scale. The result indicated a significant positive correlation between gamma power and MAAS scores. Several studies have noted the enhanced gamma power of meditators. Their neural changes are associated with enhanced attention and sensory awareness, which is comparable to the effects of Buddhism meditation.

Given the empirical evidence on the neurophysiological effects of meditation, the question should not be whether meditation fosters neural changes; rather, what do the changes actually mean? In other words, while I know that meditation can enhance my attention and awareness, how do I benefit from it? Social science studies of Buddhism, especially the application of Buddhism into mental health treatment interventions, have provided some interesting answers to these questions. The following section will summarize the most effective applications of Buddhism in professional psychology over the last 40 years.

## SOCIAL SCIENCE AND BUDDHISM

In the late 1970s, a new technique emerged in the research literature on mental health treatment. Gary Deatherage (1975) was one of the first scholars to use mindfulness techniques (as based on the *Satipaṭṭhāna Sutta*) with mental health patients, while Richard Davidson and Daniel Goleman (1977) compared the effectiveness of Buddhist meditation and hypnosis on increasing attention. Daniel Brown and Jack Engler (1980) then compared practitioners of Buddhist meditation on Rorschach[1] responses, which initiated a series of social scientific studies of Buddhist mindfulness practices by either integrating them into practices of psychology or comparing them with similar psychological constructs. However, mindfulness studies did not bring much attention in the field until the advent of Jon Kabat-Zinn.

Using chronic pain as a treatment target, Kabat-Zinn (1982) designed a ten-week stress reduction and relaxation program based on Theravāda and Mahāyāna Buddhist meditation approaches, and Zen and Yogic traditions (p. 34). Over these ten weeks, participants received instruction on mindfulness practice and then used mindfulness meditation and yoga in a group format. The result was surprisingly effective: 50% of participants reported a 50% reduction in pain symptoms after the program. Since that time, mindfulness studies have mushroomed into a hot topic of research while also inspiring a trend of integrating mindfulness practice into mental health treatment models.

Intervention models integrating Buddhism teachings—such as Mindfulness-Based Stress Reduction (MBSR; Kabat-Zinn, 1990), Dialectical Behavior Therapy (DBT; Linehan, 1993), and Mindfulness-Based Cognitive Therapy (MBCT; Segal et al., 2002) came to be known as "mindfulness-based interventions" (MBIs). Many of these MBIs, which have shown high efficacy in clinical studies, incorporate mindfulness interventions (Simiola et al., 2015). The following section will briefly review several common MBIs to elucidate their rationales for treatment while also illustrating their effectiveness.

**Mindfulness-Based Stress Reduction.** Ever since his first successful mindfulness study, Kabat-Zinn coined the term MBSR as an intervention designed to reduce distress and enhance the quality of life using mindfulness (Kabat-Zinn, 1990). It was one of the earliest psychotherapy methods to incorporate Buddhist ideas, demonstrating high efficacy in different clinical studies. Utilizing the important Buddhist concept of Right Mindfulness, this treatment program attempts to help clients achieve nonjudgment, awareness, attention, and compassion through the four mindfulness practices of sitting meditation, walking meditation, hatha yoga, and body scans (Kabat-Zinn, 1990). Through MBSR, practitioners foster greater awareness and compassion towards themselves and, consequently, reduce their suffering. MBSR effectively reduces stress, anxiety, and depression (Hofmann & Gómez, 2017; Fjorback et al., 2011; Gallegos et al., 2015). In addition, MBSR is an empirically supported intervention for reducing the symptoms of PTSD (Kimbrough et al., 2010; Kearney et al., 2013; Goldsmith et al., 2014; Gallegos et al., 2015).

**Mindfulness-Based Cognitive Therapy.** Cognitive Therapy and Cognitive Behavioral Therapy are arguably the most prevalent mental health treatments in contemporary society. Mindfulness-Based Cognitive Therapy (MBCT), a treatment that combines mindfulness techniques and cognitive therapy, was developed to treat recurrent depression (Segal et al., 2002). It aims to teach clients to gain more awareness of their thoughts, emotions, and bodies and develop improved coping mechanisms by building new relationships between their thoughts and emotions (Segal et al., 2002). Again, the notion of mindfulness in MBCT is similar to Right Mindfulness in Buddhism since both emphasize becoming more cognizant of one's mind, body, and feelings. MBCT has also proven effective in treating generalized anxiety disorder (Evans et al., 2008; Hofmann et al., 2010), residual depressive symptoms (Kingston et al., 2007), mood disorders (Hofmann et al., 2010), and bipolar disorder (Miklowitz et al., 2015).

**Dialectical Behavior Therapy.** Dialectical Behavior Therapy (DBT) is a cognitive-behavioral treatment developed to address parasuicidal behaviors among women with borderline personality disorder (BPD) (Linehan, 1993). The core treatment modes of DBT include individual therapy, skills training, client and therapist consultations, and therapist consultation meetings. DBT aims to teach clients to regulate their emotions, improve their interpersonal skills, tolerate distress more effectively, and employ self-management skills. In addition, DBT incorporates the core tenets of Zen Buddhism: mindfulness, nonjudgment, and observation (Linehan, 1993). These tenets, used to help clients increase their awareness of body, feelings, and thought processes, are similar to the notion of Right Mindfulness in Buddhism. Acceptance, a crucial component of DBT that encourages therapists to accept clients as they are while teaching them to accept themselves, resonates with the Buddhist practice of observing, accepting, and discerning internal experiences in the present moment. DBT has been demonstrated to reduce substance abuse (Linehan et al., 1999), depression, hopelessness, psychiatric distress (Iverson et al., 2009), binge eating disorders (Chen et al., 2008), emotional dysregulation (Axelrod et al., 2011), and suicidal and non-suicidal behaviors (Chen et al., 2008; McDonell et al., 2010). Some studies have also shown that DBT significantly reduces PTSD symptoms (Steil et al., 2011; Wagner et al., 2007).

**Acceptance and Commitment Therapy.** Acceptance and Commitment Therapy (ACT) starts from the assumption that psychological problems are rooted in a person's psychological rigidity. The treatment method attempts to increase the client's psychological flexibility, including one's ability to implement positive actions when faced with unfavorable emotions or experiences instead of avoiding them (Hayes et al., 1999). To enhance one's psychological flexibility, ACT emphasizes six concepts: acceptance, diffusion, self as context (observing self), contact with the present moment, values, and committed action (Hayes et al., 1999). The central assumptions about human nature behind ACT resonate with Buddhist perspectives on the causes of suffering, usually explained as rigidly clinging to the delusion of self and the craving to satisfy infinite and insatiable personal desires. The six core concepts are also similar to beliefs in Buddhism in which acceptance aligns with the idea of accepting current experiences, that diffusion aligns with detachment from the clinging to self, that the self is context-explicable in relation to the concept of non-self, that personal values align with Buddhist ethics, that contact with the present moment represents mindfulness and that committed action aligns with Right Effort in the Eightfold Path. ACT has been shown to be effective in treating obsessive-compulsive disorder symptoms (Twohig et al., 2010), depression (Twohig et al., 2010; Karlin et al., 2013), and psychosis (Bach & Hayes, 2002).

## Common Criticisms of Mindfulness-Based Interventions

MBI is empirically supported as an effective treatment program for an array of psychological symptoms. In a review of the trend of mindfulness development in psychology, William Van Gordon and Edo Shonin described these adaptations of mindfulness as first-generation mindfulness-based interventions (FG-MBIs), that is, mental health treatment interventions that adopt the Buddhist practice of mindfulness as a core component (Van Gordon & Shonin, 2020). In general, the FG-MBIs have several characteristics: (1) being silent about the spiritual or religious aspect and explicitly claiming to be a secularized approach; (2) employing particular meditative techniques; and (3) generally separating the meditative techniques from the related Buddhist framework, which emphasizes ethics. However, in the past decade, some scholars in both Buddhism and Psychology have started to show concern about the disregard for the spiritual underpinnings of Buddhist mindfulness. Let us now examine these criticisms in more detail.

(1) Contemporary models of mindfulness have tended to utilize a reductionist approach that divorces mindfulness from the spiritual paradigm of Buddhism, which may undermine the essence of Buddhist teachings (McWilliams, 2011). Some mental health professionals regarded this reductionist approach as a possible reduction in effectiveness (Huxter, 2007), diluting mindfulness into a superficial calming technique that may not bring about lasting changes (Neale, 2011), leading to a probable abandonment of the transformative potential of Buddhist-inspired mindfulness (Sun, 2014).

(2) These psychotherapies may not incorporate the essence of Buddhist principles and theories. This lack can pose potential risks to clients who are misusing Buddhist practices (Neale, 2011; Shonin, Van Gordon, Dunn, et al., 2014). First, applying mindfulness solely as a relaxation technique may lead the practitioners into dullness and hinder the progress of meditation (Britton et al., 2014). Second, certain scholars have pointed out the possible risks of practicing mindfulness without the guidance of ethics. For example, mindfulness practices can enhance the quality of awareness, but it does not naturally result in compassion or morality (Sun, 2014). In other words, one could be mindfully violent or criminally offensive. Alarmingly, even the U.S. Marine Corps utilizes mindfulness skills to optimize combat performance (Watson, 2013).

Most mindfulness research has been conducted using quantitative studies that measured symptom reduction related to short-term mindfulness-based interventions (e.g., Spinhoven et al., 2017). Little is known about the experiences of long-term practitioners of secularized versions of mindfulness or the possible differences between them and Buddhist mindfulness practitioners. Moreover, some empirical evidence has demonstrated adverse effects from such practices. Dobkin et al. (2011) conducted a literature review on the attrition and negative effects of the aforementioned mindfulness-based stress reduction (MBSR) program, a popular Buddhism-derived intervention that extracts mindfulness practice from Buddhism.

They found that participants in several studies reported significant adverse effects, such as relaxation-induced anxiety, perceived stress, and depression. Therefore, the extraction of either compassion or mindfulness from Buddhism, a holistic religion, may sabotage the approach, reduce its effectiveness, and result in potential risks.

(3) A traditional Buddhist approach to psychological healing may promote more lasting positive changes (Neale, 2011), cultivate a different, keener, wiser kind of attention (Hyland, 2015), or provide more interventions that help mental health professionals to address the needs of multiple clients better (Lee et al., 2016). Consequently, several scholars have recommended that practitioners and researchers acquire a foundation in Buddhist teachings and an understanding of the Buddhist rationale for mindfulness to deliver effective Buddhist-derived interventions (BDIs) to clients (Lee et al., 2016; McWilliams, 2011; Shonin, Van Gordon, & Griffiths, 2014; Sun, 2014).

(4) Bhikkhu Bodhi (2011), a Buddhist scholar and the president of the Buddhist Publication Society, pointed out the potential danger in integrating theories or techniques from different schools of thought. As the theoretical assumptions of each school can be different, dissonance may arise from their merger, which may produce short-term benefits but are unlikely to have long-term beneficial effects. This viewpoint implies the importance of matching techniques with theoretical assumptions in any practice.

In response to these criticisms, some scholars have started to develop treatment interventions by applying more core teachings of Buddhism. Two treatment models, in particular, have received significant research and clinical attention:

### Cognitively-Based Compassion Training

Cognitively-Based Compassion Training (CBCT) is a secularized mind training program based on Tibetan Buddhist compassion meditation practices (Negi et al., 2014, A24). The program includes six modules of meditative practices and contemplative exercises, including attentional stability and clarity, insight into the nature of mental experience, self-compassion, cultivating impartiality, appreciation and affection. Empathic concern and compassion are engaged through two meditation strategies: (1) stabilizing meditation and (2) analytical meditation (Ash et al., 2019). Moreover, the program emphasizes fostering participants' skills across three levels: content knowledge, personal insight, and embodied understanding. CBCT has shown strong efficacy for various psychological disturbances. For example, CBCT was found to increase hopefulness and decrease generalized anxiety in at-risk adolescents (Reddy et al., 2013, p. 219), reduce psychological stress in infants and young children (Poehlmann-Tynan et al., 2020, p. 126), and reduce depressive symptoms and increase self-compassion for African American suicide attempters (Sun et al., 2019).

### Awareness Training Program

Based on Mahāyāna Buddhist teachings, the Awareness Training Program (ATP) is the first group-based program to foster wisdom and compassion in participants (Wu et al., 2019). Based on the Sandhinirmochana Sūtra as a theoretical foundation, the ATP helps participants relinquish their deluded attachment to the concept of self through the development of tranquility and observation. In six three-hour workshops plus two whole-day weekend retreats, participants memorize the mantra "Oṃ maṇi padme hūṃ" and attend lectures, meditation practice, experiential and reflective learning activities, and group discussions to actualize the meaning of the mantra. Results show that participants reported experiencing a reduction of stress and improvement of coherence and psychological wellbeing. But unlike CBCT and MAT, which have already been developed over a longer period of time, the ATP is a new development, and its discoverers have only published one article indicating its effectiveness.

# FROM MINDFULNESS-BASED INTERVENTIONS TO BUDDHIST COUNSELING

Professional psychology now seems to be gradually refraining from extracting Buddhist spiritual practices from its religious framework and then incorporating them into a treatment model. Instead, there have been some attempts to take Buddhism as the core guiding principle for a treatment approach. As a comprehensive analysis of the human mind, this book suggests that Buddhism can stand alone as a theoretical counseling orientation. With its unique epistemological assumptions about human nature, psychopathology, a healthy personality ideal, and curative factors, Buddhism offers a comprehensive system of psychology to understand the human mind and human behaviors. Due to this belief, some scholars, including the author, have started proposing a new field called "Buddhist counseling."

## Definition of Buddhist Counseling and Buddhist Counselor

Several scholars are working towards definitions and parameters in this field. According to Srichannil and Prior (2014), scholars in counseling and applied psychology, Buddhist counseling is defined as a counseling process based on Buddhist teachings. The key element described in the definition seems to pinpoint the importance of a theoretical foundation for counseling instead of any interventions or techniques. Rungreangkulkij and Wongtakee (2008) applied Buddhist mindfulness training to the treatment of anxiety symptoms, yielding positive results. Although they coined their intervention "Buddhist counseling," they did not articulate a definition of this term or describe their intervention as a complete model of treatment. Instead, Rungreangkulkij and Wongtakee (2008) emphasized that Buddhist counseling strongly focuses on the "mindfulness practice" of meditation instead of using meditation as an isolated relaxation technique. This emphasis implies the importance of using mindfulness within the context of Buddhist teachings. In a conceptual paper written by the author and his research team (Lee et al., 2017, p. 113), Buddhist counseling is defined as "a process of reducing suffering in individuals using wisdom and interventions from Buddhism, which aims to train the human mind to attain a state of equanimity, joy, and liberation." From these working definitions, it seems that "Buddhist counseling" is an integrative term to apply Buddhist teachings to the framework of professional counseling, thereby providing a contemporary psychological method to reduce suffering in others.

For this first guidebook to Buddhist counseling, I define Buddhist counseling as:

A holistic treatment approach driven by Buddhist teachings as a theoretical orientation that incorporates techniques and skills from professional psychology. Applying the embodied understanding of Buddhist teachings, Buddhist counselors aim to assist clients to see reality as it is, thereby dissolving their clinging to the five aggregates, resulting in a reduction in suffering.

In this definition, Buddhist counselors are mental health professionals who adopt a Buddhist teaching-based approach to mental health treatment. Buddhist counselors aim to facilitate clients' development of realistic views to see the arising, changing, and ceasing of all phenomena by cultivating awareness of the mental activities that create emotional suffering. Once clients gain a thorough understanding of the clinging mechanisms of the mind, they can develop a stronger sense of agency when making deliberative life decisions. To achieve this goal, self-cultivation through Buddhist practices, application of Buddhist knowledge and practices to counselling, and psychological counselling skills are essential skillsets for Buddhist counselors.

## CONCLUSION

Since the emergence of mindfulness in professional psychology 30 years ago, the field has been moving towards integrating Buddhism into existing models of counseling and psychotherapy. The forefront of this trend is now moving beyond integration via the development of treatment models employing Buddhist teachings as the core theoretical foundation. At the same time, these new endeavors have tended to remain situated in the contemporary framework of professional counseling albeit substituting the treatment content with Buddhist teachings.

Buddhism has taught us that mind training is a direct experiential path to the liberation of suffering; neuroscience has taught us that training the mind can develop the brain's potential; and the social sciences have taught us that these mind training techniques can be effectively applied to therapeutic relationships and the improvement of others' psychological functioning. This book introduces a model of treatment that adopts Early Buddhist teaching as a foundation, applies psychotherapeutic techniques, and references neuroscientific understandings of the brain and mind. To modify the idiom and metaphor of "old wine in new bottles," Buddhist counseling is "new tea in an old bottle." It substitutes Buddhadhamma (tea) with extant psychological theories (wine) while using the same bottles (counseling approach).

## Contemplative Questions for Buddhist Counselors

Similar to the same steps outlined in Chapter 1, take a mindful moment to sit with your back upright while relaxing your shoulders and chest. Also relax your back, neck, and any tightened muscles in your body. Start with taking several slow and deep breaths to soothe your mind. Next, try to follow your breaths and enjoy them as they are for at least a minute. Breathe slowly and notice any thoughts, emotions, or responses coming up. Here are six follow-up contemplative questions:

- "How do I feel about the term *Buddhist counseling* according to what I have just read?"
- "How do I feel about letting go of my assumptions on science and the third-person approach and starting to think in terms of a first-person approach?"
- "How do I see myself adopting the practices and perspectives of a Buddhist counselor?"
- "How do I feel about beginning my own mindfulness practice?"
- "What is the minimal level of competency I need to attain in order to practice Buddhist counseling interventions?"
- "Am I ready for change?"

Be curious about your thoughts and assumptions. Acknowledge and be mindful of any questions, doubts, or concerns. It is helpful to write out or draw any reflections to consolidate one's thoughts, thereby deepening your personal understanding of your thought processes.

## NOTE

1. Rorschach is a projective psychological assessment tool to measure a number of characteristics, such as personality, cognitive variables, perceptions, and other domains.

## REFERENCES

Ash, M., Harrison, T., Pinto, M., DiClemente, R., & Negi, L. N. (2019, December 13). A Model for Cognitively-Based Compassion Training: Theoretical Underpinnings and Proposed Mechanisms. *Social Theory & Health*. doi:10.1057/s41285-019-00124-x

Axelrod, S. R., Perepletchikova, F., Holtzman, K., & Sinha, R. (2011). Emotion Regulation and Substance Use Frequency in Women with Substance Dependence and Borderline Personality Disorder Receiving Dialectical Behavior Therapy. *The American Journal of Drug and Alcohol Abuse*, *37*, 37–42. doi: 10.3109/00952990.2010.535582

Bach, P., & Hayes, S. C. (2002). The Use of Acceptance and Commitment Therapy to Prevent the Rehospitalization of Psychotic Patients: A Randomized Controlled Trial. *Journal of Consulting and Clinical Psychology*, *70*(5), 1129–1139. doi: 10.1037//0022-006X.70.5.1129

Barinaga, M. (2003). Buddhism and Neuroscience: Studying the Well-Trained Mind. *Science (American Association for the Advancement of Science)*, *302*(5642), 44–46.

Bodhi, B. (Ed.), (2011). *A Comprehensive Manual of Abhidhamma: The Philosophical Psychology of Buddhism*. Seattle, WA: BPS Pariyatti Editions.

Boschin, E. A., Piekema, C., & Buckley, M. J. (2015). Essential functions of primate frontopolar cortex in cognition. *Proceedings of the National Academy of Sciences – PNAS*, *112*(9), E1020–E1027.

Braboszcz, C., Cahn, B. R., Levy, J., Fernandez, M., & Delorme, A. (2017). Increased Gamma Brainwave Amplitude Compared to Control in Three Different Meditation Traditions. *PloS One*, *12*(1), E0170647.

Britton, W. B., Lindahl, J. R., Cahn, B. R., Davis, J. H., & Goldman, R. E. (2014). Awakening is Not a Metaphor: The Effects of Buddhist Meditation Practices on Basic Wakefulness. *Annals of the New York Academy of Sciences*, *1307*, 64–81. http://dx.doi.org/10.1111/nyas.12279

Brown, D. P., & Engler, J. (1980). The Stages of Mindfulness Meditation: A Validation Study. *Journal of Transpersonal Psychology*, *12*(2), 143–192.

Cahn, B. R., Delorme, A., & Polich, J. (2009). Occipital Gamma Activation During Vipassana Meditation. *Cognitive Processing*, *11*(1), 39–56.

Chen, E. Y., Matthews, L., Allen, C., Kuo, J. R., & Linehan, M. M. (2008). Dialectical Behavior Therapy for Clients with Binge-Eating Disorder or Bulimia Nervosa and Borderline Personality Disorder. *International Journal of Eating Disorders*, *41*, 505–512.

Davidson, R. J., & Goleman, D. J. (1977, October). The Role of Attention in Meditation and Hypnosis: A Psychobiological Perspective on Transformations of Consciousness. *International Journal of Clinical and Experimental Hypnosis*, *25*(4), 291–308. doi:10.1080/00207147708415986.

Davidson, R., & Kaszniak, A. (2015). Conceptual and Methodological Issues in Research on Mindfulness and Meditation. *The American Psychologist*, *70*(7), 581–592.

Deatherage, G. (1975). The Clinical Use of "Mindfulness" Meditation Techniques in Short-Term Psychotherapy. *Journal of Transpersonal Psychology*, *7*(2), 133–143.

Dobkin, P. L., Irving, J. A., & Amar, S. (2011). For Whom May Participation in a Mindfulness-Based Stress Reduction Program be Contraindicated? *Mindfulness*, *3*(1), 44–50. https://doi.org/10.1007/s12671-011-0079-9

Evans, S., Ferrando, S., Findler, M., Stowell, C., Smart, C., & Haglin, D. (2007). Mindfulness-Based Cognitive Therapy for Generalized Anxiety Disorder. *Journal of Anxiety Disorders*, *22*(4), 716–721. https://doi.org/10.1016/j.janxdis.2007.07.005

Fjorback, L. O., Arendt, M., Ørnbøl, E., Fink, P., & Walach, H. (2011). Mindfulness-Based Stress Reduction and Mindfulness-Based Cognitive Therapy – A Systematic Review of Randomized Controlled Trials. *Acta Psychiatrica Scandinavica*, *124*(2), 102–119. https://doi.org/10.1111/j.1600-0447.2011.01704.x

Gallegos, A. M., Lytle, M. C., Moynihan, J. A., & Talbot, N. L. (2015). Mindfulness-Based Stress Reduction to Enhance Psychological Functioning and Improve Inflammatory Biomarkers in Trauma-Exposed Women: A Pilot Study. *Psychological Trauma*, *7*(6), 525–532. https://doi.org/10.1037/tra0000053

Goldsmith, R. E., Gerhart, J. I., Chesney, S. A., Burns, J. W., Kleinman, B., & Hood, M. M. (2014). Mindfulness-Based Stress Reduction for Posttraumatic Stress Symptoms: Building Acceptance and Decreasing Shame. *Journal of Evidence-Based Complementary & Alternative Medicine*, *19*(4), 227–234. https://doi.org/10.1177/2156587214533703

Hanh, T. N. (1994). *Zen Keys: A Guide to Zen Practice*. Harmony: NY, New York.

Hanson, R., & Mendius, R. (2009). *Buddha's Brain: The Practical Neuroscience of Happiness, Love, and Wisdom*. New Harbinger Publications.

Hauswald, A., Übelacker, T., Leske, S., & Weisz, N. (2015). What it Means to be Zen: Marked Modulations of Local and Interareal Synchronization During Open Monitoring Meditation. *NeuroImage (Orlando, Fla.)*, *108*, 265–273.

Hayes, S. C., Strosahl, K., & Wilson, K. G. (1999). *Acceptance and Commitment Therapy: An Experiential Approach to Behavior Change.* New York: Guilford Press.

Hofmann, S. G., & Gómez, A. F. (2017). Mindfulness-Based Interventions for Anxiety and Depression. *The Psychiatric Clinics of North America, 40*(4), 739–749. https://doi.org/10.1016/j.psc.2017.08.008

Huxter, M. J. (2007). Mindfulness as Therapy from a Buddhist Perspective. In D. A. Einstein & D. A. Einstein (Eds.), *Innovations and Advances in Cognitive Behaviour Therapy* (pp. 43–55). Bowen Hills, Australia: Australian Academic Press.

Hyland, T. (2015). McMindfulness in the Workplace: Vocational Learning and the Commodification of the Present Moment. *Journal of Vocational Edu- cation and Training, 67,* 219–234. http://dx.doi.org/10.1080/13636820.2015.1022871

Iverson, K. M., Shenk, C., & Fruzzetti, A. E. (2009). Dialectical Behavior Therapy for Women Victims of Domestic Abuse: A Pilot Study. *Professional Psychology: Research and Practice, 40*(3), 242–248. doi: 10.1037/a0013476

Kabat-Zinn, J. (1982, April). An Outpatient Program in Behavioral Medicine for Chronic Pain Patients Based on the Practice of Mindfulness Meditation: Theoretical Considerations and Preliminary Results. *General Hospital Psychiatry, 4*(1), 33–47.

Kabat-Zinn, J. (1991). *Full Catastrophe Living: Using the Wisdom of Your Body and Mind to Face Stress, Pain and Illness.* Delta Trade Paperbacks.

Karlin, B. E., Walser, R. D., Yesavage, J., Zhang, A., Trockel, M., & Taylor, C. B. (2013). Effectiveness of Acceptance and Commitment Therapy for Depression: Comparison Among Older and Younger Veterans. *Aging & Mental Health, 17*(5), 555–563. doi: 10.1080/13607863.2013.789002

Karunadasa, Y. (2013). *Early Buddhist Teachings: The Middle Path Position in Theory and Practice.* Hong Kong: Centre for Buddhist Studies, Hong Kong University.

Kearney, D. J., McDermott, K., Malte, C., Martinez, M., & Simpson, T. L. (2013). Effects of Participation in a Mindfulness Program for Veterans with Posttraumatic Stress Disorder: A Randomized Controlled Pilot Study: MBSR for Veterans with PTSD. *Journal of Clinical Psychology, 69*(1), 14–27. https://doi.org/10.1002/jclp.21911

Kimbrough, E., Magyari, T., Langenberg, P., Chesney, M., & Berman, B. (2010). Mindfulness Intervention for Child Abuse Survivors. *Journal of Clinical Psychology, 66*(1), 17–33. https://doi.org/10.1002/jclp.20624

Kingston, T., Dooley, B., Bates, A., Lawlor, E., & Malone, K. (2007). Mindfulness-Based Cognitive Therapy for Residual Depressive Symptoms. *Psychology and Psychotherapy, 80*(2), 193–203. https://doi.org/10.1348/147608306X116016

Lee, K. C., Oh, A., Zhao, Q., Wu, F.-Y., Chen, S. Y., Diaz, T., & Ong, C. K. (2016). Repentance in Chinese Buddhism: Implications for Mental Health Professionals. *Journal of Spirituality in Mental Health, 18,* 1–17. http://dx.doi.org/10.1080/19349637.2016.1204258

Lee, K. C., Oh, A., Zhao, Q., Wu, F., Chen, S., Diaz, T., & Ong, C. K. (2017). Buddhist counseling: Implications for mental health professionals. *Spirituality In Clinical Practice, 4*(2), 113–128. doi:10.1037/scp0000124

Linehan, M. (1993). *Cognitive-Behavioral Treatment of Borderline Personality Disorder.* New York: Guilford Press.

Linehan, M. M., Schmidt, H., III, Dimeff, L. A., Craft, J. C., Kanter, J., & Comtois, K. A. (1999). Dialectical Behavior Therapy for Patients with Borderline Personality Disorder and Drug-Dependence. *The American Journal on Addictions, 8,* 279–292.

Lutz, A., Greischar, L. L., Rawlings, N. B., Ricard, M., & Davidson, R. J. (2004). Long-Term Meditators Self-Induce High-Amplitude Gamma Synchrony during Mental Practice. *Proceedings of the National Academy of Sciences – PNAS, 101*(46), 16369–16373. https://doi.org/10.1073/pnas.0407401101

McDonell, M. G., Tarantino, J., Dubose, A. P., Matestic, P., Steinmetz, K., Galbreath, H., & McClellan, J. M. (2010). A Pilot Evaluation of Dialectical Behavioural Therapy in Adolescent Long-Term Inpatient Care. *Child and Adolescent Mental Health, 15*(4), 193–196. doi: 10.1111/j.1475-3588.2010.00569.x

McWilliams, S. A. (2011). Contemplating a Contemporary Constructivist Buddhist Psychology. *Journal of Constructivist Psychology, 24*, 268–276. http://dx.doi.org/10.1080/10720537.2011.571566

Miklowitz, D. J., Semple, R. J., Hauser, M., Elkun, D., Weintraub, M. J., & Dimidjian, S. (2015). Mindfulness-Based Cognitive Therapy for Perinatal Women with Depression or Bipolar Spectrum Disorder. *Cognitive Therapy and Research, 39*(5), 590–600. https://doi.org/10.1007/s10608-015-9681-9

Neale, M. (2011). *McMindfulness and Frozen Yoga: Rediscovering the Essential Teachings of Ethics and Wisdom.* Retrieved from https://static1.squarespace.com/static/5a8e29ffcd39c3de866b5e14/t/5b5303d91a e6cf630b641909/1532167130908/McMindfulness.pdf

Negi, L. T., Pace, T. W. W., Wallace, B. A., Raison, C. L., & Schwartz, E. L. (2014, May). Effects of Eight-Week Meditation Training on Hippocampal Volume: A Comparison of Mindful Attention Training and Cognitively-Based Compassion Training. *Journal of Alternative & Complementary Medicine, 20*(5), A24. doi:10.1089/acm.2014.5059.abstract.

Poehlmann-Tynan, J., Engbretson, A., Vigna, A. B., Weymouth, L. A., Burnson, C., Zahn-Waxler, C., Kapoor, A., Gerstein, E. D., Fanning, K. A., & Raison, C. L. (2020, January). Cognitively-Based Compassion Training for Parents Reduces Cortisol in Infants and Young Children. *Infant Mental Health Journal, 41*(1), 126–144. doi:10.1002/imhj.21831.

Reddy, S. D., Negi, L. T., Dodson-Lavelle, B., Ozawa-de Silva, B., Pace, T. W. W., Cole, S. P., Raison, C. L., & Craighead, L. W. (2013, February). Cognitive-Based Compassion Training: A Promising Prevention Strategy for At-Risk Adolescents. *Journal of Child and Family Studies, 22*(2), 219–230. doi:10.1007/s10826-012-9571-7

Rungreangkulkij, S., & Wongtakee, W. (2008). The Psychological Impact of Buddhist Counseling for Patients Suffering From Symptoms of Anxiety. *Archives Of Psychiatric Nursing, 22*(3), 127–134. doi:10.1016/j.apnu.2007.07.004

Science Council. (2009, March). *Our Definition of Science.* https://sciencecouncil.org/about-science/our-definition-of-science/#:~:text=Science%20is%20the%20pursuit%20and,Evidence

Segal, Z. V., Williams, J. M. G., & Teasdale, J. D. (2002). *Mindfulness-Based Cognitive Therapy for Depression: A New Approach to Preventing Relapse.* New York: Guilford Press.

Shonin, E., Van Gordon, W., & Griffiths, M. D. (2014, June). Meditation Awareness Training (MAT) for Improved Psychological Well-Being: A Qualitative Examination of Participant Experiences. *Journal of Religion and Health, 53*(3), 849–863. doi:10.1007/s10943-013-9679-0

Shonin, E., Van Gordon, W., Dunn, T. J., Singh, N. N., & Griffiths, M. D. (2014, December). Meditation Awareness Training (MAT) for Work-Related Wellbeing and Job Performance: A Randomised Controlled Trial. *International Journal of Mental Health and Addiction, 12*(6), 806–823. doi:10.1007/s11469-014-9513-2

Simiola, V., Neilson, E. C., Thompson, R., & Cook, J. M. (2015). Preferences for Trauma Treatment: A Systematic Review of the Empirical Literature. *Psychological Trauma: Theory, Research, Practice, and Policy, 7*, 516–524. http://dx.doi.org/10.1037/tra0000038

Spinhoven, P., Huijbers, M. J., Ormel, J., & Speckens, A. E. (2017). Improvement of Mindfulness Skills During Mindfulness-Based Cognitive Therapy Predicts Long-Term Reductions of Neuroticism in Persons with Recurrent Depression in Remission. *Journal of Affective Disorders, 213*, 112–117. http://dx.doi.org/10.1016/j.jad.2017.02.011

Srichannil, C., & Prior, S. (2014). Practise What You Preach: Counsellors' Experience of Practising Buddhist Counselling in Thailand. *International Journal for the Advancement of Counselling, 36*(3), 243–261. doi:http://dx.doi.org.eproxy2.lib.hku.hk/10.1007/s10447-013-9204-x

Steil, R., Dyer, A., Priebe, K., Kleindienst, N., & Bohus, M. (2011). Dialectical Behavior Therapy for Posttraumatic Stress Disorder Related to Childhood Sexual Abuse: A Pilot Study of an Intensive Residential Treatment Program. *Journal of Traumatic Stress, 24*(1), 102–106. doi: 10.1002/jts.20617

Sun, J. (2014). Mindfulness in Context: A Historical Discourse Analysis. *Contemporary Buddhism, 15*, 394–415. http://dx.doi.org/10.1080/14639947.2014.978088

Sun, S., Pickover, A. M., Goldberg, S. B., Bhimji, J., Nguyen, J. K., Evans, A. E., Patterson, B., & Kaslow, N. J. (2019, August 1). For Whom Does Cognitively Based Compassion Training (Cbct) Work? An Analysis of Predictors and Moderators among African American Suicide Attempters. *Mindfulness.* doi:10.1007/s12671-019-01207-6

Tang, Y. (2017). *The Neuroscience of Mindfulness Meditation* (1st ed.). Cham: Palgrave Macmillan.

Tang, Y., Hölzel, B. K., & Posner, M. I. (2015). The Neuroscience of Mindfulness Meditation. *Nature Reviews. Neuroscience, 16*(4), 213–225. doi: https://doi.org/10.1038/nrn3916

Twohig, M. P., Hayes, S. C., Plumb, J. C., Pruitt, L. D., Collins, A. B., Hazlett-Stevens, H., & Woidneck, M. R. (2010). A Randomized Clinical Trial of Acceptance and Commitment Therapy Versus Progressive Relaxation Training for Obsessive-Compulsive Disorder. *Journal of Consulting and Clinical Psychology, 78*(5), 705–716. doi: 10.1037/a0020508

Van Gordon, W., & Shonin, E. (2020). Second-Generation Mindfulness-Based Interventions: Toward More Authentic Mindfulness Practice and Teaching. *Mindfulness, 11*, 1–4.

Varela, F., Rosch, E., & Thompson, E. (1991). *The Embodied Mind.* Cambridge, Massachusetts: MIT Press.

Wagner, A. W., Rizvi, S. L., & Harned, M. S. (2007). Applications of Dialectical Behavior Therapy to the Treatment of Complex Trauma-Related Problems: When One Case Formulation Does Not Fit All. *Journal of Traumatic Stress, 20*(4), 391–400. doi: 10.1002/jts.20268

Watson, J. (2013, January 22). Marine Corps Studying How Mindfulness Meditation Can Benefit Troops. *The Huffington Post.* Retrieved from www.huffingtonpost.com/2013/01/22/marine-corps-mindfulness-meditation_n_2526244.html

Wu, B. W. Y., Gao, J., Leung, H. K., & Sik, H. H. (2019, January 17). A Randomized Controlled Trial of Awareness Training Program (Atp), a Group-Based Mahayana Buddhist Intervention. *Mindfulness.* doi:10.1007/s12671-018-1082-1

Zak, P. J. (2017). Matthieu Ricard and Wolf Singer's Beyond the Self: Conversations between Buddhism and Neuroscience. *Cerebrum (New York, NY), 2017,* Cerebrum (New York, NY), 2017-11, Vol. 2017.

# CHAPTER 3

# Major Theoretical Assumptions in Buddhist Counseling

In a theoretical orientation, certain theoretical constructs guide the development of theory and practice. These central elements provide a paradigm to explain all human phenomena such as human nature, psychological disorders, interactions between the environment and human beings, and healing factors. This chapter discusses three elements central to Buddhism. The chapter will introduce the most fundamental constructs, namely, the theory of dependent co-arising (*paṭiccasamuppāda*), dukkha, and non-self.

## MAJOR THEORETICAL ASSUMPTIONS

With its ultimate goal of liberating human beings from suffering, early Buddhism emphasized an empiricism that involves the careful and comprehensive investigation and analysis of the mind to gain self-knowledge and knowledge of reality for the purpose of liberation. The Buddha's own realization can be summarized as resting upon three major theoretical assumptions: dependent co-arising, suffering, and non-self.

### Dependent Co-Arising

In the Buddhist worldview, a pattern of arising, changing, and ceasing characterizes all phenomena. In this flow and dissolutions of events, our mind experiences a fluid and ever-changing existence together with an awareness that everything we desire will eventually end. Ultimately, every experience—including bodily sensations, feelings, perceptions, intention, and consciousness—is interrelated and interdependent; they do not have any self-existent or self-sustaining permanent characteristics (Tirch et al., 2016). The core Buddhist teaching behind this assumption is the theory of dependent origination (*paṭiccasamuppāda*). According to the *Dasabala Sutta*, the principle of *paṭiccasamuppāda* can be summarized in the following short formula:

> When this is, that is,
> With this arising, that arises;
> When this is not, that is not,
> With this ending, that ends.
>     (Bodhi, 2003, p. 533)

DOI: 10.4324/9781003025450-3

In other words, dependent origination means that all phenomena arise only with other phenomena (Bornaetxea et al., 2014). Every phenomenon exists conditionally and interdependently because everything is mutually dependent on everything else for its existence.

Before even the simplest of phenomena occurs, numerous factors have collaboratively contributed to its existence. The phenomenon, in turn, will subside when these interdependent factors that support it are no longer present. The "phenomenon" might be anything in the world, including a lifetime, people, relationships, spaces, places, thoughts, emotions, ideas, and beliefs.

Unique among religious traditions, the Buddhist teaching of dependent origination describes the process of life without introducing any creator or created being. Instead, all phenomena are seen as emerging from a plurality of causes and conditions that co-originate and co-arise within and across lifetimes (Bornaetxea et al., 2014). Dependent origination also implies the non-existence of a permanent self and, therefore, there is no self to suffer annihilation. Instead, the self is an experience grounded in phenomena that are constantly susceptible to change. This contrasts with the impulse of the human mind to form a fixed understanding of phenomena and a belief in the intrinsic, independent, and permanent nature of existence, the result being the creation of constructs or logical abstractions based on the reification of ontological events. For example, seeing a flower is a phenomenon supported by the attention we pay to an object: our eyes receive the sensation of light and our previous knowledge of flowers recognizes the present object as similar, while the object itself is supported by sunlight, soil, oxygen, nutrients, seeds, and other elements. If any of these conditions change, the phenomenon of a "flower" can change or cease. In other words, as a constructed entity, a flower does not have a self-existent nature.

Let us see how such a principle manifests as depression. From the perspective of dependent co-arising, depression is only a mental label attached to a phenomenon. It is constructed by its interdependent conditions at a given moment, such as physical pain in the stomach and back, unpleasant sensations in the body and mind, tiredness, recognition of a mental category called "depression," the intention and urge to resist this state, inner voices and images that ruminate over past events, ill-will towards oneself, and related factors. If one or several of these conditions were to cease, the phenomenon of depression experienced at each moment may change or cease. This chain of causation can be preempted by self-compassion that dissolves self-directed ill-will and assuages strong physical discomfort.

## Non-Self

Distinct from most philosophical assumptions about the existence of a deeper, authentic, or permanent self, Buddhism describes a dependently originated self that does not inherently exist. This position stands in critical opposition to theories assuming the existence of an eternal soul, a spiritual connection with a higher power, or an intrinsic and authentic "me." For newcomers to Buddhism, a common question is, "If there is not a 'me,' then who is behind the consciousness of reading this chapter and thinking about these ideas?"

The short answer is that the Buddhist theory of non-self does not refer to the absence of self. Instead, it merely describes the mind's inclination to attribute to neutral phenomena a fantasized concrete identity. This inclination can be described as habitual energy that leads the consciousness to claim ownership of mental and bodily experiences, thereby fabricating an independent self-notion or self-identity. In other words, there is not any permanent entity called "the self" that possesses a mind. Instead, consciousness and its mental processes comprise the mind, and the mind becomes deluded when it clings to the notion that "this is my self."

*Anatta*, or non-self, is an essential concept in Buddhism. Based on the assumption of dependent co-arising, Buddhists posit that "self" is a concept without an objective reality: the experience of "self" is just a product of a logical abstraction or reification that animates and concretizes impersonal objects to mediate between the "outside" world and a delusional "personal identity." Driven by a strong desire to exist, the human mind subjectively clings to body, feelings, consciousness, experiences, values, relationships, and other conditions to convince itself of its own authentic and sustainable existence. Buddhism, however, assumes that cognitive events like thoughts do not arise in the mind; instead, the cognitive events themselves are the mind—there is not any "self" which plays the role of prime processor.

For example, one might think, "I am eating cheesecake and I love it!" However, from the viewpoint of dependent origination, "I" and "cheesecake" are not separate entities. When consciousness arises during the interaction between the taste buds and the cheesecake, there is a pleasant feeling, and the mind starts to cling to this feeling by proliferating thoughts about it: "It tastes so good," "It is so comforting and soothing for my soul," and "I have to have some cheesecake every Friday night or else I will be agitated for the whole week." Once the mind gains enough mental distance to observe how it engages in the phenomenon of eating cheesecake, it understands that the experience of eating cheesecake is just the result of various conditions (the cheesecake, the restaurant, friends in the surroundings, tiredness from work, the sensation on the tongue, the feelings that arise, the mind's inner dialogue, the thirst, the heat in the chest, the release of tension in the shoulders). It will not find a solid entity called "I." These experiences of the consciousness occurring in the moment are influenced by conditions and factors that affect the state of mind. In other words, "self" is only a label for a provisional, conceptual, and transient existence experienced by the mind instead of an intrinsic and authentic being. One of the most common Buddhist ways to describe this concept of the self is through the notion of the five aggregates.

## The Five Aggregates

According to Early Buddhist scriptures, the five aggregates (*khandhas*) model is the most commonly used across Buddhist traditions to analyze the mind as well as the concept of personal identity. Hence, this chapter will focus on the psychology of the five aggregates.

The five aggregates are five interdependent sets of processes that interact with the world, generate the idiosyncratic experiences for the human mind, and fuel our continued existence (Table 3.1). Suffering begins when an individual wrongly identifies the five aggregates as self, an independent and permanent entity. Buddhist scriptures use the metaphor of a chariot to describe a human being and illustrate the concept of the self. For example, the Buddha

TABLE 3.1 The Five Aggregates as described in Early Buddhism

| Aggregates | Description | Application |
| --- | --- | --- |
| 1. Form (*Rūpa*) | Physical body made up of the four elements and consisting of the six faculties: eye, ear, nose, tongue, body, and mind. | A healthy eye capable of seeing is led by eye-consciousness to contact an external visual object. |
| 2. Feeling Tone (*Vedanā*) | A pleasant feeling, unpleasant feeling, or neutral feeling arising from contact with form. | A pleasant visual feeling arising from sense contact. |
| 3. Perception (*Saññā*) | Based on past experiences, the mind interprets an object as a concept. | From past experiences, the visual object's features and characteristics give rise to the perception of a "tree." |
| 4. Volitional Formations (*Saṅkhāra*) | A motivational force that leads the mind in a certain direction and which fabricates and further constructs perceptions related to the notion of a self. | The notion of self identifies with and fabricates further on the "tree" and thinks of it as a "beautiful and peaceful tree." |
| 5. Consciousness (*Viññāṇa*) | Bare attention that cognizes mental experiences. | Consciousness cognizes the other aggregates and it can notice the mental experience of "I am appreciating my beautiful and peaceful tree in my garden." |

expounded the question: "What is a chariot?" One can answer by referring to the parts of a chariot, such as its axle, wheels, chariot-body, and flagstaff, yoke, reins, goad-stick; but none of these is an entity called "chariot," and each can be reduced to smaller parts or different aggregates (AN 3.15). In essence, we label the combination of constituents a "chariot," but this is nothing more than a construct or logical abstraction based on a reification of the whole (SN 5.10, Miln 2). The analogy demonstrates that there is no separate "self" that can be found in any single one, or any combination, of the five aggregates; instead, "self" is a denomination for the collective experiences of the five aggregates.

## Form

For consciousness to arise, an object needs to be present to the sense organs in order to capture the attention of the mind, such as using our eyes (sense organ) to read (consciousness) this book (sense object). This contact between sense object, sense organ, and consciousness initiates a direct sense contact, a bare sensory input devoid of any subjective inclinations (Boisvert, 1997). In this process, any external sense object is not contacted, but its mental imprint arises from the contact between sensory organs and sense objects. This arising occurs because sense objects are *potentially* perceived while sense contacts are *actually* perceived. For instance, when we are angry with somebody, we are often not mad at a physically present person in front of us; instead, we are mad at a mental impression of that person. Buddhism suggests that the solution to such psychological issues should ultimately involve transforming our internal mental processes rather than changing the external objects of perception.

## Feeling Tone

Sensation, the internal response to sensory input, arises after the entrance of the initial sensory input. Sensation is a primitive response to sense contact that manifests as three feeling tones: pleasant, unpleasant, and neutral. Sensation can be understood as a primitive and innate somatic feeling (Boisvert, 1997). Occurring without cognitive interpretation, it is our most straightforward form of direct response to sensory inputs. When we smell something pungent like rotten eggs or leaking gas, an unpleasant feeling instantly arises—we do not need to undergo lengthy interpretations to determine that it is unpleasant.

## Perception

Sensation serves as a condition for the arising of perception. Perception is a process of recognizing, classifying, and conceptualizing the incoming sensory data, followed by the naming and labeling of a perceived object based on past experiences. For example, when we recognize the redness of a shirt, we categorize its color as "red" by associating the color with our previous labels (Boisvert, 1997). As each individual has a unique concept and knowledge system, the same sensory inputs can generate different perceptions. Thus, the Buddhist understanding of perception appears to have some parallels to ideas in cognitive psychology regarding the cognitive processing of sensory information.

## Volition

Volition is a crucial concept in Buddhism because it is the core driving force of the mind that determines consequences, like the engine of a speedboat that determines direction and destination. Volition is the subtle force of intentional physical, verbal, or mental action that can generate an effect that will, in turn, become a new condition that produces a further effect. Volition is also analogous to a wheel that keeps rolling as far as the momentum that sets it in motion allows (AN 3.15). In contemporary language, it can be understood as mental and behavioral choices, and the nature of these choices will directly determine one's level of suffering. Volition tends to create a positive feedback loop. Whenever we make a volitional decision, the energy fuels itself and fosters a stronger habit.

## Consciousness

Consciousness is mere attention or pure "knowing" without any inherent content. Its content is derived from the other aggregates, that is, it is responsible for our cognizance of them. In the confluence of sense object, sense organ, and sense consciousness, sense contact arises from the conjugation of the sense organs, the sense objects, and consciousness of the sense organs. Consequently, the five aggregates are part of an interdependent cyclical process—consciousness, the last element of the five aggregates, becomes the condition for the arising of sense contact of the next cycle. Consciousness can also be seen as a faculty required for the cognizance of pure sensation and conceptualization. Buddhist scriptures explain that when one has an intention (i.e., volition) and obsesses about something, there is support for the establishment of consciousness, which then fuels the production of renewed existence (i.e., the next five-aggregate cycle; SN 12.38). In this way, the cycle of existence and human suffering repeats itself.

### Five Aggregates in Each Moment of Experience

The five aggregates work together in each and every moment of our disparate experiences. Let us use smoking as an example. When we contact an external stimulus, we label the sensation pleasant and recognize its features, such as "freshness" in the mouth and the taste of the tobacco that we label as "smoking," which captures the full awareness of our consciousness and brings us a pleasant feeling. Naming and conceptualization performed by the first three aggregates do not necessarily lead to psychological problems, but our attachment to such names, labels, or pleasures do. In other words, thoroughly enjoying a cigarette is harmless from a Buddhist perspective, but the craving for the same pleasure and holding onto a concept that "I have to smoke to enjoy a break!" instantly creates mental distress. Through repeated decisions to smoke and temporarily satiate the craving, the volitional energy grows and becomes a habit. Since every conditioned phenomenon is subject to constant changes (when the conditions cease to exist, the pleasant sensation also ceases to exist), a discrepancy between our fixated expectations and reality arises, creating deep inner dissatisfaction with the present moment. However, the intense volition energy makes it difficult to stop the craving, and this state of mind tends to resist the changes in conditions. A mental volition emerges—"Just one more cigarette would not kill me! Let's do it, and I will quit once I have kids"—and the person decides to have another cigarette regardless of health conditions, resulting in increased physical and mental suffering.

### *Dukkha* as an Innate Psychopathological Symptom

In Buddhism, *dukkha*, translated as "suffering" or "dissatisfaction," is the main target of "treatment." One significant difference between Buddhism and clinical psychology is that Buddhism understands suffering as a universal phenomenon and a common human experience instead of a psychopathology. In other words, psychological disorders are all part of *dukkha* and, to a greater or lesser extent, are an inevitable experience for every individual living in this world. In other words, Buddhism proposes that the factors that cause suffering— such as separation from loved ones, not getting what one wants, or association with people and things we dislike—are always present but that the subjective experience of suffering can be reduced. Such factors can even, in the case of enlightenment, be eliminated. In a general sense, to be liberated from suffering is to understand the laws of all things (*Dhamma*) and to cultivate the mind through consistent and progressive mindfulness practices.

In the Buddhist paradigm, the root of suffering is ignorance. The idea of ignorance in Buddhism never refers to a lack of secular knowledge or intelligence in any subject matter. Instead, it refers to a lack of understanding and acceptance of the universal laws of dependent origination. Under the law of dependent origination, every phenomenon is signified by three marks of existence: (1) impermanence (*anicca*), meaning that every phenomenon in the world is constantly arising and passing, that is, our experience is constantly changing; (2) due to (1), suffering (*dukkha*) means that every phenomenon is unsatisfactory and any object of attachment will inevitably change or cease to exist; and (3) non-self (*anatta*), referring to the fact that the existence of self is ultimately dependent on other things that are impermanent, such that the self is neither independent nor stable.

Buddhism holds that all forms of mental irregularity are derived from our over-attachment and identification of the five aggregates with a "self." The five aggregates have been compared to masses of fire (SN 35.28). They arise, pass away, and constantly change, subject to the law of dependent origination and the three marks of existence (SN 22.36), giving rise to the experiences of living, but not necessarily causing suffering. In fact, they are neutral and conditioned phenomena. Rather, the cause of suffering is the mind's clinging to the five aggregates, which results in the mental creation of an autonomous and permanent sense of self due to conceptualization and reification. Deep-rooted habits then cling to the idea that these sets of ever-changing processes equal "me," while constantly arising and ceasing thoughts and emotions are viewed as "my thoughts" and "my emotions" and grasped onto as real. From this attachment to a fixated sense of self, we begin to erroneously believe that there is a separate, inherently existing personality, and this construct is strengthened by defining ourselves through external objects, but which then causes clinging to a sense-pleasure or a wrong view (i.e., "this is mine" and "this is me"). The problem that results from such beliefs is impaired functionality.

Further, to protect the illusory existence of this self-identity, whenever the five aggregates change without our expecting them to, a habitual ego defense mechanism like a "fight-flight-freeze" reaction is automatically activated. As a result, the totality of our experience is confined to the limited perspective of ourselves, rendering us unable to accept reality as it is and present appropriate responses to the new sets of causes and conditions that meet us in the present moment. This is how suffering arises.

For example, when one witnesses the demise of loved ones, suffering results because the illusory self is disappointed by its powerlessness to control inevitable and uncontrollable life changes. Therefore, truly seeing, understanding, and accepting these three marks of existence can provide a beacon of hope in the darkness of ignorance as well as offer the remedy to suffering. However, attachment to the notion of a self makes apprehending reality difficult because our mind has a strong habitual energy to believe in its inherent existence. Fortunately, the three marks of existence imply that making changes to psychological phenomena, and therefore the elimination of mental suffering, is possible.

## PATH TO LIBERATION: CULTIVATION OF THE HIGHEST PSYCHOLOGICAL STATE

Since the root of suffering is ignorance, knowledge is the most obvious therapeutic means for eradicating suffering. The first step to proper knowledge—gaining awareness—requires a continuous process of observing and noting how one's mind engages in actions that induce suffering. A lay understanding of Buddhism is that it requires letting go of things. However, no one can let go of anything if they do not know what, or how, these things are being held. Letting go does not require the denial or rejection of clinging. Letting go, instead, is a product of having the right view towards the arising and cessation of phenomena, understanding the reason for clinging, the multiple ways and processes through which the mind clings, and the suffering that such clinging brings about. When the mind sees and accepts the true nature of phenomena, it voluntarily and momentarily chooses to release it. This act means "letting go" of the object. It results from a continuous effort to observe one's mind and cultivate a "higher mind" that can rest in a state of concentration and clarity. As a provisional understanding, the "higher mind" is a clear and stable mental state that can be trained, through self-cultivation, to see the aggregate of mind's unskilful actions and gain knowledge of which causes and conditions result in suffering. This knowledge helps people to make choices that result in less suffering.

Buddhism has developed a complete and structured framework for explaining and treating psychological problems based on the Four Noble Truths as realized by the historical Buddha, which is still applicable today. The Four Noble Truths—suffering, its origin, cessation, and path to the cessation—are the essence of the Buddha's teachings, as follows:

## Four Noble Truths

1 **Suffering.** To understand the Buddhist meaning of suffering, one needs to momentarily suspend the assumption of suffering as conceptualized by Western psychology. In general, traditional Western psychology describes suffering as a psychological pain that is an abnormal state of body and mind. For example, The Diagnostic and Statistical Manual of Mental Disorders, Fifth Edition (DSM-5) defines suffering as a mental health disorder, a psychopathological label that describes clinical symptoms as impairing a person's psychological functioning (American Psychiatric Association, 2013). In Buddhism, by contrast, suffering is a normal, inevitable, and multifaceted experience of life. Suffering, or dukkha, means dissatisfaction. The historical Buddha taught a path that can help any person cope adaptively with, but also transcend, unavoidable and painful dissatisfaction. He used his own experiences to illustrate suffering and help others see its nature and become liberated from it. We will briefly mention three explanations in this section: First, suffering is a reality of existence even though the extent and nature of suffering vary. Second, suffering can be mental or physical. Third, the human mind is "ignorant" in that it has an unskillful inclination to misinterpret experiences and aggravate the subjective experience of suffering. To liberate from suffering, one must first understand its nature and causes.

2 **Cause of suffering.** The etiology of suffering in Western psychology is usually explained by biological, psychological, environmental, social, spiritual, or other causes. Buddhism sees the ultimate cause of suffering as craving, or tanha, which is an intense desire and lust for sensual pleasure, self-existence, or self-annihilation. In short, the human mind has a powerful urge to exist continuously, so we try hard to convince ourselves of self-existence by building self-identities, personalizing belongings, developing relationships, and consolidating every encounter with a self. Explaining why craving is the cause of suffering requires understanding Buddhist assumptions about reality. Buddhism strongly asserts that we do not exist the way we want to, which is

a highly dissatisfying experience if we cannot accept this truth. According to the law of dependent origination, all phenomena—including consciousness, the concept of self, and the "I" who is typing and writing this chapter—arise through the amalgamation or co-arising of particular causes and conditions, and they cease when such causes and conditions change. In particular, the self is only viewed as the result of the interaction among five interdependent sets of processes called the five aggregates (this will be covered in-depth later). If an individual personalizes, identifies, and fabricates such ontological events to claim ownership of experiences but neglects the impermanent nature of phenomena, they will inevitably experience dissatisfaction. Infantilizing a child to feel one's ownership as a parent, repeatedly using cosmetic surgery to resist aging, or taking responsibility for something that one has no control over are some examples of denying reality.

3 **Cessation of suffering.** While traditional Western psychotherapy aims to reduce clinical symptoms, the ultimate goal of Buddhism is to achieve enlightenment or *nibbāna* (*nirvāṇa* in Sanskrit), which is regarded as the highest psychological state. Nibbāna arises from realizing the true nature of all phenomena and seeing things as they are with the help of the three marks of existence: knowing the nature of suffering, seeing phenomena as dependently originated, and not craving a notion of self. The Third Noble Truth emphasizes that there is a path to this ultimate state of mind which instills faith and assists practitioners to start the path of liberation. The Third Noble Truth also teaches us to form a different relationship with suffering. Instead of rejecting it or seeing it as a perpetual experience, the cessation of suffering can start by fostering the radical acceptance of suffering and seeking insight into the transient nature and interdependent conditions sustaining the experience of suffering. Walking towards this direction can reduce our suffering before we reach ultimate liberation.

4 **Path to the cessation of suffering.** The Historical Buddha described a methodical system to cultivate the cessation of suffering, namely the Noble Eightfold Path of eight practices categorized according to three pillars: (1) *Wisdom*: right view and right intentions, (2) *Discipline*: right speech, right action, right livelihood, and (3) *Concentration*: right effort, right mindfulness, and right concentration. Since the root of suffering is ignorance, the antidote to suffering is to raise awareness of the true nature of phenomena through this three-pillar practice of reducing the choices resulting in suffering, cultivating a stable, clear, and discerning mind through meditation, and reflecting on and contemplating the true nature of all phenomena to see reality as it is.

# A THEORETICAL ORIENTATION BASED ON NON-SELF AS A CORE THEORETICAL CONSTRUCT

In contrast to the theoretical orientation of contemporary psychotherapy models, which are based on the development of a self, a Buddhist counseling model is built on the teaching of non-self. A theoretical orientation based on non-self and the other two characteristics of existence should have several features.

First, the treatment focus should emphasize reducing the client's grasping, especially the clinging to the notion of a reified self. Buddhist counseling differs from traditional Buddhist practices, which have the ultimate goal of liberation from suffering. Clients who seek counseling are likely to aim for a reduction of suffering yet may not be interested in renunciation for the sake of liberation. Therefore, it is more appropriate to consider clients as householders who can benefit from Buddhism. Driven by the idea of non-self, a major reason for suffering is seeing self in non-self. Instead of fostering a solid sense of self, Buddhist counselors will understand the delusional nature of the self-notion and cultivate clients' mental capacity for detachment, or non-attachment. In psychological terms, this mental capacity refers to cognitive flexibility or the ability of perspective taking. In this approach, Buddhist counselors can help clients understand their self-notions, reveal and process the cravings related to those self-notions, see the dukkha arise from craving, and skilfully make wholesome decisions to pause or stop mental acts of clinging. Such treatment should follow the Four Noble Truths as a guiding principle.

In helping clients detach from clinging to self-notions, dependent co-arising should be a guiding principle. The self-notion is divisible into analyzable parts and components, and such deconstructions can challenge and dissolve clinging. Buddhist counselors can consider guiding clients to experientially break down a mental phenomenon into various support factors and conditions of the body and mind. For example, every moment of emotional suffering is a product of multiple causes and conditions. A suffering client usually holds onto a particular view, emotion, or concept, leaving most of the causal conditions unknown. In the case of a client who reports being "depressed" while staying at home during the COVID-19 pandemic of 2020/2021, the client appears to see permanence in impermanence and develops a subjective interpretation of being confined with no way out. Buddhist counselors can acknowledge the client's depression while guiding the client to raise awareness of environmental factors, sociopolitical stressors, social stressors, lifestyle changes, loss of coping strategies, bodily sensations of a depressed mood, unpleasant feelings in the mind and body, the perception of being confined, conceptual proliferations of hopelessness, and other conditions.

To help the client practice a perspective taking from the viewpoint of dependent co-arising, an effective practice is to educate the client on the impermanent nature of things and the constantly changing nature of phenomena. For example, in the 2002–2004 outbreak of SARS, a Buddhist counselor first discussed with the client how the SARS pandemic led to a depressing time. With investigation and discernment of the multiple and interdependent conditions contributing to the depressed mood, the client is less likely to become attached to concepts such as "I am depressed and I can't do anything about it," and can develop new insights such as "There are so many factors that make me feel depressed, it is reasonable to feel this way."

Last but not least, a non-self approach should aim to raise clients' awareness of dukkha in their clinging onto a self-notion. Seeing sukkha (happiness, pleasure, joy, and ease) in dukkha is another common reason for suffering. Guided by the teaching of dukkha, Buddhist counselors can help clients cultivate a more comprehensive and heedful awareness of one's experiences that result from mind acts. The goal is to help clients see the danger and aversive consequences of mental acts and skilfully decide not to delight in such cogitations. They can learn ways to stop or escape from the unwholesome stream of these mental acts. For example, one maladaptive coping strategy for stress is drinking. While alcohol consumption may induce a temporary sense of pleasure, overconsumption tends to result in insomnia, depressed mood, anxiety, physical harm to organs, addiction, and impaired judgment, leading to risk-taking behaviors. One way for Buddhist counselors to help clients see dukkha in sukkha is to collaborate with them to see the consequences of the volition to drink, discern the pleasant feelings that arise from thoughts of drinking, develop mental reminders of unpleasant consequences, explore wholesome coping strategies to replace drinking, and use mindfulness techniques to refrain from engaging in alluring fabrications. Among these techniques, the most critical initial step may be the mental reminder of the danger in drinking, which is the realization of dukkha in sukkha, and thereby to guard the mind against suffering.

In summary, non-self, dukkha, impermanence, and the Four Noble Truths are regarded as the most important theoretical constructs for Buddhist counseling, all of which guide and inform any treatment plan. Among these three, the current theoretical orientation will use non-self as the guiding principle to illustrate other components of the model. The coming chapters will sequentially introduce a Buddhist counseling approach based on the theory of non-self.

## CONCLUSION

In traditional Buddhism, there is a three-step learning process: exposure, contemplation, and practice. To reach the end goal of embodying Buddhist knowledge to liberate from suffering, one needs to begin with a gradual learning exposure of reading and listening to Buddhist wisdom. To facilitate this process, the current chapter has provided an overview of core Buddhist teachings that would prove germane to all Buddhist counseling approaches. This knowledge foundation lays the groundwork for further contemplative and experiential learning. Therefore, the first step for Buddhist counselors is to familiarize themselves with the core Buddhist assumptions of the world and human nature.

The next step is for Buddhist counselors to reflect on this worldview and try to use this perspective to inform how we should see ourselves and our clients. One common challenge is the contemplation of non-self because we generally ascribe high importance to what we are, living life with the self as the central reference point. Knowing that clinging onto this self-notion is the origin of suffering, the remedy is to detach from and dissolve this rigid grasping. Holding tight onto any view, meaning, identity, or object, regardless of how beautiful or convincing it is, will eventually result in pain. Instead of dropping it and letting it go, a tangible step is to examine whether we can ease our rigidity and hold onto it more skilfully. When we try to change our way of grasping, we free up the potential to let go, taking a step towards a life with less suffering. It is a continual process, and each time we loosen our grasp, we are wiring a new and more wholesome habit. This process needs to start with the Buddhist counselor gaining direct experience of him or herself before we can influence our clients.

## Contemplative Questions for Buddhist Counselors

To practice this chapter, we will try to connect your experience in reading this chapter with a brief experiment in perspective taking: the perspective of non-self.

Take a moment to sit with your back upright while relaxing your shoulders and chest. Take several slow and deep breaths to tranquilize your mind. Follow your breaths and enjoy them as they are. After breathing for a minute, gently focus on the following questions. Read slowly and notice your thoughts, comments, and answers that come up:

- "Who am I?"
- "What labels have I put on myself?"
- "What labels have I let other people put on me?"
- "If I say, 'I am nothing more than a defined identity,' how would that make me feel?"
- "If I can let go of all the burdens and expectations of others to be someone, how would that make me feel?"
- "If I choose to let go of who I am, how would I act differently at this moment?"

Take another moment to check in with yourself. Note any bodily sensations, thoughts, images, and feelings. Regardless of how pleasant or unpleasant they may be, just notice them and allow them to be without altering or resisting them. Take note of any strong thoughts or feelings, and try to be curious about what triggered such experiences in you. Feel free to write down any thoughts and emotions. Please remember, mindfulness aims at creating a certain mental distance. Maintain a space with these experiences, like observing a traffic jam or looking at wildfire afar from the top of a mountain. All you need to know is that these experiences are there.

# REFERENCES

American Psychiatric Association. (2013). *Diagnostic and Statistical Manual of Mental Disorders* (5th ed.). https://doi.org/10.1176/appi.books.9780890425596

AN 3.15. Rathakara (Pacetana) Sutta: The Chariot Maker, translated from the Pali by Bhikkhu, T. (2013, November 30). *Access to Insight (BCBS Edition)*. Retrieved January 5, 2020, from www.accesstoinsight.org/tipitaka/an/an03/an03.015.than.html.

Bodhi, B. (2003). *The Connected Discourses of the Buddha: A Translation of the Samyutta Nikaya*. Somerville, MA: Wisdom Publication.

Bornaetxea, F. R., Morón, D. A., Gil, A. A., & Molloy, A. A. H. (2014). Construction of reality or dependent origination? From scientific psychotherapy to responsible attention. *Contemporary Buddhism*, 15(2), 216–243. https://doi.org/10.1080/14639947.2014.934057

Boisvert, M. (1997). *The Five Aggregates: Understanding Theravāda Psychology and Soteriology* (1st Indian ed., Bibliotheca Indo-Buddhica; no. 185).Delhi, India: Sri Satguru Publications.

Miln 2. The Questions of King Milinda, translated from the Pali by Davids, T. W. R. (1890). *The Questions of King Milinda*. Oxford: The Clarendon Press.

SN 5.10.Vajira Sutta: Vajira, translated from the Pali by Bhikkhu, B. (2013, November 30). *Access to Insight (BCBS Edition)*. Retrieved January 5, 2020, from www.accesstoinsight.org/tipitaka/sn/sn05/sn05.010.bodh.html.

SN 12.38. Cetana Sutta: Intention, translated from the Pali by Bhikkhu, T. (2013, November 30). *Access to Insight (BCBS Edition)*. Retrieved January 5, 2020, from www.accesstoinsight.org/tipitaka/sn/sn12/sn12.038.than.html.

SN 22.36. Bhikkhu Sutta: The Monk, translated from the Pali by Bhikkhu, T. (2013, November 30). *Access to Insight (BCBS Edition)*. Retrieved January 5, 2020, from www.accesstoinsight.org/tipitaka/sn/sn22/sn22.036.than.html.

SN 35.28. Adittapariyaya Sutta: The Fire Sermon, translated from the Pali by Bhikkhu, T. (2013, November 30). *Access to Insight (BCBS Edition)*. Retrieved January 5, 2020, from www.accesstoinsight.org/tipitaka/sn/sn35/sn35.028.than.html.

Tirch, D., Silberstein-Tirch, L. R., & Kolts, R. L. (2016). *Buddhist Psychology and Cognitive-Behavioral Therapy: A Clinician's Guide*. New York: Guilford Press.

# CHAPTER 4

# Overview of the Note, Know, Choose Intervention Model

The essence of Buddhist practice is a process of mind training. Essentially, suffering is a product of conscious and subconscious unskillful mind acts, such as pursuing unwholesome thoughts, holding onto inaccurate views of self and others, or being dominated by urges and desires, resulting in disturbing mind states and emotions. In Buddhism, "wholesomeness" generally refers to the extent to which an activity or decision helps to reduce suffering (Karunadasa, 2013). For example, an unskillful mind craving for existence may rigidly hold onto a notion of self signified by conceit, which perpetrates the inclination to constantly ruminate over thoughts of self-importance and put down others to maintain a fabricated feeling of superiority. These mind actions are considered to be unwholesome, as any challenges to self-ascribed superiority will result in anger, resentment, and more emotional suffering. Just knowing the danger of such a craving is not enough because conceptual understanding may not necessarily lead to wholesome decisions; instead, making wholesome decisions requires persistent mind training to attend or reflect in skillful ways.

From a Buddhist perspective, the human mind is malleable and flexible, and therefore mind training can alter its inclinations. This process of mind training is parallel to training the body for martial arts, basketball, swimming, or other physical activities. Conceptually, you may understand how to shoot a ball into the rim, but the theoretical understanding is not enough to teach a weak and unskillful body in making a shot. Only through repeated muscle training and practices can the body coordinate itself to make a shot skillfully. Similarly, repeated mind training and practices will raise the capacity of the mind to observe and alter mental processes and make wholesome decisions. My application of this process to counseling is the model of *Note, Know, Choose* (NKC), and there are several reasons for this title.

First, the Buddhist Counseling Model of mind training—*Note, Know, Choose*—signifies the essence of mental processes and provides the main ingredients for therapeutic changes in behavior (Lee & Tang, 2020). I hope to develop an approach that is easy to learn and remember and explicit enough to illustrate the gist of the treatment model. To *note* is to raise awareness of the body and mind, to *know* is to analyze and understand the causes of suffering in the body and mind, and to *choose* is to make beneficial decisions in the body and mind in each present moment. Unlike many psychotherapies or counseling models, NKC is a flexible framework for mental activities ranging from a moment of awareness to a full-blown treatment process. Zooming into momentary actions of the mind, NKC can occur in a second.

DOI: 10.4324/9781003025450-4

To demonstrate this mind process, I often ask students to briefly scan their bodies and notice any muscular rigidity. As soon as students start to turn their attention inwards, I always see them doing more than just "noticing": many of them move in certain ways, such as shifting their postures, moving their shoulders, or even altering their way of breathing. Taking tight shoulders as an example, when the mind starts to *note* a strong bodily sensation and identify it as unpleasant, it labels it as undesirable. It knows that relieving the tension will help to reduce discomfort, and thereby *chooses* to stretch or move. This rather long description only captures the mind activities, including noting, knowing, and choosing, in a flash of light.

NKC describes an iterative three-phase treatment intervention to raise a client's ability to concentrate, increase their insight into the causes of and ways to reduce their suffering, and strengthen their ability to make better decisions. The ideal form of mind is the stillness and peace to note mental events, the discernment to know how these events arise and cease and how they would increase or reduce suffering, and mindfully and deliberatively choosing to think, act, or speak in ways resulting in the least suffering. In particular, the "choose" factor in this model refers to volition, a subtle mental decision that fuels actions. Volition is perhaps the most crucial starting point for making changes and can be compared to a row of dominoes.

Second, using "Note, Know, Choose" as the title instead of "Note, Know, *and* Choose" is meant to signify a continuous interdependent process (Lee & Ong, 2019). In English, "and" is a conjunction, binding different clauses, and it is used before the last connected item to represent the end of the list (e.g., "Buddhist practices have three core components: discipline, concentration, and wisdom"). The human mind is a stream of consciousness, but the result of mental cultivation is to refine its ability to become aware of the perception of potential breaking points between thoughts. While "Note, Know, and Choose" implies that the key word Choose is the end of the process, it does not adequately reflect the continuous and dynamic nature of the cyclic effort that permeates the stream of consciousness. Therefore, I coined the term "Note, Know, Choose," which may seem linguistically unusual but which symbolically represents the importance of recurrence.

Third, as NKC is a fluid concept, it is not named "Note, Know, Choose Therapy" or something equivalent because adding the idea of "therapy" may restrict its potential. To encourage a more flexible understanding of this paradigm, it is just "Note, Know, Choose" by itself. Moreover, the origin of NKC arises from Early Buddhism, which is arguably the most accepted doctrinal school. Furthermore, NKC aims to become a highly compatible concept for learning Buddhism, practicing Buddhism, or providing a Buddhist-inspired intervention in a counseling situation. For example, it can apply to secularized mindfulness training such as noting each breath, identifying distracting thoughts and ideas, and choosing to focus back on the breath. It can also apply to couples counseling in which counselors can guide a couple to note their dysfunctional communication patterns, know their unmet underlying needs, and choose to be more compassionate towards each other. In other words, NKC is a conceptual framework that can be adapted to various situations.

Finally, it is crucial to clarify the different goals of traditional Buddhist practices and a Buddhist counseling framework. In conventional Buddhist practice, the goal of practitioners is to become completely liberated from suffering through the attainment of nirvana

(*Pali: nibbāna*). In most Buddhist scriptures, reaching nirvana is associated with taking on a monastic life and cultivating discipline, wisdom, and concentration, thereby detaching from the notion of self, becoming relinquished from all defilements, and eliminating all causes and conditions of dukkha (Lee & Ng, 2020). However, a common counseling framework is not equivalent to a committed spiritual practice because clients are not expected to affiliate with a religion and believe in doctrines. The model of Buddhist counseling in this book applies Buddhist theory and practice into a counseling framework but which does not aim to bring clients to nirvana. Instead, the more mundane goal of the model is to help clients reduce their suffering through raising awareness of attachment to self. In sum, the Buddhist counseling model is a viable practice for "householders" to reduce their suffering rather than walk a path to complete liberation.

## PROCESS OF BUDDHIST COUNSELING

As discussed in Chapter 3, the Four Noble Truths are the core teaching in Buddhism. It includes an explanation of how to become liberated from suffering. Buddhist counseling integrates the Four Noble Truths as shown in Table 4.1.

### First Noble Truth as Compassionate Attunement

Early Buddhist teachings explain that the generic experience of existence through clinging to the five aggregates, or simply being "I" in the world, inevitably results in suffering. One way to apply this concept in mundane life is to understand that every person experiences suffering and has unique reasons for their suffering (Lee & Ng, 2020). Suffering is also what connects one human being to another. The most precious quality of a Buddhist counselor is one's compassionate presence to actively suffer with the person sitting across from them. Listening to a client's sorrows and lamentations, attending to the tumult of emotions, and soothing an agitated mind with warmth and regard will attune oneself with the client's suffering, thereby ameliorating it gradually. For this reason, the primary task of a Buddhist counselor is to remain compassionately and mindfully attuned to the client's suffering.

**TABLE 4.1** Application of the Four Noble Truths to Buddhist Counseling

| Noble Truths | Buddhist Counseling Procedures |
|---|---|
| First Noble Truth: **Dukkha** | **Compassionate Attunement:** To deeply and compassionately *listen* to the manifestation of suffering in a client. |
| Second Noble Truth: **Causes of Dukkha** | **Assessment:** To *assess* internal and external conditions contributing to current suffering. |
| Third Noble Truth: **Cessation of Dukkha** | **Conceptualization:** To *conceptualize* the causes of suffering to inform interventions for the reduction of suffering. |
| Fourth Noble Truth: **Path to cease Dukkha** | **Intervention:** To *intervene* using *note, know, choose* techniques to help a client raise awareness of suffering. and its causes, gain self-knowledge from analyzing the nature of mind, and make choices resulting in less suffering. |

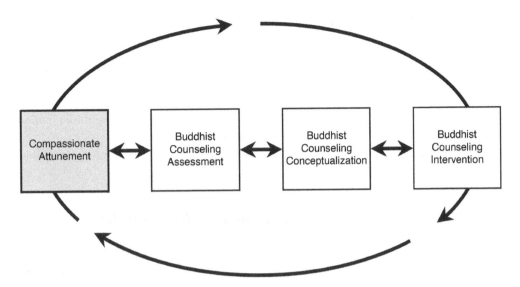

**FIGURE 4.1** Process of Buddhist Counseling

## Second Noble Truth as Assessment

The Second Noble Truth discusses the causes of suffering. According to the law of dependent origination, multiple causes and conditions contribute to a person's suffering. In mainstream counseling, meanwhile, assessment is a process of the collection of information in search of causal factors of the presenting problems and any psychopathologies. Likewise, the purpose of assessment in Buddhist counseling is to explore causes and conditions related to the client's suffering. In particular, this model divides the conditions into two parts: *external conditions*, that is, factors outside the five aggregates, such as culture, environment, and community; and *internal conditions*, that is, the five aggregates themselves, such as states of mind, feeling tones, and habits. The external conditions and internal conditions are interdependent in nature, with external conditions playing important roles in triggering or stimulating internal conditions. The assessment process can also be therapeutic because the exploring of causes and conditions tends to raise awareness of the factors affecting one's wellbeing. Identifying reasons for suffering also usually induces a moment of relief in clients.

## Third Noble Truth as Conceptualization

The Third Noble Truth concerns the cessation of suffering through the realization of the unconditioned. One aim of Buddhist counseling is to contemplate and analyze the causes and conditions, thereby gaining insights to exit from suffering. For this reason, the Third Noble Truth, in this model, is seen as a process of conceptualization to analyze and formulate *why* the client suffers and *how* to reduce that suffering. This conceptual understanding is crucial to guiding the Buddhist counselor's treatment and intervention plan.

### Forth Noble Truth as Intervention

The Fourth Noble Truth describes the path to end suffering, explaining the Noble Eightfold Path as a method of personal cultivation. In counseling, the term intervention refers to the counselors' actions to bring about changes in clients. In Buddhist counseling, the Noble Eightfold Path transforms into the NKC intervention. It helps the client to raise awareness of suffering through observing body and mind, to gain knowledge of suffering through mind analysis, and to make more skillful moment-by-moment choices.

To summarize, Figure 4.1 provides a simple illustration of the process of Buddhist counseling.

## THE THEORETICAL RATIONALE OF NOTE, KNOW, CHOOSE

The Noble Eightfold Path is the core Buddhist intervention to liberate a person from suffering. The Noble Eightfold Path includes Right View (*Samma ditthi*), Right Intention (*Samma sankappa*), Right Speech (*Samma vaca*), Right Action (*Samma kammanta*), Right Livelihood (*Samma ajiva*), Right Effort (*Samma vayama*), Right Mindfulness (*Samma sati*), and Right Concentration (*Samma samadhi*). In the Buddhist teachings, the eight paths are divided into three groups: (i) the moral discipline group (*silakkhandha*) consisting of Right Speech, Right Action, and Right Livelihood; (ii) the concentration group (*samadhikkhandha*) consisting of Right Effort, Right Mindfulness, and Right Concentration; and (iii) the wisdom group (*paññakkhandha*) consisting of Right View and Right Intention. These paths are designed to be practiced together. The following section will briefly describe each path and its application to the NKC model.

### The Concentration Group

The concentration group includes Right Effort, Right Mindfulness, and Right Concentration.

#### *Right Effort* (Samma vayama)

The principle of Right Effort refers to the practitioner's devotion to preventing any evil, negative, or unwholesome cognitive processes from arising while maintaining and nurturing wholesome cognitive processes. Right Effort means working in the right direction: towards the cessation of suffering. As a mundane person's mind does not discern between wholesome and unwholesome thoughts and has a strong capacity to dispel or sustain particular thoughts, Right Effort signifies perseverance and diligence in training the mind. For example, a practitioner can practice moment-by-moment awareness to foster single-pointedness attention to prevent the arising of craving or conceit, or one may practice loving-kindness meditation to cultivate a loving state of mind. The ultimate goal of Right Effort is to completely eradicate unwholesome cognitive processes, their latent roots, and other causes of suffering, which is considered a long-term process of gradual transformation. Right Effort signifies exertion, commitment, patience, and repeated practice in continuously shaping and upgrading the mind.

### Right Mindfulness (Samma sati)

Right Mindfulness is the attentiveness, awareness, and vigilance of a mind grounded in the present moment, such as observing and monitoring the cognitive processes. In this surveillance process, one refrains from judging, altering, fabricating, or expanding mental activities; instead, it is meant to reveal all mind activities as they are. According to the *Satipaṭṭhāna Sutta*, Right Mindfulness is used to contemplate four dimensions: body, feelings, mind, and dhammas (Anālayo, 2003). Such a practice aims to ardently and clearly comprehend, mindfully removing unwholesome qualities such as greed and distress and seeing the four foundations as they are. For example, the first foundation of mindfulness of the body as just a body is to know that it is not me, not I, not self, but just a phenomenon. One way to cultivate Right Mindfulness is to be highly aware of the in-breath and out-breath in the present moment, to the point of noting the precise moment of the rising and falling, the postures and mechanisms of each of the involved body parts and seeing how the entire process of breathing is an impersonal phenomenon rather than "I am breathing."

One significant difference between Right Mindfulness and the common concept of modern mindfulness is the "right" component. Modern mindfulness emphasizes the present moment awareness to soothe the mind without judgment, while traditional Buddhist mindfulness emphasizes the rightness of a calmed mind that realizes the true nature of things, such as non-self. Moreover, Right Mindfulness is only one part of the Noble Eightfold Path. It has to be supported by moral discipline and wisdom to reduce suffering effectively. In other words, modern mindfulness and Right Mindfulness both aim to foster a calmed mind, although practitioners of modern mindfulness can mindfully conduct either wholesome or unwholesome actions, the latter including engaging in violence, using harmful speech against others, or pursuing evil thoughts. However, a practitioner of Right Mindfulness aims to abandon all unwholesome and damaging thoughts, behaviors, and speech while at the same time fostering wholesome ones.

### Right Concentration (Samma samadhi)

While Right Mindfulness fosters heedfulness and awareness of the body and mind, Right Concentration fosters detachment from all sensual objects and unwholesome things. The Buddha categorizes Right Concentration into stages of absorption or concentration, known as *jhānas*. A *jhāna* is a meditative state of stability and concentration of a mind fully immersed into a target object of meditation. In the *Samadhanga Sutta: The Factors of Concentration*, the Buddha described four levels of *jhāna* involving the progressive abandonment of different qualities of mind, such as hindrances and thoughts, and even rapture and happiness, to finally reach a state of equanimity (AN 5.28). In this regard, right concentration is a prerequisite for wisdom as it is an essential quality to see reality as it is.

### Concentration Group as Note

In the NKC model, Note is contiguous to the concentration group, which aims to foster stillness and peace in a client's mind to enhance its capacity to observe and discern cognitive activities. Using different techniques such as mindful breathing, chanting, walking meditation, tea mediation, and other Right Mindfulness practices, the Buddhist counselor gradually helps clients to ground their minds in the present moment and develop a consistent practice outside counseling sessions. To Note is to utilize a soothed and calmed mind to observe, monitor, and polish awareness of the arising, changing, and ceasing of bodily and cognitive processes, discern wholesome and unwholesome mind acts, and notice ways to reduce unwholesome mind states and sustain wholesome mind states.

## The Wisdom Group

The wisdom group includes Right View and Right Intention.

### Right View (Samma Ditthi)

The Noble Eightfold Path is not just a sequential process; instead, it can be seen as comprising interdependent components of a holistic practice. Among the eight, Right View is the key element of the Noble Eightfold Path and a guiding principle for all other components. As ignorance is the root of suffering, it relates to an incorrect understanding, denial, or rejection of reality. As a remedy, Right View serves the purpose of seeing the true and ultimate nature of reality. This part uses two angles to discuss Right View. One important characteristic of Right View is freedom from any dogmatic and rigid attachment to any views or beliefs that "only this is right, all others are wrong" (Karunadasa, 2013, p. 34). In contrast, a Right View will reflect a flexible and open mindset that empirically examines different perspectives to find more beneficial and constructive ways of thinking. In Buddhism, all concepts and ideologies are only transitional guides to realizing goals. Like rafts, concepts are used for crossing a river to reach a destination.

From a doctrinal perspective, Right View embodies the Four Noble Truth's perspectives on self, others, and the world. In other words, one characteristic of Right View is skillfulness in understanding. In the Sutta of Right View (*Sammādiṭṭhisutta*), the Buddha stated, "A noble disciple understands the unskillful and its root, and the skillful and its root. When they've done this, they're defined as a noble disciple who has right view" (MN 9). In this sense, to view things "Right" or to be skillful is to understand: (1) how mind processes, such as mental qualities, thoughts, ideas, or behaviors, can be harmful and suffering-induced, (2) their root causes, especially delusion, hatred, and greed, and (3) the arising, changing, and ceasing of these mental phenomena, that is, a "Right" view also understands how certain mental processes, such as greed, hatred, and delusion, are beneficial. For example, in a painful breakup, a wrong view would be to keep blaming the person for leaving, ruminate over memories, and retaliate against the person. In contrast, a Right View would see how all these resentful thoughts and volitions will only bring more suffering, perpetrate hatred based on emotional injury, and understand how forgiveness, compassion for self and others, and letting go of the past will gradually reduce suffering. Although it may sound easy to know what is good for oneself, a regular person's mind is deluded, and negative thoughts and actions are incredibly tempting because they can provide instant and temporary satisfaction. Fostering Right View requires effort and practice to discern wholesome from unwholesome, nurturing direct and contemplative experiences to know what is right, and integrating support from the seven other paths.

Another vital characteristic of Right View is a non-dualistic perspective (Karunadasa, 2013). One description of the Buddha on Right View was,

> This world, Kaccāna, for the most part, depends upon a duality: 'there is' (*atthitā*) and 'there is not' (*natthitā*) … 'Everything exists': That is one extreme. 'Everything doesn't exist': That is a second extreme. Avoiding these two extremes, the Buddha (*Tathāgata*) teaches the Dhamma through the middle path.
>
> (SN 12.15)

Applying this dualistic view to human existence, individuals who cling to the absolute and immortal existence of a self or who reject self-existence each fall into duality. From the non-dualistic perspective, there is no ultimate existence, but you cannot deny that the **self "exists" in some sense**. As mentioned in Chapter 2, in a world of dependent co-arising, self is a product of causes and conditions, and this fabricated self has a provisional existence. For example, "George Lee" is a product of body, mind, culture, environment, and other factors. The phenomenon of "George Lee" exists when these causes and conditions are available, and the phenomenon will subside when the causes and conditions cease (i.e., "George Lee" dies). Moreover, different contexts and external conditions tend to give rise to different internal conditions of "George Lee," such as how he is different when he is in the family context, a classroom teacher, or in an office writing this book. Therefore, one can say "This is George Lee," a conventional identity, a label for a particular phenomenon which is not static. Mental flexibility means understanding how the two extremes make sense provisionally without becoming attached to either perspective. A view is a guide to action.

### Right Intention (Samma Sankappo)

Related to Right View, Right Intention is the mental endeavor of intending to act in wholesome and skillful ways. In other words, Right Intention is the mind's commitment to follow the path by making decisions congruent with Buddhist teachings. Intention is the motive fueling thoughts and behavioral actions and is the most impactful factor driving kamma. From a simplified kammic perspective, wholesome intention contributes to wholesome effects and vice versa. For example, an intention to alleviate the suffering of an old lady who fell on the street drives the action of gently lifting her and picking up her belongings. The immediate and more direct effort of such wholesome intention is the flourishing of a compassionate mental state of more happiness and less suffering.

In the teachings of Early Buddhism, kamma is usually not about future consequences; instead, the emphasis is on the immediate benefits to the mind. According to Karunadasa (2013), there are three types of Right Intention: (1) intention of renunciation to refrain from self-centered desires and egocentric drives; (2) intention of non-hatred to refrain from aversion; and (3) intention of nonmaleficence to refrain from harmful or cruel thoughts about self or others. Through repeated practice of these types of Right Intention, the mind will steadily nurture itself towards more wholesome states, and skillful thoughts and ideas will become more readily accessible. Right Intention follows knowing and accepting the law of kamma. It means purposefully observing, contemplating, and acting in wholesome ways to purify the mind.

### Concentration Group as Know

In Buddhism, wisdom is the knowledge of the true nature of things, such as the suffering caused by clinging to the existence of the self. Following on from enhanced awareness via Note, the next factor of Know analyzes and contemplates *how* and *why* suffering arises, changes, and ceases in the mind. In this process, Right Intention seeks to continually analyze, contemplate, and reflect on the right view of each phenomenon. For example, a wrong view of depression is that it exists as a powerful and enduring energy that will never end. The right view of depression is that it is a phenomenon consisting of different causes and conditions, such as rigidity in some body parts, fatigue or pain in some muscles, unpleasant sensations in the body and mind, the labeling of an experience as depression, ruminative thoughts on how depression is always there, immersive attention to negative feelings and thoughts, and other conditions. To Know is to foster mental distance from this phenomenon temporarily to observe the body and mind moment-by-moment, thereby gaining insight into how depression is actually an interdependent experience supported by distinct yet related factors. The right view guides us to understand that depression is an impermanent ontological experience if we have developed a capacity to detach from body-and-mind acts and sustain wholesome acts.

## Moral Discipline Group

The moral discipline group consists of Right Speech, Right Action, and Right Livelihood.

### Right Speech (Samma vayama)

Vocal actions, physical actions, and life choices all constitute areas of moral discipline. Speech is a process of concretizing and organizing thoughts and intentions into sounds, resulting in social effects. Right Speech is the verbal manifestation of Right Intention, in which one strives to speak in a truthful, meaningful, benevolent, and timely way. Right Speech is also to refrain from lying, slandering, being hateful or abusive in language, and speaking frivolously. In essence, right speech is the vocal aspect of Buddhist practice.

### Right Action (Samma kammanta)

Right Action refers to behavioral choices based on Right Views and Right Intention. It refers to the prevention of harm to any beings in any form. In particular, to have Right Action is to refrain from killing, stealing, and sexual misconduct. Intention serves as a root cause for action, and action reciprocally fuels intention in a positive feedback loop. For example, if you intend to eat chocolate cheesecake and transform the intention into the actual behavior of eating, the physical behavior of enjoying chocolate cheesecake tends to reinforce the intention, driving the next craving for this particular food. Alternatively, behavioral choices can shape intention. For example, constantly choosing to eat an apple and not feed the craving for chocolate cheesecake tends to mitigate such craving from a Buddhist perspective. For this reason, enforcing wholesome behavioral choices tends to facilitate the cultivation of wholesome mind acts and states.

### *Right Livelihood* (Samma ajiva)

Livelihood concerns how we secure the necessities of life. It usually refers to the choice of financially or vocationally supporting one's life. Right Livelihood means living a life in congruence with the moral expectations of Buddhism. Specifically, there are several aspects of vocation to avoid, including making a living in weapons, in human beings (such as slavery), in living beings (such as fisherman and meat production), in poisons (such as the production of chemical weapons), and in intoxicating substances (such as selling drugs) (Karunadasa, 2013). Regardless of the materialistic values of these choices, practitioners should not become involved in them, as doing so will result in harmful consequences for themselves and others.

## Moral Discipline Group as Choose

Discipline is usually the starting point of Buddhist practice. Discipline emphasizes the mind enforcing wholesome behavioral choices, thereby molding external choices. This sequence is mainly applicable to individuals who identify as Buddhist and commit to Buddhist practice and for whom the starting point is usually the receiving of Buddhist precepts. Of course, clients in mental health practices may not see the value of or be ready to take Buddhist precepts or follow Buddhist discipline. However, if we take a deeper look at the value of Buddhist moral discipline, we see the profound implications of kamma: refraining from an action not to avoid punishment but to avoid immediate negative and unwholesome mental consequences.

As discussed, unwholesome actions and decisions perpetuate delusions, fuel craving and desire, and result in more suffering. Therefore, unwholesome actions start with benefits to oneself. The Choose component helps clients to make wholesome decisions that result in positive kamma. In any event, there are numerous mind choices at any given moment. From

**TABLE 4.2** Application of the Noble Eightfold Path to Note, Know, Choose

| Focus of Counseling | Parallel Concepts in Buddhism | Treatment Focus |
|---|---|---|
| **Note** | **Concentration** | **Goal:** Raise awareness of the five aggregates (sense contact/body, feeling, perception, examination, volition) by:<br>1. Re-centering.<br>2. Sustaining.<br>3. Observing. |
| **Know** | **Wisdom** | **Goal:** Cultivate clients' capacity to see what, how, and why the mind is clinging by:<br>1. Detaching.<br>2. Deconstructing.<br>3. Discerning. |
| **Choose** | **Discipline** | **Goal:** Shape future kamma (mindfully decide on body, speech, and mind actions) using knowledge of self and mindfulness of the moment by:<br>1. Identifying choice points.<br>2. Checking-in with realistic conditions.<br>3. Making skillful decisions. |

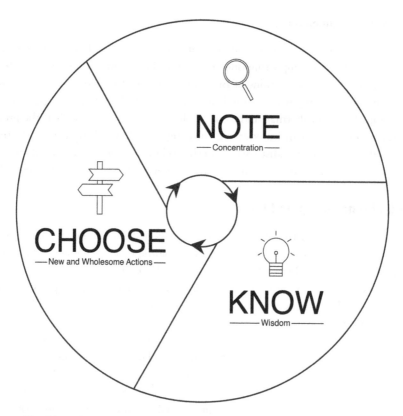

**FIGURE 4.2** The Note, Know, Choose Model

insights gained from Know, an individual contemplates the nature of consequences associated with a different intention. A mind with concentration and knowledge can identify the decision points and choose an action resulting in less suffering. The goal is to help clients identify decision points and develop the skillful means needed to shape future kamma by mindfully choosing body, speech, and mind actions using knowledge of self and mindfulness to inform wholesome decisions in each moment.

Table 4.2 presents the application of the threefold training in the NKC model.

### Note, Know, Choose Altogether

Concentration, Wisdom, and Moral Discipline are interdependent and mutually progressive in the cultivation of the mind. NKC endorses this Threefold Training in Buddhism as the guiding principle. Figure 4.2 provides an illustrative view of NKC to indicate its continuous and interdependent nature. The coming chapters will discuss this model in more detail.

## PRACTICAL ISSUES

For students in mental health fields, the process of counseling may not be self-explanatory, so this session briefly introduces the practical aspects of counseling.

## Documentation

Documentation refers to a process of ethical and professional recordkeeping of the counseling process, which usually involves recording informed consent, progress notes, initial assessment forms, a treatment plan, and a closing summary. The purposes of documentation are many: it offers direct evidence of treatment, tracks treatment progress, ensures clients' safety, enhances communication among peer professionals, meets reimbursement compliance, and others. In essence, good documentation is a criterion of professional counseling, including Buddhist counseling, so Buddhist counselors should develop an effective documentation system.

Each client has a folder to record all documentation; the folder can be in paper form, electronic, or both. This section will provide an overview of standard documents in a client's folder together with samples of Buddhist counseling.

### Informed Consent

Informed consent refers to the client's voluntary agreement to participate in the counseling process based on the client's understanding of its nature, its potential benefits, its possible risks, and available alternatives to treatment (American Psychological Association, 2007). Informed consent usually signifies the beginning of a treatment process and is conducted in the first session with a client. A common standard is to collect a written and signed informed consent to store in the client's file (either a paper or electronic version). Chapter 6 will provide more details.

### Progress Note

A progress note is a written record to document the care delivered to clients, including any clinical event that occurs, treatments provided, diagnosis, or other relevant information (Aghili et al., 1997). It is designed to be concise and readable, accurately reflecting the course of treatment. Appendix 4.1 provides a sample progress note by a Buddhist counselor as a reference for the reader.

### Initial Assessment Form

Initial assessment, or intake assessment, is usually the first phase in counseling. As discussed in this chapter, assessment is a process of information collection to investigate causes and conditions contributing to a client's suffering. Initial assessment forms are documents created to guide the assessment process and capture significant areas of the client's background. Chapter 6 will provide more details on this topic together with a sample Buddhist counseling initial assessment form.

### Treatment Plan

A treatment plan is a documented plan with information about clients' presenting problems, goals and objectives of treatment, proposed stages and steps, and other information about the treatment process. It is similar to a blueprint of what is expected to happen to help the client reduce their suffering.

### Summary

When a client ends counseling, the closing summary concludes with the services provided, the treatment outcome, and plans for the next steps, such as termination of care or referral to other professional services. It is usually the last document in a client's folder (see Appendix 4.2).

Each setting will have a set of forms developed for the specific needs of the counselors and clients. New counselors must become familiar with these forms before seeing clients.

## Counseling Session Structure

The NKC model can be used for different mental health professionals in various settings, such as hospitals, schools, the military, and field-based counseling settings. However, the structure and nature of sessions can vary from setting to setting. To give a sense of what a regular session looks like, a breakdown of a sample session now follows. A NKC session in a traditional clinical setting usually takes 75 mins. It includes:

1 15 minutes of guided meditation to foster a mindful haven or deepened meditative state.
2 Checking-in with the client (including reviewing homework if necessary).
3 Conducting the NKC Process.
4 10 minutes of closing mindfulness activities to introduce the practice for the following week and/or to foster a mindful haven.
5 Discussion of a homework assignment (i.e., practicing the Note, Know, or Choose technique between sessions).

Unlike traditional counseling, which lasts for 50–60 minutes per session, a NKC session is long enough to allow Buddhist counselors to help clients learn meditation. The topic of meditation can vary according to the needs of the client and the stage of treatment. For example, the Note phase emphasizes concentration meditation to help clients develop a mindful haven, while the Know phase focuses on contemplation and insight meditation to help clients understand how they are clinging to a self-notion. It is also possible to structure the session in a more flexible and unstructured way to meet a client's needs at any particular moment. The three crucial and perhaps unchangeable components in this model are to (1) help the client develop an effective practice to raise awareness and concentration through in-session practice in addition to daily regular practice, (2) practice meditation with clients in sessions and provide tailor-made guidance to help them develop and improve their practice, and (3) apply the NKC approach to foster more skillful decision making in and outside of sessions.

Depending on the severity of a client's disturbance, the treatment duration usually lasts from one to three months for clients who aim to resolve more immediate presenting problems but who are not yet ready for or interested in transformation. For clients who are committed to mind cultivation, the treatment duration can last six months or even more.

## CONCLUSION

Every Buddhist school and tradition follows the Four Noble Truths, and this should be the same for any Buddhist counseling model. In particular, the NKC intervention model attempts to integrate the Noble Eightfold Path as treatment principles, repackaging Buddhist teachings to the frame of professional counseling. Introducing my model of Buddhist counseling to you is similar to buying groceries in a market and making a dish to share with others. I believe that the ingredients (Buddhist teachings) are of the highest quality, so I can only use my limited skills in cooking (the interpreted model) to create a dish that tastes good to me. My dish is open for tasting. As every person has a different preference for food, you may take as much or as little as you like, you may reference the recipe to create your own dish, or you may prefer your own recipe.

---

### Contemplative Questions for Buddhist Counselors

As the Four Noble Truths are the guiding principles for the Note, Know, Choose model, Buddhist counselors need to contemplate this Buddhist worldview for themselves so that they can apply the insights gained to help others. Please read slowly and answer the following contemplative questions, maintaining an open attitude to your reactions in body and mind:

*First Noble Truth:*

- "Where is my suffering right now?"
- "How does suffering manifest in my body and mind?"
- "How much do I want to reduce my suffering?"

*Second Noble Truth:*

- "How do I contribute to my suffering?"
- "What causes of suffering are under my control?"
- "What causes of suffering are out of my control?"

*Third Noble Truth:*

- "What are my innermost urges and desires in life?"
- "How have these urges and needs been driving me to act harmfully to myself and others?"
- "Can I genuinely love and accept myself, including all pleasant and unpleasant parts of me?"

*Fourth Noble Truth*:

- "How do I feel about establishing discipline in my life to reduce suffering?"
- "How do I feel about fully immersing myself into the present moment without attending to my thoughts, worries, fear, or fantasies regardless of how tempting they are?"
- "How do I feel about learning to detach from who I am or who I wish to become?"

I know that some of the questions can be challenging to answer. One important set of qualities of a Buddhist counselor are the 3Cs: *courage, compassion*, and *commitment*. Be courageous in turning towards any dark or unwanted side of yourself because running away from it will only give it more power; be compassionate enough to love and accept yourself because the relationship with yourself is a mirror of your relationship with others, including your clients; and be committed to change because you have had enough of suffering, and you genuinely want to have more sustainable happiness. I hope that you can become the most containing and accepting Buddhist counselor for yourself and then be able to transfer this wholesome relationship to your clients.

## REFERENCES

Aghili, H., Mushlin, R. A, Williams, R. M, & Rose, J. S. (1997). Progress Notes Model. *Journal of the American Medical Informatics Association: JAMIA, 4*, 12–16.

American Psychological Association. (2007). *APA Dictionary of Psychology*. Washington, DC: American Psychological Association.

AN 5.28.Samadhanga Sutta: The Factors of Concentration. Aṅguttara Nikāya, translated by Bhikkhu, T. (1997). Access to Insight (BCBS Edition). Retrieved from www.accesstoinsight.org/tipitaka/an/an05/an05.028.than.html

Anālayo, B. (2003). *Satipatthāna: the Direct Path to Realization*. Cambridge, UK: Windhorse Publications.

Karunadasa, Y. (2013). *Early Buddhist Teachings: The Middle Path Position in Theory and Practice*. Centre for Buddhist Studies, Hong Kong University.

Lee, K. C., & Ng, C. F. (2020). An Indigenous Perspective on Buddhism. Invited chapter in T. A. Sisemore & J. J. Knabb (Ed.), *The Psychology of World Religions and Spiritualities: An Indigenous Perspective* (pp. 137–164). West Conshohocken, Pennsylvania: Templeton Press.

Lee, K. C. & Ong, C. K. (2019). The Satipaṭṭhāna Sutta: An Application of Buddhist Mindfulness for Counsellors. *Journal of Contemporary Buddhism, 19*(2), 327–341. https://doi.org/10.1080/14639947.2018.1576292

Lee, K. C., & Tang, J. (2020). Note, Know, Choose: A Psychospiritual Treatment Model based on Early Buddhist Teachings. *Spirituality in Clinical Practice*. Advanced online publication. https://doi.org/10.1037/scp0000220

MN 9. Sammādiṭṭhi Sutta: The Discourse on Right View. Majjhima Nikaya, translated by Thera, N. & Bodhi, B. (1998). *Access to Insight (BCBS Edition)*. Retrieved from www.accesstoinsight.org/tipitaka/mn/mn.009.ntbb.html

SN 12.15.Kaccayanagotta Sutta: To Kaccayana Gotta. Samyutta Nikaya, translated by Bhikkhu, T. (1997). *Access to Insight (BCBS Edition)*. Retrieved from www.accesstoinsight.org/tipitaka/sn/sn12/sn12.015.than.html

## APPENDIX 4.1

### Note, Know, Choose Progress Note

| Name of Client: Cindy | Progress Note No.: 3 |
|---|---|
| | Case No.: BC210499 |
| Date: July 16th, 2021 | Duration (mins): 73 |

**Type of Service:**
✓ Individual ☐ Couple ☐ Family ☐ Child ☐ Group ☐ Field (Loc.: _____ ) ☐ Others: _____

**Present in Session:**
✓ Client ☐ Parent: _____ ☐ Family: _____ ☐ Counselor 2 ☐ Others: _____

**Client's Presentation and Mind States:**
Client showed up online to session and was well-groomed. Her cognition and perception appeared to be intact. Her affect was depressed and she cried when discussing how her mother put her down. It seems that client keeps dwelling into ruminating about the absence of validation from her mother. Client also presents with an aversive mind state that she becomes irritable when talking about a recent incident of her mother criticizing the way she dresses. At the end of the session, client appeared to have more energy and be more at ease.

**(G) Treatment Goal(s):**
Continue to help client develop a mindful haven to foster concentration and equanimity. Raise awareness of her self-notion and emotional needs of the self-notion.

**(I) Intervention:**
Note: Started session with a guided meditation to help client learn to follow and observe breaths without manipulation. Ended with a short breathing exercising to contemplate on insights gained in the session.

Know: Used an expressive art activity to help client gain insight to her self-notion. Provided a detachment to describe the artwork as a stranger to client and invite client to reflect from a detached perspective to see herself as a person. Processed client's feelings and thoughts.

Choose: Briefly explored potential choices to deal with oneself and the needs of oneself.

Others: Addressed client's questions about regular mindfulness practice.

**(R) Response and Changes:**
Client reported that she has started regular mindfulness practice which has helped her stabilize her emotions at times. She also stated that mindful breathing is an effective mindful haven as long as her mother is not around. When discussing the recent interactions with her mother, client cried during her description of how her mother said, "you are so ugly!" to her. After processing her feelings and thoughts, she stated that she may be "expecting something that is never there" and "it is exhausting." In the art exercise, client described an outer layer of her as striving for attention and success while the inner layer of her just hopes to rest and be at peace. After the exercise, client reported that she may actually "just a normal person with normal needs."

**(P) Plan:**
Client will continue to practice mindful breathing for 15 minutes everyday. Client will also try to notice triggering point of her negative emotions during interactions with her mother.

**Time and Date of next session**: July 24th, 2021

| Signature of Trainee and Date: | Signature of Supervisor and Date: |
|---|---|
| July 23th, 2021 | July 23th, 2021 |
| **Name of Student Trainee:** | **Name of Supervisor:** |
| Dorothy Fu | Kin Cheung (George) Lee, Ph.D. |

# APPENDIX 4.2

## Note, Know, Choose Termination Summary

| | |
|---|---|
| **Name of Client:** Cindy | **Case No.:** BC210499 |
| **Date of Report:** September 27th, 2021 | **Number of Sessions Attended:** 19 |

**Type(s) of Service Provided:**
✓ Individual ☐ Couple ☐ Family ☐ Child ☐ Group ☐ Field (Loc.: _____) ☐ Others:_____

**Reason(s) for Termination:**
☐ Client ☐ Parent: _____ ☐ Family: _____ ☐ Counselor 2 ☐ Others:_____

**Treatment Summary:**
Client is a 48-year-old Chinese lesbian suffering from depression and irritability due to the loss of a long-term job and relational problems with her mother. Client has a history of depression since the passing of her father. Client sought counseling for an overarching goal to cope with her depressive symptoms. After the five months of Note, Know, Choose treatment, client reported to experience a significant reduction of depressive symptoms as well as a higher satisfaction in life.

**Summary of Goals and Objectives:**
1) Note: Foster concentration and equanimity to guard client's mind against depression.
2) Know: Foster insights to client's inner desire to be loved by her mother as well as the realistic condition that her mother may not be able to love her the way she ever wanted.
3) Choose: making a more skillful decision to manage her self-notion, craving for love, and her mother.

**Progress Made:**
According to clinical observations and client's description, client has made progress in:
1) Reducing depressed mood, becoming less irritable to her mother, increasing sleeping quality, and increasing motivation in work.
2) Increasing compassion for herself, thereby taking more self-care and letting go of her clinging of a loving mother.
3) Improving communication with her mother.

**Recommendation:**
Should depressive symptoms arise again, client will contact the center for counseling.
Client will continue her regular practice after treatment.

| **Signature of Trainee and Date:** | **Signature of Supervisor and Date:** |
|---|---|
| October 12th, 2021 | October 12th, 2021 |
| **Name of Student Trainee:**<br>Dorothy Fu | **Name of Supervisor:**<br>Kin Cheung (George) Lee, Ph.D. |

CHAPTER 5

# Buddhist Spiritual Formation as a Counselor

In the Aṅguttara Nikāya, the *Kalama Sutta* documented an intriguing dialogue between the residents of the town of the Kalamas and the Buddha. The story opened with some Brahmins and ascetics who came into the town to glorify their doctrines and deprecate the doctrines of others. After a while, another group of Brahmins and ascetics came to revile those doctrines and expound their new doctrines as the only truth. The residents were confused, so they brought their doubts on which teaching to follow to the Buddha. Instead of telling the residents what to believe, the Buddha taught them a new attitude towards learning: Do not go by reports, traditions, or important people, but directly experience the teaching yourself to generate your own conclusions because only a practitioner who has gained empirical and direct experience via their own effort can accurately judge whether a practice is beneficial to wellbeing.

When teaching the course on spiritual formation for Buddhist counselors and explaining why this course is a core foundation in the program, I usually start with the question, "Does anyone want to see a counselor more miserable than you are?" Unsurprisingly, all students hope to see counselors who seem happier than them and come across as compassionate, nonjudgmental, caring, and peaceful. Instead of assuming these are innate positive qualities of a person, Buddhist practices have let us know that we can nurture and cultivate these qualities to become happier counselors. Through our direct experience with Buddhist practice we can foster clarity and stability, seeing and letting go of burning and disturbing desires and needs, and mindfully making more wholesome decisions. Applying this knowledge and experience, we can learn to be more accurate in understanding how to guide clients in soothing the mind, grasping the nature and conditions of their desires and urges, and contemplating better life decisions. In short, Buddhist counselors should be the first to benefit from the Dharma, and these benefits are major ingredients in fostering the spiritual growth and counseling competency of Buddhist counselors. In doing so, I believe practitioners of Buddhist counseling do not have to become Buddhists; however, there are two important provisos: (1) counselling practitioners should understand and accept the worldview of Buddhism (as when a counselor who adopts any other theoretical orientation would also need to understand and accept the worldview of that particular school of thought), and (2) the practitioners should develop spiritual practices for mind cultivation and be able to benefit from the process. These two prerequisites are likely to enhance the effectiveness of Buddhist counseling interventions as well as the therapeutic presence of the counselor.

DOI: 10.4324/9781003025450-5

# BUDDHIST SPIRITUAL FORMATION

Spiritual formation is a widespread practice in different schools of theology, especially Christianity. Wilhoit and Howard (2020) defined spiritual formation as an active endeavor to receive from and follow the person and work of Christ as documented in the Scriptures. Similarly, The Portland Seminary (2020) of George Fox University uses the Bible to define Christian spiritual formation as the "process of being conformed to the image of Jesus Christ for the glory of God and for the sake of others" (II Corinthians 3:17–18). In this process of walking the path of Christ, spiritual formation is an important commitment to advance and deepen one's spiritual practice. In this regard, Jones (2003) argued that Christian spirituality starts with practices rather than beliefs, such that "a deeper spirituality required a deeper spiritual practice" (p. 1).

Similarly, Keating (1994) promotes the spiritual practice of the Centering Prayer for Christians to cultivate the loving presence of God and diminish the obstructions in the current environment. With this strong emphasis on spiritual practice to form individual spirituality, many training programs put spiritual formation as a core foundation in training chaplains, ministry care providers, and other spiritual care providers. It is a common belief that the ability to form and flourish personal and congregational spiritual lives enhances one's capacity to foster the spiritual lives of others.

Spiritual formation is thus a common process of cultivation for practitioners and care providers in chaplaincy and other disciplines. Although spiritual formation for Buddhist counselors is not limited to Buddhist practices, the current chapter introduces some Buddhist spiritual formation methods in Buddhist counseling as a process of contemplative development in concentration, wisdom, and compassion. For this purpose, contemplation in this book generally refers to the Buddhist methods of cultivation that readers of different faiths or spiritual backgrounds can explore and apply to their traditions. The self-cultivation of Buddhist counselors is essential for enhancing the quality of mind necessary to provide effective Buddhist counseling. Self-cultivation constitutes the spiritual nutrients required to drive and enhance the counselor's competency to practice all the other components. Therefore, this model recommends that all Buddhist counselors develop a devoted Buddhist practice within their chosen tradition. In other words, the self-cultivation of Buddhist counselors should be the fundamental step in preparing them for counseling. Buddhist counselors should also abide by Buddhist ethics and take vows to follow at least the five precepts to guide their Buddhist counseling practices. The calming and therapeutic presence of a cultivated Buddhist counselor can be one of the most therapeutic factors in the process of counseling. In particular, such a counselor will have an enhanced capacity to notice the personal causes of suffering in clients.

Although there is a lack of literature on the training of Buddhist counselors, we shall refer to the training of Buddhist chaplains, which has a considerably longer history. Buddhist chaplains are usually trained through an interfaith approach and connected with a contemplative tradition (Buddhist, non-Buddhist, or an integration) in their professional training, such as a particular Buddhist school and community. In these traditions, they receive rigorous training in contemplative practices, which enhances their capacity to provide spiritual services. In the counseling process, Buddhist counselors need to use their skillful qualities to help clients learn to rectify their personal qualities, which implies that practitioners have attained a certain level of cultivation to offer help (Lee et al., 2017). In other words, contemplative practices are a necessary training requirement for Buddhist chaplains to increase their competency in providing contemplative care. Gauthier (2017) has also explained that Buddhist chaplaincy students have to develop and practice meditation techniques, constantly introspect and reflect on their practice while discerning areas of pathology in the self, and study and apply the Dharma into their practice if they wish to become competent chaplains. The rationale is clear—contemplative practices help to cultivate compassion and kindness for others and deepen interpersonal connections (Haynes, 2004). Watts and Jin (2016) summarized the experiences of several Buddhist chaplains who have attested to how contemplative practices helped them promote inner awareness, increase their sensitivity to clients' emotions, and provide spiritual support for their work. Moreover, Lee et al. (2017) proposed that the efficacy of a Buddhist chaplain is directly proportionate to one's level of self-cultivation, that is, the more cultivated chaplains are, the more skillfully they can note their mind and body states in reaction to clients, discern clients' mind and body states, and choose effective strategies to promote calmness and relaxation in clients. A Buddhist counselor, like a Buddhist chaplain, is a trained professional, with both professions requiring the embodiment of Buddhism in practice. This chapter will now discuss how to use contemplative practices to prepare for Buddhist counseling.

## AN INDIVIDUALIZED MIND WORKOUT PLAN

One way to understand Buddhist practice is to examine its approach to mind training. Through gradual and repetitive training to contemplate the three characteristics of existence—namely, suffering, impermanence, and non-self—the mind will progressively develop qualities and skills to reduce suffering. For example, radiating compassion to a person we dislike is an advanced skill. One way to train the mind to achieve this is to begin by recollecting life experiences of receiving compassion, which can then sustain the growth of a compassionate mind. Using this experience, we can gradually spread compassion to people we care for, people we feel neutral towards, and even towards people we dislike. Through continual practice and insights gained from overcoming struggles, we will develop a more compassionate attitude towards those we dislike. Like muscle training when working out at a gym, this process is a long-term and committed endeavor that is ideally a lifelong pursuit.

Good Buddhist counselors should develop a semi-structured plan to train the mind systemically. Being inspired by the *Satipaṭṭhāna Sutta* and the contemporary application of compassion into psychotherapeutic interventions, I have designed a model for Buddhist spiritual formation for those who can modify it and adapt it into their personal and professional lives. It is important to note that all of these interventions can be transformed into Buddhist counseling techniques for clients but it requires the Buddhist counselors' own direct experiences with these practices as an essential ingredient for treatment implementation. Let us now examine some Buddhist practices.

First of all, effective Buddhist cultivation should include both on-cushion and off-cushion practices (Lee, 2019).

## On-Cushion Practice

On-Cushion practice is a monastic term to describe traditional sitting meditation. In general, good Buddhist counselors should develop a habit of daily meditation of at least 20 minutes, in a safe and undisturbed physical space, and at a regular time of the day.

### Foundational Mindfulness

An essential skill for a Buddhist counselor is to increase one's ability to sustain a concentrated mind onto an objective of meditation, to gain deeper and clearer awareness into the nature and mechanisms of body and mind, and to gain insight into the interactions between body, mind, and environment (Lee, 2019). The *Satipaṭṭhāna Sutta* summarized this part of the practice as "perceiving again and again the body as just the body (not 'my body' but a body) with diligence, clear understanding, and mindfulness, thus keeping away covetousness and mental pain in the world" (DN 22). This refined ability to concentrate is requisite to the mind's ability to engage and sustain wholesome thoughts, disengage from and relinquish unwholesome thoughts, soothe heightened emotionality, or notice deeper clinging and craving. For to this reason, it is worthwhile to make the effort and time to develop foundational mindfulness skills. As a guidebook to Buddhist counseling, the following section describes five required steps in order for a beginning Buddhist counselor to establish a practice of meditation (Figure 5.1):

1 **Physical Preparation:** Many individuals have locked stress or negative emotions in their bodies, manifesting as tension or rigidity. To enter a meditative state, relaxing bodily tension is essential. Wearing loose clothes, moving or massaging tense body parts, or engaging in simple stretching or yoga will relax one's body and focus the mind. The key to the posture is to sit in an upright position with the spine straight but not stiff. The spine should be 70–80% upright. The shoulders are relaxed and the hands are centered on the lap, one palm on top of the other. For the legs, depending on each person's physical condition, one can decide to sit in such postures as a full-lotus, half-lotus, Burmese style, or on a chair. It is most important to allow the body to sustain balance and reasonable comfort throughout the practice.

2 **Mind Preparation:** Let yourself know that it is a time to rest the mind and gently train it, and that nothing is more important than that. Set all potential physical and mental distractions aside, knowing that you will ground your mind in the present moment with the body, reminding yourself of the goal of practice: "Breathing in, knowing it's breathing in; breathing out, knowing it's breathing out."

3 **Choosing an Object of Meditation:** An object of meditation is the target of focus during meditation. An uncultivated mind inclines to attractive or strong objects, but they are often unwholesome and result in more suffering. The practice of mindfulness training intentionally applies the mind to a chosen object that is wholesome or neutral, even though sustaining attention on these objects can be boring. Wholesome objects of meditation, especially during an initial stage of mind training, include the in- and out-breaths or movements of the abdomen in the process of breathing. It is also possible to

use wholesome mental objects such as pleasant images or experiences, the recollection of memories, or a feeling tone. However, it is easier and more beneficial for beginning meditators to start by focusing on breath and body. Searching for a stable object of meditation is an important early task for practitioners, one which involves a constant process of dealing with distracting mental states. For example, a practitioner may have a good experience using the nostril sensations as an object of meditation. When feeling anxious during meditation, they can try switching the object to the rising and falling of the abdomen before going back to the breath.

4  **Observing Breaths:** After using an object of meditation to anchor the mind, one can start to get to know the breath. We breathe every day, but that does not mean we understand each breath's process, mechanism, and changes. The beginning level of meditation involves refining our awareness of how the breath arises and changes in our bodies. In this process, abdominal breathing can provide a more sustainable and relaxing experience. One way to start meditation is to intentionally breathe in and out at a slower and deeper pace. The practitioner can then relax the mind and mentally "sit back" to observe one's breath, such as noticing the breathing sensations, the coldness of the in-breath, an itch, the expansion of the nostrils, or other sensations. Mentally, the practitioner can use an inner voice to label the sensations of the in-breath as "in" and label the sensations of the out-breath as "out." In addition, some practitioners find it helpful to count their breaths by labeling each in- and out-breath, counting back to one after finishing a set of eight. This process is meant to synchronize the mind with the physical sensations to achieve a stable mental state.

5  **Developing Skills Through Experimentation:** Given that distraction is an inevitable experience for all practitioners, training one's mind is highly idiosyncratic. Each person has to find a way to soothe and ground the mind, but there are several ways that many practitioners find helpful. First, should disturbing thoughts or urges arise, the practitioner can acknowledge these experiences, purposefully disengage from them, and search for a sustainable object of meditation again. Each attempt to bring the mind back is a step closer to taming the mind. Second, although many objects of meditation may seem boring to focus on at the beginning, the process also involves joy and pleasant sensations. For example, realizing pleasant feelings of breathing, such as the joy of breathing in and out from the nostrils, can help to attract and ground the mind. Another feature of foundational mindfulness is to foster a higher sensitivity to pleasant feelings by becoming aware of them in our mundane life. Third, when the mind is agitated or easily distracted, one may try using different styles or rhythms of breathing to soothe it and then resume attention to the original object of meditation. As pointed out in the *Kalamas Sutta*, practitioners should be proactive in gaining direct and empirical experiences to find the most optimal personal way to ground and train their own minds. A more advanced practice is to surrender or let go of our grasping to the breath instead of just observing it as it is. This way of observing the breath helps to tranquilize a practitioner's mind further. Readers can search for the free guided meditation online by Dr. Gil Fronsdal for such a systematic practice. This chapter also includes a sample foundational mindfulness script for readers to practise.

**Commitment:** How I sit on this cushion is how I want to live my life. At this designated time for myself, I promise to mindfully and unconditionally care for myself. I will sit in a way that balances between being alert and being relaxed; I will sit in a way that I can comfortably sustain myself for some time; and I will sit in a way that I don't let any disturbances hinder my attempt to care for myself.

**Invitation:** We breathe all the time, but we rarely pay attention to how we breathe. Many studies have proven that paying attention to our breath in a particular way can be very effective in soothing and calming ourselves.

**Introduction:** Now, we're going to practice a short breathing exercise that may allow us to reconnect with the present moment.
Try to find a comfortable, upright position. Get yourself in what feels like a stable and alert posture, which hopefully feels somewhat relaxed. There is a balance between being alert and relaxed. This balance is an important issue. Gently close your eyes (or focus on a spot in front of you). Please remember that the most basic thing we're doing is simply noticing and knowing what is happening in the present moment. It's really simple.
Before you have any ideas about getting concentrated or being peaceful or making something happen—**just notice**. So, you might take a moment now just to notice how you are and what's going on for you, in the here and now.
And as you pay attention to the here and now, how easy is it to stay there? Are you operating on any ideas that something is supposed to happen? Trying to accomplish something, more than just notice?

**Controlled Breathing:** Take a few long, slow, deep breaths to bring yourself into the present moment. Breathe in deeply and then, as you exhale, relax in your body [pause five seconds]. Let go of whatever tension you can easily let go of.
Notice any sensations, be they of discomfort or tension. Notice your feet on the ground, notice whatever you are sitting on, notice your clothes against your body and the air against the skin. [Pause five seconds.] Briefly scan through your body. It might be possible to soften your forehead, your eyes, your jaw, your shoulders, your chest, your belly, and your entire body. [Pause five seconds.]

**Following Breath:** Now allow your breathing to return to normal. For this mindfulness meditation, we are not making any effort at all to breathe in any particular way. We just let ourselves breathe in whatever way we wish. Gently bring your attention to your breath. Notice the cool air flowing in through your nose as you inhale and the warm air as you exhale [pause], as you breathe in and out. [Pause.] Very softly in the mind, label the in-breath "in," the out-breath "out." Just a very quiet whisper in the mind that just encourages you to hang in there, stay present, instead of getting distracted. [Pause five seconds.]

**Reminder:** If you find your mind wandering away from your breath, simply bring it back to noticing each breath, in and out, as they follow, one after the other. [Pause five seconds.]

**Ending:** Now, bring your attention back to the room; open your eyes if they are closed. Notice what you can see; notice what you can hear. Push your feet into the ground and have a stretch; notice yourself stretching. Experience the difference in your body and mind.

Welcome back.

**FIGURE 5.1** Sample Guidance for Foundational Mindfulness Practice

### Compassion Meditation

Another important inner quality that Buddhist counselors should cultivate is compassion. In this book, compassion is defined as a mental quality of goodwill, kindness, and benevolence with an intention to deeply understand and remove suffering in others. It is a selfless volition to alleviate pain and suffering in other beings without any agenda for self-gain (Lee & Oh, 2018). Moreover, genuine compassion is not sympathy, leniency, or pity. It is selfless love without attachments or afflictions. It also involves accurate empathy for the pain and distress of others by letting go of personal judgments, stereotypes, and assumptions to see and experience suffering from another person's perspective.

Compassion is an intrinsic quality in everyone, but an uncultivated mind does not know how to access it resourcefully. In a typical state of mind, we tend to:

- Assume reality is worse than our fears.
- Underrate the power of love and disconnect from spiritual friends, loved ones, and other beneficial persons physically and mentally.
- Overrate what "I" can do and assume that "I" am the key in any relationship.
- Underrate what we can do to compassionately love ourselves to unconditionally understand, accept, and love who we are.

Self-compassion is a good starting point for Buddhist counselors in cultivating undifferentiated compassion for others. Such undifferentiated compassion will enhance the Buddhist counselors' ability to connect with their clients, cope with negative emotional reactivity, prevent burnout, and see reality as it is (Lee & Oh, 2018). Self-compassion meditation or compassionate view meditation includes several steps:

1 **Recollection of resources of compassion:** Calling upon previous experiences of receiving kind acts, empathy, and compassionate offering is one of the most direct ways to generate a compassionate mind state. Depending on the practitioner's experience, recollecting experiences of compassion can be difficult. The practitioner can visualize unconditional love sent by one's parents or caregivers, remember a difficult time in life in which a compassionate friend offered selfless help, recall a memory of bonding with pets or children, or any other experience. This person is usually referred to as a benefactor who has role-modeled a selfless act.

2 **Sustaining a compassionate state of mind:** When the recollection of a compassionate experience is successful, the practitioner can pay attention to the nature of the thoughts, feelings, emotions, and other mental processes during this state. In particular, observing and noticing the happiness, gratitude, and pleasant sensations in mind and body can help sustain the mind state. So can maintaining mindful breathing and becoming immersed in the present experience while disengaging from distracting thoughts. Once the feeling of compassion is consolidated, the practitioner can start visualizing the radiation of compassion to others.

3 **Radiating compassion to others:** A vital step to fostering compassion is intentionally visualizing and generating compassion for others. It is usually easier to start by

reciprocating compassion to the benefactor. After visualizing this person standing in front of the practitioner and sending compassionate wishes to them, the practitioner can return the compassion by reciting certain statements of compassion indicated in the sample script (Figure 5.2). After reciting these kind words, the practitioner can use the same process to send compassion sequentially to (1) family and friends, (2) neutral people, and (3) the practitioner himself or herself. In more advanced training, the practitioner can try visualizing difficult people and sending them compassionate wishes or even radiating compassion to all beings. To facilitate this practice for Buddhist counselors, Figure 5.2 is a sample script of a compassion meditation session.

---

In this sitting meditation session, we will cultivate compassion, a natural capacity that we all have within us. It is a spontaneous opening of our hearts to wish everyone, including ourselves, safety, wellness, and happiness. It is also an action of kindness to remove suffering in ourselves and others.

We will gently start by focusing on the breath for a few moments to quiet and calm our minds. Allow ourselves to remember and open up to our basic goodness, kindness, and compassion.

While keeping eyes closed, think of a person who has loved you the most. It could be someone from the past or the present, a friend, a family member, or a spiritual mentor. Think about an incident where the person was compassionate to you, has sent you unconditional love, caring, and compassion. The compassionate act has protected you from harm, consoled your sorrow, and given you peace and calm. That person continues to send you wishes for your safety, for your wellbeing, and happiness. Feel the warm wishes and loving-kindness coming from that person towards you. Experience the compassion. Get to know the mental feeling, bodily feeling, and the present experience of compassion.

Now in your mind invite this person to come to you. Visualize this person standing in front of you. Begin to send the love, warmth, and compassion that you feel back to that person. You and this person are similar. Just like you, this person wishes to be happy and safe. Send all your compassionate wishes to that person:

*May you be free from harm and danger.*
*May you be free from mental suffering.*
*May you be free from physical suffering.*
*May you take care of yourself happily.*
*May you be safe and peaceful.*
*May you be free from suffering.*
*May you be free from suffering.*
*May you be free from suffering.*

We will continue to radiate compassion for the people around us. Think of people who are not too close to you, maybe a friend or colleague you are not particularly familiar with.

Visualize this person standing in front of you. Begin to send love, warmth, and compassion to this person. With an open heart, wish this person wellness and happiness. This

---

**FIGURE 5.2** Sample Guidance for Self-Compassion Meditation Practice *(Continued)*

person wishes to be happy and safe, just like yourself. Send all your compassionate wishes to that person:

> *May you be free from harm and danger.*
> *May you be free from mental suffering.*
> *May you be free from physical suffering.*
> *May you take care of yourself happily.*
> *May you be safe and peaceful.*
> *May you be free from suffering.*
> *May you be free from suffering.*
> *May you be free from suffering.*

Finally, we will call upon the most important person in your life. I would like you to visualize yourself standing here. Look at the hair, the face, the eyes, and the body. See the brightness on your face, experience the compassion you have for this person. From the bottom of your heart, transmit unconditional love, warmth, and compassion to this person. Send all your compassionate wishes to yourself:

> *May you be free from harm and danger.*
> *May you be free from mental suffering.*
> *May you be free from physical suffering.*
> *May you take care of yourself happily.*
> *May you be safe and peaceful.*
> *May you be free from suffering.*
> *May you be free from suffering.*
> *May you be free from suffering.*

**FIGURE 5.2** *(Continued)*

## Off-Cushion Practice

Off-cushion practice is a term to describe meditative practices outside of traditional sitting meditation. In other words, meditation practice is applicable in daily life by constantly reflecting on the body and mind and the analysis of causes, conditions, and consequences (Lee, 2019). In fact, one core purpose of meditation is to guard the mind against unwholesome cognitive acts; in addition, there are numerous opportunities for the daily practice of maintaining peace, clarity, and stability of mind. This session introduces three such standard methods of practice.

### Mindful Eating

In principle, any daily activity can be used as an opportunity for meditation as every moment is a window through which to observe and understand the dynamics of body and mind. Mindful eating can be an effective way to assess the quality of attention and awareness using daily meals and a more concrete opportunity to observe body–mind interactions (Kristeller et al., 2014). Practitioners may designate one meal during the day or the week and try the following steps, which are an adaptation of the Mindfulness–Based Training developed by

Dr. Jean Kristeller, although practitioners can modify the following steps and details according to their practice:

1   Choose a designated time in a quiet and undisturbed environment.
2   Mindfully decide on a type of food that is reasonably healthy and tasty for the practitioner.
3   Start by taking several deep breaths, closing the eyes, and thanking the food. For example, one can reflect on the effort required to bring food to the practitioner, considering how it arrived on the table.
4   Pay mindful attention to the entire experience of eating by mindfully experiencing different senses in the present moment. Appreciate the visual presentation of food, smell the savory aroma, feel the tactile sensation of the plate, bowl, or the food, taste the food slowly and gradually, and let the body and mind become immersed in eating.
5   Notice and enjoy each moment of eating and continually redirect attention to the present experience if the practitioner is distracted.
6   Breathe mindfully throughout the process and reflect on bodily sensations before, during, and after eating.
7   After the meal, humbly express one's gratitude to the food. One suggestion is to say to oneself, "I appreciate this food which supports the good health of my body and mind. I thank every condition and person who brought this food to me. I wish that all beings could be liberated from hunger, sickness, and all forms of suffering."

### Mindful Walking

Although mindful walking is usually interspersed with sitting meditation in longer meditation sessions, walking meditation is another common practice in Buddhism which fosters another level of bodily awareness through movement (Kabat-Zinn, 2017). Compared to regular walking, which usually has an aim in terms of a destination, mindful walking aims to train attention to the body, cultivating a deeper awareness of its various parts, their movement, and their coordination, especially the feet (Amaro, 2019). If we pay attention to our steps, we will realize the different mind acts, foot movements, and muscle coordination required to complete each step: standing with both feet on the ground with balance, intentionally lifting one foot with the front part of the foot as support, moving that foot and leg forward, placing that foot on the ground again, usually with the heel, and then shifting the balance to the other foot and repeating the process. Mindful walking is usually done slowly to help practitioners attend to, observe, and understand each phase and to use this cultivation of concentration to pacify the mind. To practice, one can consider the following steps as adapted from Kabat-Zinn (2017):

1   Designate about ten minutes in a safe and reasonably undisturbed environment.
2   Start by mindfully breathing for a minute and then turning one's attention to the feet. Experience the feeling of stepping firmly on the ground.
3   Start walking by slowly:
    a   lifting one heel and bringing awareness to the feet,
    b   moving the foot and heel forward,

    c  placing the foot on the ground and noticing the first contact point on the ground,

    d  shifting the weight of the body onto the forward foot, with the toes of the other foot remaining on the ground,

    e  repeating the cyclic movement of lifting, moving, and placing the feet and legs mindfully.

### Befriend the Daily Breath

One of the daily practices in *Plum Village* is to regularly pause all activities and take three enjoyable and mindful breaths. It is an effective technique to stop the mind in its daily hustle and bustle and just "be" in the present moment. Throughout the day, a practitioner can fully immerse in the three breaths by noticing the temperature, rhythm, strength, and other sensations of the in- and out-breath. In this process, having a reminder is helpful. Some practitioners find it beneficial to set an alarm clock in the office with a singing bowl sound every 15 minutes. Other practitioners may spontaneously return to mindful breathing whenever they remember to do so. Writing a note as a reminder, setting smartphone reminders, or practicing mental reminders are all possible. The key is to breathe mindfully as much as possible during the day.

To develop a habit of committed practice, it is helpful for practitioners to consider developing a personalized plan for daily practice. Besides the techniques mentioned in this chapter, a practitioner can choose to incorporate various practices into a daily plan. Working with a meditation teacher on designing a plan that focuses on a personal struggle can also be highly beneficial.

## CONCLUSION

Good Buddhist counselors are good practitioners in that they can embody Buddhist teachings for the benefit of self and others. The advanced meditative practice of Buddhist counselors is likely to strengthen their effectiveness when using mindfulness interventions to understand clients' conditions, address their questions, and provide tailor-made instructions to meet their particular needs. For example, some clients find it difficult to breathe mindfully during mindful breathing, struggling to calm down from anger, feeling drowsy, or letting go of thoughts and images in the mind. Experienced meditators can address these questions and use them as reference points to raise clients' awareness of their causes of suffering. Moreover, a commitment to spiritual practice and formation is likely to become a protective factor for burnout and empathy fatigue. The profession of counseling is challenging work, so each Buddhist counselor should start mindfully and care compassionately for themselves in order to foster and radiate this power to clients.

## REFERENCES

Amaro, A. (2019). Guided Sitting and Walking Meditations on Emotion. *Mindfulness*, *10*(6), 1186–1187. https://doi.org/10.1007/s12671-019-01144-4

DN 22. Maha-satipatthana Sutta: The Great Frames of Reference. Dīgha Nikāya, translated by Bhikkhu, T. (2000). *Access to Insight (BCBS Edition)*. Retrieved from www.accesstoinsight.org/tipitaka/dn/dn.22.0.than.html

Gauthier, T. J. (2017). Formation and Supervision in Buddhist Chaplaincy. *Reflective Practice: Formation and Supervision in Ministry, 37*(1).

Jones, J. (2003). *The Mirror of God: Christian Faith as Spiritual Practice—Lessons from Buddhism and Psychotherapy*. New York: Palgrave

Kabat-Zinn, J. (2017). Walking Meditations. *Mindfulness, 8*(1), 249–250. https://doi.org/10.1007/s12671-016-0638-1

Keating, T. (1994). *Intimacy with God: An Introduction to Centering Prayer*. New York: Crossroad.

Kristeller, J., Wolever, R. Q., & Sheets, V. (2014). Mindfulness-Based Eating Awareness Training (MB-EAT) for Binge Eating: A Randomized Clinical Trial. *Mindfulness, 5*(3), 282–297. https://doi.org/10.1007/s12671-012-0179-1

Haynes, D. (2004). Contemplative Practice and the Education of the Whole Person. *ARTS: The Arts in Religious and Theological Studies, 16*(2), 8–10.

Lee, K. C. (2019). A Clinical Psychologist as a Beginning Buddhist: A Personal Reflection on the Buddhist Path. *Journal of Psychotherapy and Counselling Psychology Reflections, 4*(1), 11–18.

Lee, K. C., & Oh, A. (2018). Introduction to Compassionate View Intervention: A Buddhist Counseling Technique Based on Mahāyāna Buddhist Teachings. *Journal of Spirituality in Mental Health*. https://doi.org/10.1080/19349637.2018.1464422

Lee, K. C. (G.), Oh, A., Zhao, Q., Wu, F.-Y., Chen, S., Diaz, T., & Ong, C. K. (2017). Buddhist Counseling: Implications for Mental Health Professionals. *Spirituality in Clinical Practice (Washington, D.C.), 4*(2), 113–128. https://doi.org/10.1037/scp0000124

Portland Seminary. (2020). *What Is Spiritual Formation?* Portland Seminary. Retrieved October 15, 2020, from www.georgefox.edu/seminary/about/formation.html

Watts, J., & Jin, H. (2016, August 21). Contemplative Engagement: The Development of Buddhist Chaplaincy in the United States & Its Meaning for Japan. Retrieved from http://jneb.jp/english/japan/rinbutsuken/contemplative-engagement1/contemplative-engagement-part-3

Wilhoit, J. C., & Howard, E. B. (2020). The Wisdom of Christian Spiritual Formation. *Journal of Spiritual Formation & Soul Care, 13*(1), 5–21. https://doi.org/10.1177/1939790920903841

CHAPTER 6

# Assessment in Buddhist Counseling

Initial assessment, also referred to as the intake evaluation or initial clinical interview, is an information-gathering process that gives mental health professionals an overall understanding of a client's concerns, history, culture, and background information. It is usually the first contact between clients and counselors and is a significant step in laying the foundation of counseling. Several considerations in this beginning process are highly relevant to Buddhist counseling and this chapter will introduce initial assessment in psychology, followed by the Buddhist conuseling components in the process. The term "counselors" here refers to mental health professionals and spiritual care providers who are interested in adopting this Buddhist counseling model in their practice.

## INTRODUCTION TO THE PROCESS OF COUNSELING

Counselors should explain to a client the purpose of assessment and the counseling process. In this process, one of the first things to discuss is confidentiality and limitations to confidentiality. According to the ethical discipline of the profession, criteria of confidentiality and limitations to confidentiality can be different, so I suggest that readers refer to the ethical guidelines of their professions and practice settings. For example, to explain confidentiality to clients, one may consider the following disclosure:

> Everything you discuss with me is confidential, meaning that everything we talk about in counseling is just between us. I cannot disclose your information to others without your permission. However, there are a few circumstances that I may need to break confidentiality. For example, when we know of imminent danger to you or someone else, any minor, elderly, or dependent adult who are victims of abuse, or in the case of a court order, we may have to pass certain information on to other parties. Should these circumstances arise, we will try to sit down with you and talk with you about it and work together with you. Do you have any questions about this?

Counselors need to address clients' questions and explain the process of counseling to help clients understand what to expect. Moreover, getting familiar with this opening is particularly

DOI: 10.4324/9781003025450-6

important for new counselors. It is one of the first steps in laying the foundations of a professional counseling relationship and establishing a safe therapeutic space for clients.

## Therapeutic Alliance

In this initial session (or sometimes the first few sessions), good counselors will establish a therapeutic alliance with clients and build a trusting, safe environment. A therapeutic alliance is a professional, collaborative relationship between a mental health professional and a client. The research literature has consistently shown that the therapeutic alliance is the key to successful psychotherapy and effective care (Da Costa et al., 2020). Imagine the anxiety and worries of a client coming to a counselor for the first time. This suffering individual is concerned about whether friends and family may label him or her as a "crazy person," fear becoming vulnerable to a stranger who is seen as having more knowledge and power, and uncertain of what to expect in this mysterious counseling process.

In the face of a person in deep suffering, the role of spiritual friends (*kalyāṇa-mittatā*) in Buddhism seems to resonate with the role of Buddhist counselors. When asked about the importance of friendship in the path of cultivation, the Buddha described spiritual friends as crucial components of successful practice (SN 12.15). The good influence from a friend who diligently cultivates one's mental qualities plays an important role in motivating others to diligently practice. Moreover, spiritual friends strive to embody the Buddhist path and in turn apply the learnings to benefit others, such as facilitate others on their path of cultivation, compassionately offering assistance, and sharing insights gained on the path for the benefit of others. Buddhist counselors can be considered as taking up the role of spiritual friendships who diligently commit to mind cultivation, compassionately attune to clients' suffering, and humbly using different interventions in fostering insights in clients. Moreover, many clients see professional mental health services as a last resort for their problems, while many do not know what counseling can offer them. For these reasons, initial assessment serves as a crucial entry point to the client's feelings about counseling. The counselor should address any questions or worries that the client may have and provide a genuine, compassionate, welcoming, and non-judgmental presence for clients.

For example, KB is a gay man who has not come out to his family, and he has many self-criticizing thoughts about being gay in a conservative family. He has high self-esteem about his sexual identity and physical appearance, but he experiences others in his life as rejecting and unreliable. He came to counseling to address his interpersonal conflict with a male colleague.

KB: Do you know how hard it is for me to come to you?

COUNSELOR: (in a calm and neutral tone) What makes it so hard?

KB: I always hated to see doctors, and you are like a doctor. Doctors are judgmental. Last time I went to a doctor for my skin allergy, I still remember he looked at me disgustedly and insisted on opening the door for me as if I am contagious and my germs would stay on his door handle.

COUNSELOR: It sounds like it was an awful experience!

KB: Yes, but he has a point. If I am contagious, then he needs to take precautions.

COUNSELOR: How do you feel in this session thus far?

KB: I feel alright. At least I know you are listening to me, but I'm still a little nervous.

COUNSELOR: Seeing a stranger for the first time and having to talk about some of your deepest secrets that you have never told anyone—of course, it's nerve-wracking. I do think it is challenging for anyone, and I would be nervous if I were in your seat, too.

KB: Thank you for understanding how it feels for me.

In this example, the counselor patiently listened to the client and openly inquired into the client's feelings about the therapeutic alliance. This inviting gesture usually eases clients' discomfort by acknowledging their feelings, which shows a readiness to address potential issues in the professional relationship. The counselor communicated an understanding of the client's discomfort and validated those feelings.

## Intake Style

Depending on a counselor's theoretical orientation and personal style, the initial assessment process may be different. Some counselors prefer a more structured style in assessing clients' information and may supplement the intake process with measurement scales, such as the Patient Health Questionnaire-9 or the BDI-II Beck Depression Inventory-II, to evaluate the client's severity of clinical symptoms. Another potential measure for wisdom in Buddhism is the Nonattachment Scale (NAS-7) which serves to measure a client's nonattachment to one's notion of self (Whitehead et al., 2018). In this approach, counselors may systemically ask a list of questions and gently interrupt and redirect the client to gather answers to the intended questions. This approach usually results in a greater breadth of information and provides an overall portrayal of the client.

On the other hand, some counselors prefer a more naturalistic and unstructured style to deepen their understanding of clients' responses, and they use questions flexibly to explore meanings and values. It is also common that beginning counselors will use more structured forms to supplement their assessment process and regularly refer to them. At the same time, seasoned counselors tend to have embodied the assessment areas and can skillfully ask questions in a dialogue. For this guidebook to Buddhist counseling, I will introduce an initial assessment form that provides a concrete example for beginning counselors. For counselors interested in using measurement scales to gauge a client's progress throughout treatment, I would recommend the Nonattachment Scale-Short Form (NAS-SF), an 8-item scale to measure Buddhist nonattachment (Chio et al., 2018). This valid and reliable measure correlates with mindfulness, mental wellbeing, psychological distress, and interpersonal relationships; it can be used as either a standalone or a supplement scale.

## Theoretical Framework for Assessment

Counselors conduct an initial assessment to obtain crucial information about clients to guide case conceptualization and treatment planning. Information collected directly influences the counselors' understanding of clients' mental health diagnoses and the subsequent clinical course of action. In Buddhist counseling, the initial assessment is a data collection process intended to understand and analyze a client's conditions that contribute to suffering. Suffering is a conditioned state in which the mind clings to the ontological nature of an event and continuously constructs it while remaining ignorant of the underlying conditions. As the Buddha pointed out in one of his first discourses, liberation from suffering allows the mind to reach an unconditioned state (visaṅkhāragataṃ), which in turn allows the deconstruction of events into analyzable components (Dhammapada Verse 154). In other words, analyzing supporting conditions of a conditioned experience generates insights into its fabricated and impermanent nature, thereby letting go of the grasping onto the event. A Buddhist counseling assessment thus aims to assess the multiple conditions contributing to a client's suffering and deconstruct this experience for them. This model takes the three postulates of dependent co-arising as stated in Abhidhamma as the theoretical guide for the initial assessment (Karunadasa, 2013):

Nothing arises without the appropriate causes and conditions.
Nothing arises from a single, solitary cause.
Nothing arises as a single, solitary phenomenon.

In this postulation, the counselor's introspective question when assessing a client's suffering should always be, "What are the causes and conditions sustaining this client's suffering?" Every ontological experience at a given moment is a product of the interplay among multiple interdependent conditions. In this plural causality, the arising and ceasing of an experience directly depends on the interrelationships among various conditions. However, most individuals can only see the ontological event but not the conditions behind it. Taking a client's concern of anxiety as an example, "anxiety" is a mental label associated with a phenomenon sustained by internal and external conditions. If we analyze the internal conditions giving rise to the experience of "anxiety," we see bodily sensations such as muscle tension, butterflies in the stomach, and heat in the body. These unpleasant sensations in the body create thoughts and mental images of fear and worry. If one or several of these conditions were to cease through an increase in self-compassion that dissolves self-directed ill-will while soothing physical discomfort, the phenomenon of depression being experienced at the moment may change or end. In other words, once an individual can penetrate through an ontological experience into its sustaining components and mechanism, one may alter specific causes or conditions to cope with, dissolve, or avoid an experience.

However, the idea of the plurality of conditions is challenging to comprehend and apply to counseling. To facilitate understanding of conditions, the current model will divide the multiple conditions into two categories: *internal conditions* and *external conditions*. Internal conditions refer to mind conditions or the intrapsychic elements and cognitive tendencies. The current assessment model focuses on several psychological constituents, including characteristics of self, views, states of mind, and habitual patterns of thought. External conditions refer to any condition outside of the mind, and various conditions of a client's lived system, subsystems, and interactions between them. These include a person's physical body and the outer environment as well as the client's history, demographic background, interconnectedness, culture, and related factors outside the client's mind. The internal conditions and external conditions are interdependent in nature and mutually influential to each other in a spiral manner: how external conditions of environmental impacts play a role in fostering the internal conditions of self-notion and view of the world while such constructed notions and views affect one's interactions with the environment, thereby eliciting certain responsive conditions in the environment. For example, a boy growing up in poverty (external condition) develops a low self-esteem as he sees himself as a "less-than" (internal condition) when compared to his classmates. This poor self-image makes him shy, timid, and afraid of voicing out his needs and this presence makes other classmates further reject him or tease him (external condition). As a result, the external reinforces and concretizes the boy's self-notion of being a "less-than" (internal condition). For the assessment purpose, conditions are divided this way to help Buddhist counselors get a quick grasp of the interdependent conditions contributing to a client's suffering at a given period and the coming sections will discuss the practicality of this concept.

## THE PRACTICE OF BUDDHIST COUNSELING ASSESSMENT

Given the centrality of the Buddhist concept of causation, the author has integrated the core principle of dependent co-arising in to an intake assessment. The intake interview takes 60 to 90 minutes, depending on the client's presentation and the counselor's style. Counselors of various theoretical approaches may wish to extract relevant components of the assessment to supplement their existing practice.

The assessment form covers six categories: (a) a client's reported concerns, (b) assessment of internal conditions, (c) assessment of external conditions, (d) assessment of habits, (e) assessment of potential risks, and (f) preliminary case formulation. The following section will discuss each area of assessment with a fictional case example, Cindy, to illustrate how to put the form into practice (see Appendix 6.1 for an example of a Buddhist Counseling Assessment Form). (Note that in the next three chapters, "Cindy" will continue to be the case study to illustrate each step of Buddhist counseling.)

> Cindy is a Chinese 48-year-old female, a seasoned counselor who is well established in her professional field. She identifies as a lesbian and has been cohabitating with her girlfriend for over a decade. Cindy has been working as a counselor for more than 20 years; she works full time as a senior counselor and supervisor for new counselors, teaches part-time for a Master of Counseling program, and regularly gives presentations to the public. Regardless of her achievement and recognition in the field, she reports that she has been suffering from depression for a long time, and she is self-referred to counseling for her recent depressive episode. Cindy states that the recent depressive feelings arise directly from her recent loss of job.

### Introduction

Depending on the counselor's work setting and board of licensure or registration, counseling usually starts with obtaining the client's informed consent to document that clients are informed about the treatment and voluntarily agree to participate. Informed consent is usually signed during the first session to explain the course of treatment, the nature and limits of confidentiality, any fees involved, and to answer questions from clients. After completing the informed consent and other necessary paperwork, the counselor may briefly introduce the goal of the intake session:

COUNSELOR:  Hello Cindy, the first session of counseling will be what we call an intake session. I will use this form to ask you some questions regarding what has happened to you and your past experiences to know more about you and possible ways to help. Do you have any questions before we proceed?

CINDY:  No, not at this moment.

## Clients' Reported Concerns

The first section focuses on clients' perspectives and concerns, motivating them to seek professional help. In Buddhist counseling, counselors usually do not take clients' assumptions of problems as concrete and definitive in nature. It is common for clients to assume an event is a problem and mentally fixate on it. Many clients have narrowed down their interpretation of events into a particular view and subconsciously try to convince the counselor that, "This is what I need, but I can't get it, so it is a problem." It is easy for new counselors to be convinced by the client that this is the only available view of the situation. It also helps to explain why new counselors often feel helpless, as though they have bought into the client's attachment to a particular perspective.

Some clients may even provide some specific solutions for their identified problem and ask the counselor to help them reach those solutions. However, the concept of dependent co-arising suggests that a problem is a mental construct based on multiple conditions; when one gains insight into the sustaining conditions, assumptions about the problem may change. This idea does not refer to judging or rejecting clients' perspectives. Instead, counselors should practice a dependently co-arising view while attentively and compassionately understanding *what makes the situation a problem from the client's perspective*. Moreover, counselors will inquire about clients' expectations for counseling, allowing both the counselors and clients to set realistic expectations in the therapeutic relationship. It is important to note that counselors will need to supplement the clinical interviewing process with basic micro-skills, such as paraphrasing, summarizing, clarification, reflecting on feelings, and considering meaning.

COUNSELOR:  So Cindy, what brings you to counseling?

CINDY:  (*Start with a sigh*) I got let go by my agency, meaning that I didn't get a new contract. It is like firing me.... I have been working with them for over 20 years. I can't believe they can just fire me like that.

COUNSELOR:  I notice you started with a big sigh, which conveys how disappointed you feel about being let go from a long-term employer. Can you tell me more about what happened?

CINDY:  Well, they said it's a budget cut. Perhaps you know that many agencies are undergoing financial difficulties, so part of me can understand why it happened. I receive higher pay than many of my colleagues, so I guess they decided to use my salary for others. I understand why they did it during this kind of economic crisis, but it's just so cold not to renew a contract with a faithful and long-term employee like me. So, the other part of me is pretty frustrated and perhaps sad about how uncaring they can be. Wouldn't they try to discuss with me first?

COUNSELOR: Would it be fair to say you feel disrespected by them?

CINDY: Yes, it's huge disrespect!

COUNSELOR: How has this incident been impacting you?

CINDY: Economically, not that much. Emotionally, quite a lot. The thing is, I've actually been suffering from depression for a long time. There is almost like a switch that is 'turning on and off.' I realize that it is coming back again.... I see myself having problems sleeping, eating, and focusing at work.

COUNSELOR: I see. So, at first, there was some frustration about how the agency handled your contract. Gradually, you recognize your mood and the problems eating, sleeping, and concentrating, which hint that this long-term depression may be coming back. When did you start noticing these problems?

CINDY: I was let go about a month ago.... I think the first one-to-two days, I was kind of shocked and frustrated, and then I started having problems sleeping a few days afterwards. As I don't have that much work and am tired from being sleep-deprived, I also tend to stay at home most of the time.

COUNSELOR: After the incident, what is a regular day like for you now?

CINDY: That's a good question.... I wake up at about 5 am, trying to fall asleep again, but it usually doesn't work. I lie on my bed and sometimes play with my phone until 7 am. Then I get up, wash, and get something to eat. Sometimes I eat with my mother. If I have a class that day, I will prepare for it. Usually, noon to early afternoon is pretty quiet. Sometimes, I counsel clients or supervisees to meet in the late afternoon or at night. Yeah, that's the kind of regular day I have.

COUNSELOR: What time do you usually sleep?

CINDY: I actually get into bed around 11pm since I want to force myself to sleep a little more. I avoid using my phone or watching TV for at least an hour before I sleep. I used to sleep pretty well, but I started to have sleeping problems again after last month.

COUNSELOR: Let me summarize a bit. When the agency let go of you by not renewing your contract about a month ago, you felt disrespected and frustrated at first, but those feelings gradually manifested as depression, which is a familiar feeling to you since it's not the first time you've been feeling that way. Then you start to have problems eating, sleeping, and concentrating, and you find yourself getting more tired, even though you can still manage your daily work. Did I miss anything?

CINDY: Yes, that's pretty much what I am going through right now.

COUNSELOR: How would you like counseling to help you?

CINDY: I don't want to fall back into the depressive loop, and I really want to get help with my depression before it gets too bad.

COUNSELOR: I hear you. We will certainly work together to manage this depression. Today, I will start by asking you some questions regarding your background so that I know how best to help you.

## Assessment of External Conditions

After getting a sense of clients' reported concerns, the counselor can move onward to gather information on their external conditions. Again, external conditions are environmental and systemic factors contributing to their suffering. The main areas are the client's interconnectedness with others, bodily conditions, and environmental factors. The counselor will sequentially address each domain to get an overview of the client's background. The following example captures the essence of the transactions, but the actual dialogue may be much longer.

## Assessment of Basic Family Background

COUNSELOR: Who are you living with now?

CINDY: It's only my mother and me. My father passed away more than ... I think it's 13 years ago already.

COUNSELOR: You have been living with your mother since your father's passing?

CINDY: That's right.

COUNSELOR: How would you describe your relationship with your mother?

CINDY: Hmm.... Complicated, I guess?

COUNSELOR: How so?

CINDY: [*Smiling with bitterness.*] How should I frame it? For as long as I can remember, she has always tried very hard to care for our family. She cooks, cleans, and makes sure everything is fine at home. But to me ... she's just demanding.

COUNSELOR: I sense some bitterness on your face and some hesitation when talking about your mother.

CINDY: Yes, it's not easy to talk about her. She has always wanted a boy. My family is a traditional Chao Zhou (潮洲) family, meaning that males are much more preferred than females. Since I was young, my mother said many times things like, 'If you were a boy, you would probably be ...', and 'If you were a boy, I wouldn't have to worry.' She constantly compares me with my male cousins and thinks they are better. Almost like no matter what I do, I'm not worthy because I'm a female.

COUNSELOR: So probably because of the Chao Zhou (潮洲) cultural values regarding family, there is a favoritism towards boys, and according to what you described, your mother is somewhat rejecting of your gender identity and the fact that you are not the boy that she wanted. Is it correct?

CINDY: That's correct. Sadly.

COUNSELOR: How about your father? How was your relationship with him?

CINDY: We were really close.

COUNSELOR: Please, tell me more if you don't mind.

CINDY: My mother is a dominant and harsh person who always takes the lead at home. My father was the opposite. He was very kind, timid, and caring. They were like yin and yang. Every time my mother got angry, my father would remain silent and take the blame. Then, he would comfort her and apologize.

COUNSELOR: Uh-huh. How did you feel about this dynamic?

CINDY: I used to feel very bad for my father. I think my mom didn't make sense a lot of the time, but my father never talked back. Thinking about him now, I still remember his warm smile.

COUNSELOR: Even though your father has been gone for some time, you still miss him.

CINDY: Definitely. I think I had my first depressive episode when he died. It was devastating for me.

COUNSELOR: I can imagine how painful it can be to lose such an important person in your life.

CINDY: Yes … and I had to live with my mother. Just my mother and myself. That's another big reason to be depressed, if not crazy!

The assessment dialogue here revealed the basic dynamic of Cindy's family relationship, especially her close relationship with her father and her conflicted relationship with her mother. Counselors can also assess for other familial conditions, such as relationships with extended family (it is common for Chinese families to have influential family members out of the immediate family). Moreover, the client might still be experiencing unresolved grief for her father, which the counselor can process in later sessions.

## Assessment of Social Relationships

COUNSELOR: Let's switch gears a little to talk about your current relationships. Are you currently dating or in a relationship?

CINDY: Yes, I have a girlfriend.

COUNSELOR: I see. How would you identify your sexual orientation?

CINDY: Lesbian.

COUNSELOR: What's she like?

CINDY: Hmm…. Her name is Kathy. She is a very nice person. She is caring and understanding. To be honest, I am really lucky to have met her.

COUNSELOR: I see a glee on your face when talking about her.

CINDY: Yes, I guess she is my main support in life now.

COUNSELOR: How long have you two been dating?

CINDY: Let me think … it's going to be the 14th year already.

COUNSELOR: It seems to be a very serious and committed relationship!

CINDY: It is. Although we are not living together, we feel like a married couple.

COUNSELOR: As you mentioned that you come from a traditional family, how does your sexual orientation affect your relationship with your family?

CINDY: You know what? I never told my parents about it. My parents knew that I never really dated any men, and my mother kept forcing me to date. I guess my father kind of knew, and there were some occasions that I brought Kathy to see my father. And he was very welcoming to Kathy. He even thanked Kathy for taking care of his daughter. It was very touching for me.

COUNSELOR: I can imagine how much it meant to you. It seems to be a sign of acceptance from him.

CINDY:  Certainly. But my mother will never accept it, so I don't bother bringing Kathy to see her.

COUNSELOR:  I see. Besides family, are there any problems or discrimination you have faced for being a lesbian in Hong Kong?

CINDY:  There are occasions that people may give a weird look when I go out with Kathy. There was also a time that we passed by a wet market, an old lady was saying something like, 'See those two women, it's just disgusting!' Other than that, I think most of my problems came from my mother.

COUNSELOR:  How did you feel about those incidents of discrimination?

CINDY:  I was pretty frustrated when I was younger.

COUNSELOR:  Of course, what that lady said was a really rude comment to make to anyone.

CINDY:  Well, that's the way it is in Hong Kong. I have now learned that I am not wrong, and I have the right to choose a way of living. Maybe because I work in the counseling profession and have encountered many people who are open to different sexual orientations! Actually, the job that let me go was an organization supporting the LGBTIQ populations in Hong Kong, and we have done lots of work in the community.

COUNSELOR:  So to summarize, there were some challenges with being a lesbian in Hong Kong, but you have coped with them pretty well, and you are happily in love in a committed relationship. However, the main problem tends to revolve around your mother's attitude towards you. Is that correct?

CINDY:  That's correct.

In this social relationship assessment, one important condition revealed to the counselor is Cindy's sexual identity as a lesbian and the discrimination against this identity in Hong Kong. First, it is essential for counselors not to assume that all clients are part of the "mainstream" culture, such as born and raised in the country of your practice, having the same ethnic background as most of the individuals in your country, being heterosexual, or not having any visible or invisible disabilities. Second, good Buddhist counselors should always respect cultural differences and put themselves in the clients' shoes to see their perspectives and hear their voices.

## Assessment of Challenging Experiences

COUNSELOR:  As a part of the initial assessment, there are some other questions that I hope to ask you, but some of them may sound a little awkward.

CINDY:  No problem.

COUNSELOR:  Were there any domestic violence, abuse, or other challenging experiences while growing up, besides what you have described?

CINDY:  Well … I can't think of any. My mother may yell or scold, but there was not any physical fighting. The only thing might be that my mother used to use corporal punishment when I did not do well enough at school.

COUNSELOR:  How did she usually punish you?

CINDY:  She would use a hanger to hit my buttocks.

COUNSELOR: It sounds pretty scary. How old were you?

CINDY: Yes, it was really scary. I think I was in primary school, so I was about 8 to 12 years old. She no longer did it when I went to secondary school.

COUNSELOR: What do you notice in your body and mind when recollecting these scary incidents?

CINDY: Let me see … a part of me is still a little scared, but I think it's more sad than scared now.

COUNSELOR: Sad?

CINDY: Yes. Thinking about how a girl cannot really feel safe going home is pretty sad.

In this exchange, the client revealed some abusive experiences from her mother. Even though corporal punishment was culturally acceptable during that time in Hong Kong, it does not mean that we can underestimate the psychological harm to the client. In this example, Cindy did not present with post-traumatic stress symptoms; instead, she expressed sadness about this challenging experience. It might be related to her deep yearnings to be loved and accepted, but at this point, the counselor will remember this information and continue with the intake process.

## Assessment of Education and Work

COUNSELOR: How you described your parents react to your grades seems to reflect their high expectations about your academic performance.

CINDY: Definitely. Similar to many other families in Hong Kong and other Chinese cities, they are strong believers in academic achievement, and they expect me to be a high achiever.

COUNSELOR: I am just wondering, how do they convey this message, or value, to you that you have to be a high achiever?

CINDY: My parents actually didn't get much education, and my father often talked about how he was looked down on because of how poorly educated he was. So, since I was young, my parents wanted me to rank among the top students in school. If I didn't do well, my mother would hit me sometimes.

COUNSELOR: What do you think about that?

CINDY: It's good in a way. I used to get really good grades when I was in school. I think my parents' values really pushed me forward.

COUNSELOR: Do these values impact you later in life, including your work?

CINDY: I think I have developed very high expectations of myself, which motivated me to get a higher education, to become a supervisor and a university lecturer, and to give my best in every role at work.

COUNSELOR: It seems like you did fulfill their expectations of becoming a high achiever. Did/do your parents think so?

CINDY: It is so ironic that since I was young, my teachers saw me as a superstar at school, yet when I arrived home I was seen as mere trash. Basically, she never praised me for anything I did. I gradually realized that my mother still thinks I am not good enough no matter how well I do. She just kept asking me to learn from my male cousins, who actually didn't do as well as I did. Of course, my father was a lot happier with me, and he took me out to eat every time I got good grades.

COUNSELOR: 'Trash' is a really strong word! I sensed some frustration when you talked about it.

CINDY: I guess I don't see her seeing any value in me no matter how hard I try. I have always tried my best to make her happy, and sometimes it involves sacrificing what I like.

COUNSELOR: Can you give me an example?

CINDY: You know, I didn't want to be a counselor at first. I wanted to become a jewelry designer. They wanted me to be a professional, like an accountant, a lawyer, or a medical doctor, but I had no interest in any of those fields. I was fortunate to find psychology and finally got into a master's program for counseling. From my parents' perspective, becoming a counselor is more like a 'doctor,' so they kind of allowed me to do it.

COUNSELOR: So what you meant is, you had to sacrifice your passion for art and jewelry design to fulfill their expectations of you.

CINDY: Yes, but to be fair, I like my current job, and it is satisfying to see how I can help my clients and help my students become good counselors. At the same time, I worked very hard for this. I am a 'workaholic' who always gives my best in the service of advancing my career. As you may know, it's not easy to become an established counselor in Hong Kong, and it's hard to make money in this profession, but I never give up.

COUNSELOR: And you have become a successful counselor as well as an expert in the field.

CINDY: Thank you. I think so, but maybe that's why I find it so difficult to accept the fact that I got 'let go' at this age, after serving them for 12 years and working so hard. And the worst part is, when I told my mother about it, she just assumed I was fired because I am not good enough. She didn't even bother to listen.

This exchange focused on the interconnectedness of the client in terms of her family relationships and meaningful experiences while growing up. Crucial to shaping a person's notion of self, the nature of these relationships and experiences provides information on a person's clinging. In particular, the relationship between Cindy and her parents possibly shaped her expectations of herself, such as "Only boys are good," "You are not good enough because you are not a boy," and "Achievement is important." Another important finding is that Cindy's primary emotional support, her father, passed away a long time previously, and Cindy may still be grieving this loss. As Cindy's responses begin gravitating towards her issues with her mother, it is time for a Buddhist counselor to dig deeper in this direction and assess her internal conditions.

## Assessment of Internal Conditions

The assessment of external conditions in Buddhist counseling is somewhat like the practices of contemporary counseling. However, the assessment of internal conditions involves applying several Buddhist psychological concepts. The form focuses on three areas: notions of self, views, and cognitive processes.

### Notion of Self and Views

As mentioned in previous chapters, every person has fabricated a concept of the self according to the five aggregates. This notion of self concerns subjective clinging, and most experiential suffering comes from dissatisfaction with sustaining this notion of self. If a person can understand the nature and characteristics of this notion and how one clings onto it, their mind will have increased flexibility when deciding whether to continue clinging or to let go. Therefore, knowing about the client's notion of self is a crucial step; it is also a continual process that takes time, effort, and acumen.

One manifestation of attachment to a self-notion is the habit of clinging to different views. Views arise from craving, and holding onto them gives the illusion of the satisfying of desires (Analayo, 2003, p. 161). In psychological nomenclature, views are the core beliefs or values of a person that give meaning to and guide their decisions in life. Some views may appear inspiring, profound, and beautiful such as honor, integrity, or justice. Nonetheless, attachment to these views only provides rationalizations to fulfill our self-centered desires and deep-rooted yearnings and urges. Buddhist practice aims to transcend all views and ideologies, thereby relinquishing oneself from the bondage of concepts. To this end, counselors will need to let clients get in touch with their views to reveal the innermost yearnings and desires associated with such views.

During the initial assessment, counselors can consider using the following approach to start the process of examining self-notion and related views:

COUNSELOR: After hearing quite a lot about your family background and your history, I hope to learn more about you. You once described yourself as a 'workaholic,' so what does it mean to be one?

CINDY: It's a good question. As I value achievements, I think work has been a top priority in my life. Sometimes, I am a perfectionist. I can be pretty self-critical. Yes, sometimes I can be very harsh to myself. I guess this is what it means to be a workaholic.

COUNSELOR: What about choosing counseling as a life career? Are there any values or vision driving this direction other than that it sounds more professional than becoming a jewelry designer in your parents' eyes?

CINDY: Let me think…. I've liked having deeper talks with others since I was young. You know, my father was a very good listener, and I always find this way of listening quite healing. I hoped to become someone like him, listening to others to make them feel better.

COUNSELOR: So another characteristic of you is you genuinely care about people, is that right?

CINDY: I do; that's a big reason why I became a counselor.

COUNSELOR: Summarizing what you have said, you tend to see yourself as a high achiever who can be self-critical and harsh to yourself. At the same time, you value deep listening to others, and you care about others, which seems to be another motivation for you to work hard. Moreover, as you mentioned earlier, you strive to become a successful professional to fulfill your parents' expectations. You label all these characteristics as 'workaholic.' Would that be a fair description?

CINDY: That's fair. I think that's probably why I work so hard and feel so disappointed about losing the chance to work more.

Asking how clients describe themselves helps counselors raise awareness of clients' self-notions and reveals how and why they cling onto them. In Cindy's descriptions, clients may consciously or subconsciously portray a desirable self-image to the counselor, and perhaps clinging onto this desirable image satisfies Cindy's deeper needs.

COUNSELOR: Let me go a step further: How happy are you in holding onto this identity as a 'workaholic'? Imagine a scale from 0–10, 0 being the worst and 10 being the happiest, where do you fall by being this 'workaholic'?

CINDY: I have never thought about it. I guess it is an ambivalent feeling. On the one hand, I am happy to be respected. On the other hand, it is very exhausting to be a 'workaholic.' I would say a 3?

COUNSELOR: That does not seem to be very happy.

CINDY: No, it doesn't. Maybe I just don't know how else to live.

COUNSELOR: If it is not very satisfying to become a 'workaholic' while you have been trying hard to be one for a long time, does this identity fulfill certain needs in you?

CINDY: What kind of needs?

COUNSELOR: It could be emotional needs, a need to feel that we exist, a need to be acknowledged, a need to be accepted, or something else. It is a question to ask our heart.

CINDY: Your question made me think of something. When I told my mother about being 'let go,' she just assumed I am not good enough, and I guess being a 'workaholic' makes me feel that I am good?

COUNSELOR: That's a deep reflection. But do you want to convince yourself that you are good, or do you want to convince your mother that you are good?

CINDY: (*pondered for a while*) Myself? No, I think it's about my mother?

COUNSELOR: So perhaps being a 'workaholic' has something to do with your mother's need.

CINDY: I think so.

In exploring the client's views, counselors can examine the reasons sustaining these views and the needs fulfilled by them. In this example, Cindy may have deep yearnings for unconditional love and acceptance from her mother. In response, Cindy keeps trying to become successful, hoping to earn her mother's love and attention, but that hope has been disappointed all these years. This helpless and disappointed feeling may be a causal condition for her depression.

## Assessment of Habits

By understanding clients' interpretations of events and past decisions, counselors can get a sense of their yearnings and their habitual attempts to fulfill these yearnings. There are three main areas assessed in this section of the intake interview: potential yearnings, unskillful habits, and skillful habits. Potential yearnings refer to clients' innermost needs, which drive clients' actions. Yearnings can also be understood as idealistic expectations that lead to disappointment in reality. (Indeed, clients usually would not seek help if these expectations were met in reality.) For example, in her dialogue, Cindy began to acknowledge the potential to be accepted and loved by her mother. She expects that when she can achieve a certain level, such as becoming more respectable and competent than boys, her mother will eventually acknowledge her. Unskillful habits are not beneficial, or even harmful, ways that clients try to meet their expectations in life, often just creating dysfunctional patterns. Since she was young, Cindy has been trying to tolerate her mother and continually work harder to prove that she is good enough. However, getting good grades, becoming a top student, and becoming a respected professional as her parents wanted did not get her needs met. This cycle and unskillful habit of attempting to earn love has repeatedly failed, resulting in long-term disappointment and suffering. One job of a Buddhist counselor is to notice this kind of habit pattern and reflect it to the client in order to raise their awareness.

Moreover, skillful habits are an essential criterion in this assessment form, as every client will have some strengths, skillful means, or protective factors. Acknowledging such factors can help to alleviate the client's suffering. For example, Cindy is a compassionate, intelligent, responsible, and diligent person who has overcome numerous life challenges, but she may not be aware of these strengths.

COUNSELOR: What kind of strengths do you have?

CINDY: Well, besides being as hardworking as an ox, I am not sure if I have any particular strengths.

COUNSELOR: Can I share my observation?

CINDY: Sure.

COUNSELOR: From what you have told me, you seem to try very hard at fulfilling your parents' expectations, which is a sign of filial piety. You have exceeded in all your studies, which is a sign of diligence and intelligence. You have become a successful expert in counseling with lots of students, which speaks of your work ethic. You have devoted a lot of effort to help the LGBTIQ population in Hong Kong, which speaks of your compassion for others. What do you think about these strengths?

CINDY: Thanks…. When you put it in that way … that's right. Perhaps I do have some strengths.

## Short Note on Assessment of Risks

The last part of the data collection assesses potential risk factors. This section of the assessment form reflects the common practice of all counselors in that it covers severe mental health disorders, risk of suicidality or homicidality, past or current experience of abuse or trauma, and other potential risk factors that clients may mention during sessions. As the purpose of this book is to focus on the specifics of Buddhist counseling, interested readers can use other professional counseling guidebooks to learn about the assessment of risks, such as Chapter 6 in *Counseling Assessment and Evaluation: Fundamentals of Applied Practice* by Watson and Flamez (2014) and Chapters 4 to 7 of *Working with Risk in Counselling and Psychotherapy* by Reeves (2015).

## CONCLUSION

Assessment is usually conducted in a spiral manner such that a question in one category will likely elicit answers in other categories. For example, when Cindy talked about work and dating, she actually focused on her mother and revealed more information. Counselors need to be flexible in evaluating different conditions and organize them into a coherent report after the session. Instead of a one-off gesture, Buddhist counselors should consider assessment a continual process, like treatment, because the counselors' and clients' realizations of how conditions contribute to suffering continue to develop throughout the sessions. This chapter has only pinpointed major areas of the assessment form, and readers can refer to the completed form as a reference.

After the initial assessment, the following steps involve formulating a Buddhist understanding of the case and deciding on the course of treatment. The next chapter will discuss a Buddhist counseling case conceptualization together with the beginning of a discussion on treatment planning.

### Contemplative Questions for Buddhist Counselors

Using Figure 6.1, we will try a contemplative exercise to apply a dependent co-arising perspective on suffering. This exercise can be used with clients to pinpoint the experience of suffering and then to gradually deconstruct it to its supporting conditions.

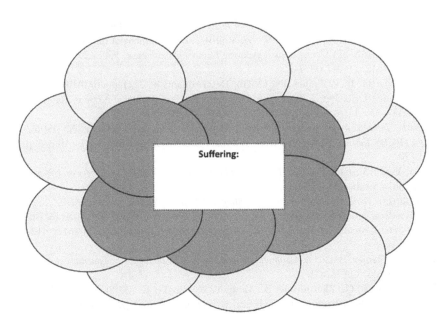

**FIGURE 6.1** An Application of Dependent Co-Arising to Cognitively Deconstruct Conditions of Suffering

First, identify a recent experience of suffering and write it down in the middle label.

Second, reflect and write down all external conditions contributing to your suffering at that moment on the *lighter* outer circles.

Third, reflect on your body and mind. Write all the internal conditions contributing to your suffering at that moment on the *darker* and inner circles.

After you are done, contemplate the following questions:

- "How do I feel when I see that my suffering can be divisible into different conditions?"
- "Which conditions are the most influential, contributing to my suffering?"
- "What conditions are changeable? Why?"
- "What conditions are unchangeable? Why?"
- "Close my eyes and take three mindful deep breaths. How would I feel if I take off the label of suffering and just see the conditions as they are?"

Jot down any feelings, thoughts, ideas, and body sensations. Check with your body and mind to see if the level of suffering changes after this exercise. Again, if this dependent co-arising exercise is helpful to you, you can embody and integrate it as one of your Buddhist counseling techniques.

# REFERENCES

Analayo, B. (2003). *Satipatthana: The Direct Path to Realization*. Cambridge: Windhorse Publications.

Chio, F. H. N., Lai, M. H. C., & Mak, W. W. S. (2018). Development of the Nonattachment Scale-Short Form (NAS-SF) Using Item Response Theory. *Mindfulness*, 9(4), 1299–1308. https://doi.org/10.1007/s12671-017-0874-z

da Costa, H., Martin, B., & Franck, N. (2020). Determinants of Therapeutic Alliance with People with Psychotic Disorders: A Systematic Literature Review. *Journal of Nervous and Mental Disease*, 208(4), 329–339. https://doi.org/10.1097/NMD.0000000000001125

Dhammapada Verse 154. Jaravagga: Old Age, translated by Buddharakkhita, A. (1996). *Access to Insight (BCBS Edition)*. Retrieved from www.accesstoinsight.org/tipitaka/kn/dhp/dhp.11.budd.html%20.

Karunadasa, Y. (2013). *Early Buddhist Teachings: The Middle Path Position in Theory and Practice*. Centre for Buddhist Studies, Hong Kong University.

Reeves, A. (2015). *Working with Risk in Counselling and Psychotherapy*. London: SAGE.

SN 12.15. Kaccayanagotta Sutta: To Kaccayana Gotta. Samyutta Nikaya, translated by Bhikkhu, T. (1997). *Sutta Central*. Retrieved from www.accesstoinsight.org/tipitaka/sn/sn12/sn12.015.than.html

Watson, J. C., & Flamez, B. (2014). *Counseling Assessment and Evaluation: Fundamentals of Applied Practice*. Thousand Oaks, CA: SAGE

Whitehead, R., Bates, G., Elphinstone, B., Yang, Y., & Murray, G. (2018). Letting Go of Self: The Creation of the Nonattachment to Self Scale. *Frontiers in Psychology*, 9, 2544.

## APPENDIX 6.1

### Buddhist Counseling Initial Assessment Form Template

| | |
|---|---|
| Client Name: _____ | Date of Intake: _____ |
| Gender: _____  Age: _____ | Case Number: _____ |

| **1. Client's Reported Concerns** | |
|---|---|
| **Reported Concerns**<br><br>• What makes client decide to seek treatment at this time point? **(The Phenomenon)** Current Complaints: onset, duration, intensity, and frequency?<br><br>• Client's **expectations** of counseling | |

| **2. Assessment of External Conditions** | |
|---|---|
| 1. **Interconnectedness:**<br>*Family*<br>What's client's family composition?<br>How's client's current living situation?<br>How's client's family relationships and experience growing up in this family?<br>Any domestic violence, abuse, or safety issues?<br><br>*Social*<br>What's client's relationship status?<br>How's client's social relationships?<br><br>2. **Body:**<br>How's client's physical health?<br>Any major illnesses or problems?<br>Any current medication or treatment?<br>Any substance use?<br><br>3. **Environment:**<br>*Sociopolitical Influences*<br>How does current sociopolitical issues impact client's wellbeing as a member of the community?<br><br>*Culture*<br>How would client describe one's ethnic identity and culture?<br>How would client describe one's sexual orientation identity?<br>What's client's experience with discrimination or oppression?<br><br>*Education/Work*<br>What's client's education level?<br>What does client do for a living?<br>How's client handling work?<br><br>*Financial situation*<br>How's client's financial situation?<br><br>*Spirituality/Religiosity*:<br>Does client have any spiritual or religious affiliation? | |

| 3. Assessment of Internal Conditions | |
|---|---|
| **1. Notion of Self**<br>What ways, characteristics, or manners do client use to describe himself or herself? | |
| **2. Views**<br><br>**Expectations:**<br>What are client's major expectations in life?<br><br>**Values/Views:**<br>What are client's important beliefs and values?<br><br>**Craving under Values:**<br>What craving does client satisfy by holding onto these values? | |
| **3. Yearnings**<br><br>**Potential yearnings**<br>• What may be some innermost yearnings driving client's actions?<br>• What are client's delusional or unrealistic expectations to try to fulfill yearnings?<br><br>**Unskillful habits**<br>• What kinds of unskillful means are client using to try to fulfill expectations?<br><br>**Skillful habits**<br>• What are client's strengths?<br>• What is client's level of insights to the suffering?<br>• What are some current skillful means?<br><br>**Other Relevant Conditions:** | |
| 4. Assessment of Risks | |
| **Severe Mental Health Disorders (e.g. psychosis, bipolar, PTSD etc.):**<br>Does client have any diagnosis or signs of severe mental illness?<br><br>Any history of mental health treatment?<br><br>**Suicidality/Homicidality:** Does client show any thoughts, behavior, stated intent, risks to self or others?<br><br>**Abuse and Trauma:** Does client report any experiences of being abused or traumatized?<br><br>**Other risk factors:** Is there any other potential harm to self or others? | |

## 5. Case Formulation

**I. Summary & Formulation:** Please use the following questions to help you complete a case formulation to explain client's causes of suffering.
a. How would you describe client's notion of self?
b. What are the discrepancies between unfulfilled expectations and reality?
c. How would you describe client's type and nature of suffering?
d. What are the causes for client's suffering?

## Signatures

_____          _____

Buddhist Counselor's          Date          Supervisor's          Date
Signature                                    Signature

# CHAPTER 7

# Buddhist Counseling Case Conceptualization

In professional psychology, a theoretical orientation or theoretical approach is a standard nomenclature to describe the theory behind a psychotherapeutic practice. Under the assumption that counseling or psychotherapy is a theory-driven practice, the practitioner employs a particular theoretical lens to conceptualize a client's presenting problems, analyze the reasons for suffering, intervene to reduce or eliminate the presenting problem, and make clinical decisions in a process commonly known as case conceptualization or case formulation.

New counselors often have problems understanding the term *case conceptualization* or *case formulation*. Case conceptualization is a multilevel theoretical explanation of a client's psychological presentation that conveys information on how to facilitate therapeutic gains (Ridley et al., 2017). In other words, it is a theory-driven answer to the *why* question after assessment: based on all the information I have gathered, why does my client suffer? It is also a conceptual framework for creating and making sense of a picture of raw data, and can be compared to buying all of the essential ingredients in a grocery store during the assessment phase and cooking them to make a single dish during the conceptualization phase. As different theories have different worldviews and values, theoretical orientations often match a mental health professional's attitudes, beliefs, and preferences.

To briefly illustrate different approaches driven by different theoretical orientations, we will use a hypothetical case involving Lisa to show how different counselors' conceptualizations may vary significantly. The background of Lisa is as follows:

> Lisa is a 25-year-old Thai graduate student in a Master program in Social Science in Accountancy in Singapore. She was referred to you for her presenting problem of anxiety and a depressed mood. She describes herself as having problems sleeping, loss of concentration, low appetite, suffering from intense worries about not being able to finish her thesis on time, feeling sad sometimes, and starting to avoid her thesis supervisor. She hopes to find ways to cope with her anxiety so that she can complete her thesis and graduate on time. In addition, she has a strong interest in jewelry design, but she gave up pursuing this path because her family, especially her father (a successful accountant in Thailand), does not see it as a proper profession.

DOI: 10.4324/9781003025450-7

First, psychodynamic theories focus on how early relationships influence the formation of a person's self-concept and a relationship blueprint for life so that individuals' unmet needs and the development of negative feelings in current relationships are believed to replicate unhealthy relationships with primary caregivers (parents). Thus, a psychodynamic counselor may assess Lisa's relationships with and perceptions of her parents to examine whether she has been reenacting unhealthy relational patterns in current relationships, e.g., with her supervisor, classmate, partner, friend, etc. For example, Lisa may subconsciously experience her dissertation supervisor as her critical and rejecting father and transfer the negative relational experience with her father to her supervisor–supervisee relationship, which provokes an overwhelming sense of anxiety in her. Moreover, Lisa's pursuit of higher education may aim to fulfill her family's expectation of being a successful professional, which squashed any desire to follow her aspiration for jewelry design. Furthermore, her need to satisfy her family's expectations to become a child worthy of love and care created lots of anxiety, and the sadness may come from her inability to follow her aspirations. Psychodynamic interventions would aim to help Lisa contain her anxiety while relating her personal narrative and facilitating an underlying catharsis, supporting her to activate her defenses, transference, and (unmet) needs.

Person-centered therapy generally focuses on providing an unconditional and accepting environment for the growth of the authentic self. A counselor practicing person-centered therapy would explore Lisa's reasons for getting a master's degree, especially the related internal needs and environmental demands, and to understand any incongruence between Lisa's authentic and ideal self. For instance, Lisa's pursuit of higher education fulfilled her family's expectation of being a perfectly successful professional, although this had squashed any desires to follow her aspiration for jewelry design. Her need to satisfy her family's expectations to become a child worthy of love and care (i.e., conditional love) created much anxiety. Her subsequent sadness may come from her inability to follow her aspirations (self-actualization). Person-centered therapy aims to create a therapeutic environment characterized by empathy, congruence (genuineness), and unconditional positive regard. Such an approach will facilitate Lisa to get in touch with her intrinsic values and help her to explore her life decisions together with a higher congruence between her needs and environmental demands.

Finally, cognitive behavioral therapy focuses on adopting rational and helpful beliefs and thinking. A counselor using a cognitive behavioral therapy approach may explore Lisa's thoughts, assumptions, and beliefs contributing to her anxiety symptoms. For example, Lisa may have frequent, negative, and irrational thoughts of "I am not smart enough to manage a master's thesis" when needing to start her thesis, resulting in worries, anxiety, ruminations, and physiological problems. Cognitive-behavioral interventions may focus on teaching Lisa behavioral techniques to cope with her anxiety symptoms, raising Lisa's awareness of her thought processes and fostering more helpful and rational thoughts and beliefs.

So how would a Buddhist theoretical orientation understand any client's psychological presentation? To answer this question, this chapter will now utilize the teachings of Buddhism to conceptualize the client's suffering and thereby lay the foundation for the reduction of suffering in coming chapters.

## CASE CONCEPTUALIZATION BASED ON BUDDHIST TEACHING

In Buddhism, we suffer because "what should be" does not align with "what is" in the world. As stated in the First Noble Truth, *dukkha* is an inevitable experience in life. The root of the word *dukkha* implies the axle of a wheel that is out of alignment, which may also be interpreted as the mismatch between our expectations and reality, resulting in unsatisfactoriness. Most of us are driven by a state of ignorance that fails to see and accept what is actually happening. Instead, we are prone to follow our cravings and desires, expecting our needs to be satisfied, and we consequently tend to distort or deny actual happenings when reality does not satisfy us. This distortion may bring about temporary satisfaction, but it will eventually result in greater suffering. Ignorance describes our lack of insight into this process of resisting reality, perpetuating suffering through our re-conceptualizations of what actually is. From a Buddhist perspective, ignorance manifests in many forms. In the Note, Know, Choose model, we use the concepts of craving, clinging, and expectations to illustrate the major causes of suffering (Figure 7.1 and Table 7.1).

### Craving

The historical Buddha provided a complete and structured framework for explaining and treating suffering called the Four Noble Truths, which is the foundation of basically all Buddhist Teachings. In Buddhist counseling, the Four Noble Truths—suffering, its causes, the cessation of suffering, and the path to cessation—guides conceptualization and treatment. According to the second Noble Truth, craving (*Taṇhā*) is the root cause of suffering (Karunadasa, 2013). *Taṇhā* refers to a powerful lust or a strong mental or physical thirst and longing for one of three experiences: craving for sensual pleasures (*kāma-taṇhā*), craving for existence (*bhava-taṇhā*), and craving for annihilation (*vibhava-taṇhā*). Craving for sensual

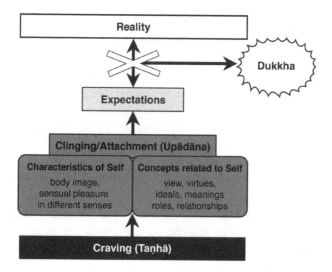

**FIGURE 7.1** Diagram of Conceptualization of the Note, Know, Choose Model

**TABLE 7.1** Diagram of Initial Conceptualization of Cindy

| Conceptualization Domains | Description |
|---|---|
| *Dukkha* | Nature and type of suffering. |
| *Reality* | Realistic and objective conditions according to the understanding of counselor and client. |
| *Expectations* | Client's expectation of conditions to fulfill his or her needs. |
| *Notion of Self* | Client's creation of a self-identity as a subjective agent to satisfy innermost cravings. |
| *Clinging* | Concretized attachment to specific physical or metaphysical objects such as concepts, relationships, or self-identities, in the wish to satisfy cravings. |
| *Craving* | A primitive drive of yearning impelled by ignorance in the belief that "I" exists. |

pleasures results from the mind's inclination to indulge in pleasant feelings of the six senses: (1) sight—pleasurable visual experiences, such as appreciating beautiful paintings; (2) sound—pleasurable auditory experiences, such as listening to melodious music; (3) taste—pleasurable eating experiences, such as enjoying flavorful food; (4) smell—pleasurable aromatic experiences, such as smelling fragrance; (5) touch—pleasurable tactile experiences, such as intimate touch during sex; and (6) mind—pleasurable mental experiences, such as creative thinking, solving intellectual problems, and recollecting favorable memories. In Buddhism, experiencing pleasure is not a problem in itself, but the craving for pleasure creates suffering (Karunadasa, 2013). For most individuals, the pursuit of sensual pleasure is an attempt to satiate cravings that leads to short-term gratification while also fueling the desire to repeat the same action. Progressively, the magnitude of the craving will be strengthened until it becomes a habit, wiring the mind with a rigid pattern of pursuing pleasure that ultimately results in suffering.

Craving for existence refers to a longing for continuity in a physical body that is sustained by ascribed identities, interpersonal relationships, views and values, meanings of life and other endeavors, in the pursuit of which we attempt to personalize neutral objects, people, or events. This effort to convince oneself that "I exist" creates the illusion of a permanent and continuous existence. In daily life, the experience of existence can stem, for example, from building up the personal identity of a successful, wealthy, and likable person, from attachment to a marriage bond between two unrelated individuals for the rest of their lives, from treating children as a continuation or fulfillment of parental wishes, or from building fame and reputation to ensure that one's name is remembered. No matter how vivid or convincing these experiences appear, every achievement and relationship will eventually fade away or collapse because none of these has a self-sustaining nature. In other words, these costly, draining, and unproductive endeavors only lead to provisional and transient experiences that cannot satiate the mind's unrealistic desire for permanence. The result is disappointment and dissatisfaction.

Both the craving for sensual pleasure and the craving for existence are embedded within the poison of greed. While the craving for sensuality overemphasizes the positivity of existence, the craving for annihilation exaggerates the negativity of existence and drives a strong, usually transient, desire to resist life. It leads to a drive for self-destruction in reaction to unbearable and unavoidable pain in life based on the view that the self is a source of suffering that should be destroyed. Some explanations have described craving for annihilation as an extreme reaction to disappointment with existence that develops into an intense hatred towards life, oneself, and others. Individuals who have shaped a negative self-identity or experienced intolerable suffering may have a craving to reject their own existence through self-destruction, believing that such destruction will bring an end to suffering. In life, this craving for annihilation often manifests as suicide attempts or self-destructive behaviors. It creates a strong urge to declare, "That's it! My life sucks, and I don't want it anymore!" However, neither resistance to a painful experience nor destroying oneself will end suffering because a mind of hatred and aversion towards itself is irritating and disturbing.

All three types of craving fuel the notion of self, which perpetuates unhealthy habits that eventually result in greater dissatisfaction.

## Clinging

Driven by craving, the human minds cling to the external world and fabricate a permanent relationship between the mind and objects (Bodhi, 2003). This attempt to satiate desire is a process called clinging (*upādāna*), commonly translated as "attachment." The three types of craving lead one's mind to grasp onto environmental factors. This grasping/clinging helps the mind to concretize and materialize its habitual drive for permanence, which in turn functions to fuel craving further. Clinging is a strong psychological attachment to, identification with, and immersion in mental or physical objects, coupled with the delusion that possessing those objects can satisfy one's craving. For example, a woman born and raised in a family culture of rigidly defined gender roles will naturally believe that being a mother is the only way to be recognized and valued. Her craving for existence drives her to meet this social expectation, and she clings to the role of a mother, after which she clings to her relationship with her son, which further feeds her craving to sustain the identity of a good mother. This mother may then ignore the emerging independence of her three-year-old son, striving to infantilize him, which serves to make her feel needed. From the perspective of dependent origination, the son's conditions are constantly changing as he experiences continuous physical-motor development as well as socioemotional and cognitive changes. Her son today has grown to be different from her son of yesterday. However, the mother may fixate on the previous concept of a "son" who is highly dependent on her, thereby ignoring his changes while grasping an unrealistic concept that fulfills her need for existence.

## Notion of Self

Distinct from most philosophical assumptions about the existence of a more in-depth, authentic, or permanent self, Buddhism describes a self that—due to dependent origination—does not inherently exist. This position stands in critical opposition to theories assuming the existence of an eternal soul, a spiritual connection with a higher power, or an intrinsic and authentic "me." For novices of Buddhism, a common question is, "If there is not a 'me,' then who is behind the consciousness of reading this chapter and thinking about these ideas?"

The short answer is that the Buddhist theory of non-self does not refer to the absence of self. Instead, it merely describes the mind's inclination to attribute to neutral phenomena a fantasized concrete identity. This inclination can be described as habitual energy that leads the consciousness to claim ownership of mental and bodily experiences, thereby fabricating an independent self-notion or self-identity. In other words, there is not any permanent entity called "the self" that possesses a mind. Instead, consciousness itself and its mental processes compose the mind, and the mind becomes deluded when it becomes convinced of the notion that "this is my self."

Although such a self-notion is not an inherently existing entity, the mind's repeated attempts to reify and concretize its existence have made it seem highly authentic. Since birth, every person, or each set of the five aggregates, continuously interacts with the external environment and internalized messages from others to formulate a sense of "I." In this process, the role of primary caregivers—usually one's father and mother—has a significant impact. Children create their notion of self through the direct and interactive influences of their parents and family, especially how their parents behave as role models, the extent to which they value their children's presence, and the quality of emotional bonding made available to them. For example, parents who show love to children by spending quality time with them, soothing and protecting them when they are scared, and physically caring for them are likely to send messages of "You are lovable" or "You are important." Their children will internalize such messages and transform them into lovable and essential parts of their self-notion. On the other hand, parents who are abusive, neglectful, extremely critical, and rejecting are telling their children that "you are not worthy of love" and "you are not important." In turn, these children are likely to form a notion of self characterized by vulnerability and being unlovable. Together with a self-notion, there are several everyday psychological needs for which a self usually yearns.

Clinging (Pāli: Upādāna) is an attempt to grasp onto and attach to the created self-notion as the mind's effort to convince itself of existence. Fueled by craving (Pāli: Taṇhā), one yearns to satisfy innermost needs and desires through clinging onto such self-notions. Some common needs and desires to sustain a self-notion include (1) *existential needs*, such as a sense of identity, sense of control, sense of competence, and sense of meaning; (2) *emotional needs*, such as love, respect, acceptance and acknowledgment, and emotional security; and (3) *biological needs*, such as sensual pleasure and physical safety. Human beings tend to have these needs from birth onwards, and the needs are likely to last until the end of life for mundane persons.

Further, individuals who did not fulfill specific needs from primary caregivers may seek fulfillment from others in different relationships. At the same time, some of the desires can be highly ambivalent. For example, an individual with a weak and vulnerable self-notion may want to be with a partner who is perceived as powerful and competent. This pursuit of togetherness may grant a temporary sense of being powerful and safe. However, the weak and vulnerable self-notion may develop jealousy of the powerful and competent person, believing that the partner took away love and attention from those close to them, and then push them away. Afterwards, loneliness and the insecurity of being weak and vulnerable are highly disturbing, so the individual with a weak and vulnerable self-notion seeks to be with another person who is perceived as powerful and competent. Then, the cycle repeats itself.

The self-notion is like a main character: it includes multiple layers and facets such as personalities, history, relationships, needs, problems, and context. To understand the self-notion is to reveal a person's story from his or her idiosyncratic perspective. However, every person's clinging to a self-notion is unique and each of our stories is qualitatively distinctive. Therefore, it is crucial to genuinely understand a person's whole story without overgeneralizations and assumptions. In my experience of teaching Buddhist counseling, many students learning the concept of self-notion become confused with a core premise of cognitive-behavioral therapy (CBT): that each person has a robust cognitive schema for self-labeling (such as "I am unlovable" or "I am incompetent"), although it may be true that many individuals have one or two self-attached labels that contribute actively to suffering. In my understanding, a self-notion usually includes a comprehensive, multilayered, and multi-faceted story. First, there can be different layers of self-notions. For example, a person may believe oneself to be competent and likable, which can be a defensive coat to fend against inner insecurity and inadequacy. When failure or formidable life challenges impinge on such outer layers of self-notion, the deeper self-notion of being vulnerable, weak, and unlovable may emerge. The person may collapse and be accused of being weak and vulnerable.

To conceptualize the self-notion concept, this model applies another core Buddhist teaching: self-view (SN 22.49). Delusionally believing in the existence of self, one tends to compare oneself to others and cling to one of the following three conclusions: "I am better," "I am equal to/as good as," or "I am worse." Each of these views is rooted in conceit (*māna*). An uncultivated person tends to be born with an inclination to believe that "I" exist and have importance in this world. While it is easy to imagine how ascribing superiority to oneself would explain clinging to "I am superior," it may be more difficult to understand clinging to equality and inferiority. However, these three views are each a product of conceit, taking "I" as the central reference point. It is a highly self-centered attitude by itself.

Moreover, some scholars believe that the self-notion is a multilayered psychological complex, meaning that the views may not be mutually exclusive. For example, a person who believes that "I am inferior" may have a protective layer of superiority. When external events and people boost and pamper the self, a dormant sense of superiority may emerge. Again, the commonality among the three is that of self-importance, which usually manifests through comparison with others. When one compares, one differentiates and categorizes. Thus, the existence of self gets continuously validated through reified differentiations and categorizations (i.e., "I am this, you are that, then I am this … on and on and on …").

Usually, there is a habitually attached view, but the other two views, with their related thoughts and behaviors, can also emerge. For example, for persons attached to "I am equal," there are several tendencies. First, when a person is being regarded as a "less than," the root thought for proliferations might be "I'm as good as you," but the underlying implication might be "and a good deal better!" (Ashby & Fawcett, 1994). In this way, the person may try hard to prove that he or she is not worse than the other. Second, when there is a sense of unfairness or injustice that triggers the person's attachment, the person becomes emotionally reactive and seeks fairness.

It is different from an ideal of justice because this person tends to personalize the event instead of perceiving justice as beneficial for an interconnected world. One thought might be, "How dare you discriminate against one of us! My group represents 'I' and 'I' am not worse than you, so you should treat my group fairly." Using social justice or other beautiful views as a rationalization, the person continues to prove themself equal to their targets. But in actuality, the self-notion is an interdependently constructed experience based on the aggregates of causes and conditions and countless conditions that make every human existence unique. Attaching to "I am equal" reflects ignorance about the interdependent conditions supporting a phenomenon and assumes everyone is the same. For example, when a person sees another not being able to achieve a task, he or she may think, "If I can do it, so can you." In other situations, when the person cannot achieve a task, he or she may think, "If you can do it, I should be able to do it too." This view can easily become an expectation of self and others. Here is a brief description of each view:

1 "*I am superior to you*": So I need to keep on proving my superiority by achievements and recognitions.
2 "*I am equal to you*": So I need to make sure it is absolutely fair.
3 "*I am inferior to you*": So I need to fend off this inferiority by working extra hard to get recognition, relying on others or, paradoxically, ruining this self.

Different self-notions can manifest as similar needs, and clients may even behave similarly in certain situations while there are subtle and fundamental differences at the core. This section will discuss two illustrative real-life examples of successful psychologists, albeit with altered biographical information to ensure confidentiality.

The first psychologist, Peggy, grew up in an environment where both of her parents were demanding but, despite Peggy's best efforts, still not meeting their expectations. But the background causes and conditions were complex. Her father has had multiple affairs, and her mother is emotionally abusive to Peggy as an outlet for resentment towards her husband. Peggy did not receive much attention at school, and there were very few loving and attentive role models in her life to assure her of her importance. Moreover, she was born and raised in a patriarchal cultural background in which girls are less important than boys.

The second psychologist, Donald, also grew up in an environment where the parents are demanding, with subsequent very high expectations for their son, who nevertheless believes that he has never been able to satisfy those expectations. However, Donald's mother is a loving and warm person who spends a lot of quality time caring for him. His parents also have a stable and satisfying relationship. Moreover, many relatives and mentors think highly of Donald, the firstborn son in a cultural tradition that values boys highly.

Perhaps due to the failure in meeting their parents' expectations, Donald and Peggy grew up becoming high-achieving psychologists in the field. Both are self-critical, have high expectations of themselves, and hope to earn acknowledgment and recognition from others. However, their self-notions and ways of clinging are different. Donald has formed a self-notion as a superior person with a sense of grandiosity. He strives to convince himself that this existence is desirable and must be lived continuously. In contrast, Peggy has formed a self-notion as an inferior person, so she tries very hard to fend off this undesirable sense of self via her achievements and recognition.

If a counselor mindfully explores the thoughts and decisions occurring between these two individuals, there will be clear differences in motivation, reliance, and sense of control. In particular, Donald is motivated to sustain his desirable self-notion, while Peggy is trying hard to deny or hide her undesirable self-notion. In addition, Donald is very self-reliant and believes that he can muddle through failures, while Peggy is very other-reliant, tending to depend on others to get through challenges. Lastly, Donald believes that he can make deliberative decisions, while Peggy thinks that most things are out of her control so that being with someone powerful is the only way she can gain back some influence.

It will not help Buddhist counselors to assume that the high achieving and self-critical characteristics of these two have roots in the same notion of self. An inaccurate interpretation can be a hindrance to awareness and insight. The importance of self-notion does not aim to find a definitive answer because there will never be a valid answer for a fabricated question. Instead, the value of exploration lies in becoming aware of how we continue to fabricate self-notions to meet specific needs and how suffering arises in the process. Clinical exploration aims to train one's mind to gain insights into the dissatisfying nature of the process and differentiate the fabricated self-notion and the realistic sense of self as the five aggregates living in the world (i.e., Who I wish I am vs. Who I am objectively). Such "self" understanding is a crucial first step in the reduction of suffering.

## Expectations

Driven by craving and solidified by clinging, the mind tends to form assumptions of the world and place expectations on self, others, relationships, and the nature of things, to assure the mind that those expectations will be met. This conceptualization of expectations is derived from the Buddhist concept of clinging as it describes the mind's preference for what should happen over what is happening. The mother clinging to her role may expect her son to depend on her despite his maturity. The mother may come to expect her son to live close to home, talk to her regularly, seek emotional comfort from her, and ask her to do his chores. When her son finally starts to launch his life and become autonomous, this support for her identity collapses, which challenges her craving for existence.

## Realistic Conditions

In previous chapters, we discussed the Buddhist reality of dukkha, impermanence, dependent co-arising, and non-self. Another way to define reality in Buddhism is "things as they are." While it sounds abstract, most mundane people, like you and me, tend to distort or fabricate reality to satisfy our egoistic needs. This unacceptance of reality will eventually lead to suffering, while the way out of suffering is to see and accept reality, regardless of how undesirable it may be. For example, the famous *Sallatha Sutta: The Arrow* (SN 36.6) discusses two different reactions to the suffering of a layperson versus an advanced practitioner: in both individuals, there is inevitable suffering, such as physical pain, which is regarded as the first arrow (Figure 7.2). A layperson's mind inclines to sorrow, lamentation, aggravation,

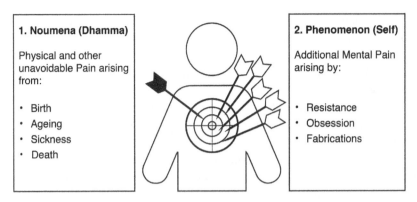

**FIGURE 7.2** Reality vs. Fabrications: The Two Arrows

and to expand the pain through psychological resistance, obsession, or both. Such added self-inflicted pain is regarded as the second arrow. However, a cultivated practitioner sees and accepts the physical pain without resistance, obsession, or distortion, thereby refraining from stabbing himself with the second arrow.

In this sutta, Buddhist reality is regarded as an objective and depersonalized noumenon instead of a phenomenon (composed of observer experiences). Again, to reduce suffering is to see and accept the noumenon without grasping the phenomenon, which is tainted by craving. It is common to see clients suffering from the unacceptance of reality because that reality disappoints their expectations, thereby suffering from both the original pain as well as the distress of pain. For example, they desire a partner to be more emotionally caring, that their parent will eventually adore them instead of other siblings, hold firmly onto the ideal of justice and equality in society, or wish themselves or significant others to be free from chronic illnesses.

## Dukkha

There are several ways to define and classify dukkha in Buddhism. The current model chooses two clinically relevant systems. First, according to the *Mahaparinibbana Sutta* (DN 16), there are eight categories of dukkha to help us understand how suffering manifests when reality clashes with expectations. Since an uncultivated mind assumes a self and clings to one's self-notion, most of us expect to live happily and continuously until reality clashes with our expectations. These eight types of suffering (Trungpa, 2009) are:

- *Birth*: Traditionally, a volition to be born carries an expectation for happiness in human life. However, the suffering of birth initiates from the suffering inside the mother's womb, a small bounded place, and continues through the formidable challenges and demands after birth. Another interpretation is to consider birth the initiation of desire, clinging, or other mental phenomena that will eventually clash with reality.
- *Old age*: A subtle expectation in life is to live continuously, while the reality is that aging always comes after birth, and there is inevitable psychological and physiological suffering along with the aging process.

- *Sickness*: Similarly, the reality of living includes the sufferings of physiological or psychological disorders as a part of life, which challenges the expectation of a healthy and happy life.
- *Death*: Death is another major cause of suffering because it bluntly confronts one's desire for and expectation of self-continuity.
- *Getting what you don't want*: This is one of the three common daily sufferings associated with undesirable people and situations, such as harsh supervisors, punitive parents, anxious partners, political conflicts, or an undesirable occupation.
- *Not being able to hold onto what is desirable*: This is the second common daily suffering. It involves losing important persons, things, or events and being unable to keep these unchanged. The reality is that change is a natural and unavoidable process in an impermanent world.
- *Not getting what you want*: This is the last common daily suffering, in which the expectation of getting one's wishes granted clashes with reality. The cravings might be for love, acceptance, achievement, recognition, or any other desired object in life.
- *Suffering between the periods of birth and death in the five aggregates*: This suffering is more abstract. It refers to the suffering associated with the five aggregates. In theory, any clinging to the five aggregates, including pleasant and neutral feelings, has a taste of dukkha. However, only cultivated practitioners can discern this level of suffering. The current conceptualization is primarily for analyzing regular individuals, so this dukkha is included.

From my clinical experience, another helpful way to classify dukkha is to use the Three Marks of Existence (namely, non-self, impermanence, dukkha). These types of dukkha are related to a Wrong View of reality as well as the drive from the three poisons to satisfy egoistic needs, as follows:

- *Seeing self in a non-self*: For many clients, suffering originates from a self-view that interprets any event using the self as a central reference point. Some examples include, "I am the one who works the hardest in this agency, how come those who don't do much get all the recognition," a view which narrows down what one sees according to what one's self does and thinks, regardless of multiple causes and conditions. For example, a person could say: "I would rather have my daughter abort her fetus with Down's syndrome because it makes my life and my family imperfect," which identifies and personalizes the daughter's child as "mine"; and "I have to have a really skinny body, and I don't care about forcing myself to vomit," a view which clings onto one's body and identifies it as self or "me." These rigid expectations of self-relevance usually manifest as lack of empathy for others, dissatisfactions in relationships, self- and other-blaming, and other disturbances when they clash with the reality that the self is not the center of the world.
- *Seeing permanence in impermanence*: Holding onto things and assuming that they will last forever can be a common experience for clients suffering from long-term mental disorders such as depression. For example, a female client with multiple major depressive episodes due to the tragic death of her father and fiancé said, "I can never get out of my depression. All the important men in my life left me. It may be a curse. This pain is

so overwhelming that I cannot see any way out. I just feel ... no matter what I do, this depressing pain will always be here." In the Buddhist view, depression is impermanent, as any experience of depression is an interactive and interdependent phenomenon of bodily sensations, feelings, thoughts, volitions, and consciousness. That is, the reality of depression is that it can arise, change, and cease. At the same time, the client holds onto previous experiences and assigns a permanent nature to depression, resulting in an intense level of suffering.

- *Seeing pleasure in dukkha:* Suffering can be masked behind temporarily satisfying choices, one source of suffering being to assume that transient satisfying choices are lasting ways to sustain happiness. For example, a 40-year-old male married client believes that flirting with female colleagues is a sustainable way to be happy, but reality hits him when his wife discovers the texts and wants a divorce. Another example is the pursuit of pleasurable feelings when drinking and ingesting chemical substances without noticing the long-term damage to body and mind. The common ground in these examples is the mind's narrow focus on the fleeting pleasant feelings without seeing a more realistic and objective picture of associated suffering.

Classifying dukkha in these 11 ways can shed light on how a client's expectations collide with reality. It is possible to discuss the types of dukkha with clients, especially clients who affiliate with Buddhism and collaboratively become mindful and categorize the experiences of suffering. This process may normalize the client's suffering, help the client see dukkha as more tangible and explainable, and empower the client with adaptive ways to reduce dukkha.

The following vignette illustrates the matured "Cindy," who sought Buddhist counseling for her depressed mood. We can also see how she has changed in the last 23 years while some core unfulfilled yearnings remained the same.

## Case Vignette Conceptualization: the 48-year-old "Cindy"

From the perspective of dependent origination, Cindy's suffering is a phenomenon attributable to multiple factors and conditions, beginning with her environmental and familial conditions. Cindy was born into a Chinese subculture that has a strong preference for sons over daughters and which also highly values academic achievement. Her mother, the parental figure with the most authority in the family, failed to accept and value her as a daughter and became highly critical of Cindy at an early age. Her father, by contrast, was a kind and loving parental figure who offered some warmth and support, although he did not oppose his wife's rejecting attitude towards Cindy not providing her with the powerful affirmative acceptance she needed.

Cindy's mother has constantly made her feel less important than her male cousins. She has openly expressed feeling ashamed for not giving birth to a son, has rejected emotional closeness with Cindy, and wished that Cindy would conform to a masculine stereotype, such as becoming independent, hiding her emotional vulnerability, and being competitive. At the same time, Cindy has several close relatives who empathize with her situation and think highly of her. The fact that Cindy was the first in the family to attend university and complete a master's degree brought some pride to the extended family. Since Cindy started

| **Craving** |
| Sensuality, Existence, Non-existence |
| Craving for existence. |

⇓

| **Created Notion of Self: Who am "I"?** | **Clinging and Yearnings: What do "I" need?** |
| --- | --- |
| Cindy has formed a self-notion as a competent and lovable daughter, with a superior sense of self, who can persevere through challenges to get her needs met. Cindy has overcome numerous formidable challenges in her life to become a seasoned lesbian counselor who is well-known in the community. However, the current loss of her job together with put-downs by her mother has squashed her superior notion of self, resulting in doubts, helplessness, and a depressed mood. | This notion of self is based on her Clinging to maternal love signified by acceptance, acknowledgment, and warmth. This notion of self yearns for love and recognition from her mother. |

⇓

| **Expectations: What do "I" expect in daily life?** |
| She expects her mother to love and accept her unconditionally. |
| **Related Realistic Conditions: What actually happens?** |
| Cindy's mother does not acknowledge that a daughter could be competent and lovable. |

⇓

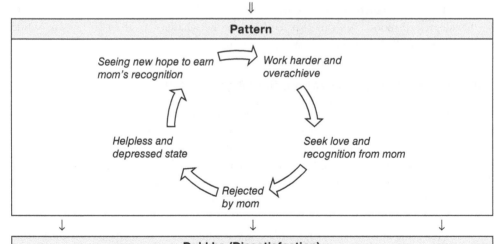

| **Dukkha (Dissatisfaction)** |
| *e.g. Birth, Ageing, Sickness, Dying, association with dislike, separation from like, not getting what you want* |
| *Association with dislike, Not getting what you want* |

**FIGURE 7.3** Case Conceptualization Diagram of Cindy

school, her intelligence, sense of responsibility, and motivation to learn have made her a favorite student of many teachers and mentors. Combined with her father's unconditional love, these factors have formed in Cindy a superior belief about herself that has fueled her perseverance through challenges and rejections.

However, Cindy's mother has never accepted the existence of her daughter. In response, driven by a craving for existence, Cindy has developed a yearning to foster and sustain her notion of self and she has therefore developed a clinging relationship with a mother who loves and accepts her. As her mother always emphasizes the achievements and accolades of Cindy's male cousins, Cindy believes that changing her mother's attitude about her will result in a potential breakthrough. Cindy has sought, and received, professional recognition as a seasoned counselor and has developed a subsequent clinging to her professional role to support her notion of self as a lovable daughter. In the quest to change her mother's perception of her, she ended up becoming more successful than her male cousins. When Cindy was "let go of" from her position at her agency, her hope of changing the reality of her mother's rejection collapsed, and a sense of helplessness and sadness arose. More importantly, Cindy realizes that she has a powerful sense of frustration with herself because her attempt to earn love from her mother puts her continuously in states of disappointment and suffering.

Cindy has a fervent desire to resist this reality by overachieving to change her mother's view of her and convince her mother to acknowledge her as a worthy child. In other words, a significant cause of Cindy's suffering is her strong attachment to an image of a loving and accepting mother, even as reality continues to fail to meet her expectations. This experience of not obtaining what she has been yearning for causes significant suffering, which then manifests as frustration and depression. Moreover, these failed attempts have formed a habitual pattern of false hope and disappointments, thereby continually aggravating Cindy's suffering. To facilitate case conceptualization, a specific diagram can be used in Buddhist counseling (Figure 7.3). (A blank form is included in Appendix 7.1).

## Brief Note on Treatment Planning

After gaining a deeper understanding of the clients' causes of suffering in the case conceptualization, the next step is for counselors to formulate a treatment plan to reduce clients' suffering. A treatment plan is a customized, clear, and structured outline of the course of treatment created to help clients reach specific therapeutic goals (Figure 7.4). Like assessment forms, different theoretical orientations and treatment models tend to have different treatment plans. For example, the current Buddhist counseling model uses Note, Know, Choose as a basis for strategizing a client's treatment process while also serving as a conceptual guide for the direction of counseling.

There are three components in the Buddhist counseling treatment plan: an overarching long-term goal, a plan for each phase, and interventions under each short-term goal. The long-term goal is to dissolve the client's clinging to her mother and the need for her approval, thereby reducing her suffering. Cindy's depressive feelings, for instance, are a manifestation of her failure to receive acknowledgment and love from her mother while also not getting her work contract renewed. The long-term goal will be for Cindy to let go of her clinging to a non-existent mother who unconditionally acknowledges and loves her. However,

---

**Treatment Plan: Cindy**

**Overarching Goal:** To let go of clinging onto a perceived loving mother.

### Initial Phase of Treatment

**Note Plan:** Raise awareness of body and mind.
*Note Interventions:*
1  Develop daily practice of mindful breathing for 15 minutes to develop concentration.
2  Practice recentering techniques to soothe conceptual proliferations.
3  Use journaling to notice internal mental dialogues.

**Know Plan:** Revealing clinging and craving.
*Know Interventions:*
1  Examine influences from past and present conditions.
2  Reflect on clinging and desire through exploration of choices and needs in relationships with parents and other important figures in her life.

### Working Phase of Treatment

**Note Plan:** Foster concentration of mind.
*Note Interventions:*
1  Applying Note techniques to cope with strong emotional reactivity.

**Know Plan:** Seeing realistic conditions.
*Know Interventions:*
1  Explore and process the realistic "mother" and the expectation of a "mother."
2  Use detachment visualization to further process the experience of clinging.
3  Practice Mind Moment Analysis to realize and highlight moments of choice in one's life.

**Choose Plan:** Choosing to let go of an innermost urge for a loving mother in daily life.
*Choose Interventions:*
1  Practice weekly self-compassion meditation and exercises.
2  Explore internal mental decisions with the realistic "mother."
3  Practice making new decisions with mother in daily encounters.

### Closing Phase of Treatment

**Note Plan:** Foster equanimity of mind.
*Note Interventions:*
1  Continue regular Note practice to foster equanimity.

**Know Plan:** Accepting realistic conditions.
*Know Interventions:*
1  Get insights in to bodily and mental triggers causing relapse.
2  Develop a care plan for relapse situations.

**Choose Plan:** Choosing to let go of innermost urge for a loving mother in daily life.
*Choose Interventions:*
1  Practice compassion choices for self and others in suffering.
2  Choosing new directions and meanings for life.

**FIGURE 7.4** Treatment Plan for Cindy

meeting these types of goals is challenging, so counselors may design plans using the steps in each phase of the Note, Know, Choose model.

For the specific plan for each phase and intervention, subsequent chapters will discuss each of the Note, Know, Choose components with an appropriate array of goals, techniques, and examples.

## CONCLUSION

Along with assessment, case conceptualization is a continual process to help a counselor and client progressively understand the latter's causes of suffering. Just as we gain new insights into our sensations whenever we pay attention to our breathing, revisiting and contemplating a client's manifestations and causes of suffering will shed light and self-understanding. In the next step, counselors will take the information analyzed in case conceptualization to make a treatment plan. Contrary to many psychological approaches which focus on symptom reduction, Buddhist counseling focuses on mind cultivation. Cultivating a skillful mind with heightened concentration, the ability to discern the causes and conditions of suffering, and the wisdom to make decisions leading to less suffering is the goal of Buddhist counseling. With a mind characterized by clarity and insight, clients will gradually see the suffering in clinging on and choose to let go of the illusory "I." The following three chapters will discuss how the Note, Know, Choose model achieves this goal.

---

### Contemplative Questions for Buddhist Counselors

A counselor's own attainment and use of wisdom is directly proportional to the level of wisdom we can help our clients to attain. For this reason, it is important for Buddhist counselors to foster wisdom via self-contemplation and reflection, thereby transforming our own self-notion as well as any associated clinging and desires for such an identity. To this end, we will now make use of a conceptualization exercise to reveal our self-notion using the diagram in Figure 7.5.

The assumption here is that a part of one's self-notion is shaped by internalizing the relationship with and characteristics of one's father, mother, major events, and a formative environment. To conceptualize such a self-notion, Figure 7.5 is divided into quadrants, each with two points of focus: (1) how you see the present condition and (2) how this condition influences you and becomes a part of you.

To start with, please relax your body, breathing, and mind. Adjust your sitting position to an upright and relaxed posture. Try to let go of any tension in your muscles while holding your back straight to support your body. Observe your breathing in this present moment and try to let it just be. Notice the in- and out-breaths without any intention to alter or manipulate them. Just simply enjoy each mindful breath.

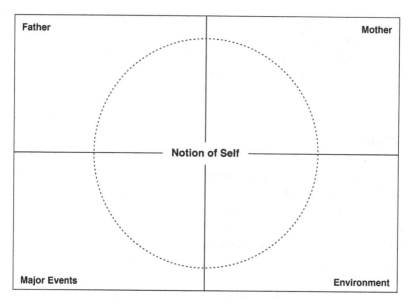

**FIGURE 7.5** Self-Notion Conceptualization Diagram

Next, take a moment to reflect on how you have become who you are. First, think of your father and contemplate the following questions:

- "How would you describe him as a father?"
- "Which three words would you choose to describe him as a person?"
- "What are the most memorable things, good or bad, that he has done for you?"

Please write down all your thoughts and answers on the outer layer of the father quadrant.

After that, let's move into the area of self-notion of the father. Read and contemplate mindfully the following questions:

- "How did your father influence your thinking of yourself as a child?"
- "What messages did your father tell you about who you are and who you should be?"
- "What have you learned from this person to become who you are now?"

Please write down all your thoughts and answers in the inner layer of the father quadrant.

Second, we will switch to the next quadrant, the mother figure, and contemplate the following questions:

- "How would you describe her as a mother?"
- "Which three words would you choose to describe her as a person?"
- "What are the most memorable things, good or bad, that she has done for you?"

Please write down all your thoughts and answers in the outer layer of the mother quadrant.

After that, move into the area of self-notion in the mother quadrant. Read and contemplate mindfully on the following questions:

- "How did your mother influence your thinking of yourself as a child?"
- "What messages did your mother tell you about who you are and who you should be?"
- "What have you learned from this person to become who you are now?"

Please write down all your thoughts and answers in the inner layer of the mother quadrant.

Third, we will move to the major events quadrant. Contemplate the following questions:

- "What were the most important and influential events in your life?"
- "What were the most challenging or even traumatic events in your life?"
- "What were the greatest things that happened to you?"

Please write down all your thoughts and answers in the outer layer of the major events block.

After that, move into the area of self-notion of the major events quadrant. Read and contemplate mindfully on the following questions:

- "What have I learned about the world, others, and myself during these events?"
- "How did all these events shape me into whom I am today?"

Finally, let us move to the environment block. Use the following questions for contemplation:

- "What role did my environment, such as culture, customs, social norms, values, or other factors, play in my life?"
- "What were the privileges, power, stereotypes, and labels assigned to me?"
- "How did my surrounding environment influence me in how I see myself as a person?"

Please write down all your thoughts and answers in the outer layer of the environment quadrant.

After that, move into the boundary of self-notion of the environment quadrant. Read and contemplate mindfully on the following questions:

- "What labels from the environment have I integrated into my identity?"
- "How did all these environmental and systemic factors shape me into whom I am today?"

Finally, notice and reflect on your thoughts, emotions, and bodily sensations. Remember, the self-notion is not an ultimate existent, so we are not confined to any rigid definition of who we actually are. In Buddhism, every moment of awareness is a new beginning of life. In this moment, you have all you need to make new choices: to accept your self-notion, to shape a better self-notion, or to let go of clinging to this self-notion.

## REFERENCES

Ashby, E. & Fawcett, B. (1994). Pride and Conceit. *Access to Insight (BCBS Edition)*. Retrieved from www.accesstoinsight.org/lib/authors/various/bl014.html

Bodhi, B. (2003). *The Connected Discourses of the Buddha: A Translation of the Samyutta Nikaya*. Somerville, MA: Wisdom Publication.

DN 16.Mahāparinibbānasutta: Last Days of the Buddha. Dīgha Nikāya, translated by Vajira, S. & Story, F. (1998). *Access to Insight (BCBS Edition)*. Retrieved from www.accesstoinsight.org/tipitaka/dn/dn.16.1-6.vaji.html.

Karunadasa, Y. (2013). *Early Buddhist Teachings: The Middle Path Position in Theory and Practice*. Hong Kong: Centre for Buddhist Studies, Hong Kong University.

Ridley, C. R., Jeffrey, C. E., & Roberson, R. B. (2017). Case Mis-Conceptualization in Psychological Treatment: An Enduring Clinical Problem. *Journal of Clinical Psychology*, 73(4), 359–375. https://doi.org/10.1002/jclp.22354

SN 22.49.Conceit. Samyutta Nikaya, translated by Walshe, M. O. (2007). *Access to Insight (BCBS Edition)*. Retrieved from www.accesstoinsight.org/tipitaka/sn/sn22/sn22.049.wlsh.html%20

SN 36.6. Sallatha Sutta: The Dart. Samyutta Nikaya, translated by Thera, N. (1998). *Access to Insight (BCBS Edition)*. Retrieved from www.accesstoinsight.org/tipitaka/sn/sn36/sn36.006.nypo.html.

Trungpa, C. (2009). *The Truth of Suffering and the Path of Liberation*. J. Leif (Ed.). London, MA: Shambhala.

# APPENDIX 7.1

## Dukkha Analysis Diagram

Client Name:                                    Date:

| **Craving**<br>*e.g. Sensuality, Existence, Non-existence* |
| --- |

↓

| **Created Notion of Self: Who am "I"?** | **Clinging and Yearnings: What do "I" need?** |
| --- | --- |
|  |  |

↓

| **Expectations: What do "I" expect in daily life?** |
| --- |
| **Related Realistic Conditions: What actually happens?** |

↓

| **Pattern** |
| --- |

↓                         ↓                         ↓

| **Dukkha (Dissatisfaction)** |
| --- |
| *e.g., Birth, Ageing, Sickness, Dying, Association with dislike, Separation from like, Not getting what you want* |

# CHAPTER 8

# Intervention and Techniques

## *Note*

According to Buddhist teachings, awareness is one of the most important factors in attaining liberation from suffering. In general, cultivating awareness refers to noticing the interdependent relationships between the external world, body, and mind, thereby informing us what stimuli, bodily sensations, cognitive acts, or other conditions increase or reduce suffering. With heightened awareness, one can better understand the causes and conditions of any event, leading to acceptance, compassion, and better knowledge in making decisions conducive to self and others. For example, noticing that stress tends to make us tighten our shoulders and hold onto such tension, we can choose to start relaxation by first loosening tension in the shoulders; second, by noticing how our volition to pursue anxiety-provoking thoughts tend to increase our level of anxiety, we can choose to let go of or distract ourselves from those thoughts; third, by noticing how we repeatedly get hurt by trying to seek love and acknowledgment from individuals who do not appreciate us, we can choose to befriend people who value us. While it may be easy to understand the beneficial effect of such awareness, it can be challenging to gauge how much we are aware of at this moment. Most of us are not aware of the subtle cognitive acts we make from moment to moment.

To *note* is to cultivate awareness through concentration practices and see how conditions affect the present moment. This mind training process is like lifting weights for muscle training or running for cardio. When a counselor directs a client's mind to focus on the present moment, it is like a trainer guiding a trainee in lifting a dumbbell: the mind "muscle" strengthens through each intentional application. This mental strength is a crucial protection against highly disturbing emotions, anchoring itself back to the present moment, which is a mental ground characterized by equanimity. Imagine when a highly anxious client comes to a counselor who listens with a compassionate presence, reflects with a soothing tone of voice, and guides the client to breathe mindfully and re-center their attention to the sensations in the nostrils. These are all techniques for protecting a client's mind from conceptually proliferating emotions. It is usually the starting point of the Note, Know, Choose model to ground the client's mind and strengthen its capacity to focus.

DOI: 10.4324/9781003025450-8

# THE THEORETICAL RATIONALE OF NOTE

When I teach Buddhist counseling, I usually start with a contemplative question: holding a pen in my hand, showing it to the class, and asking, "How do I let go of this pen?" My answer is simple: to let go of the pen, you first need to become aware that you are grasping the pen. If we do not know that we are holding onto an object, there is no way we can put it down. Therefore, to note is to discern *how* and *why* we are grasping onto something via consistent awareness training, thereby laying a foundation for the potential choice of letting go.

The Note phase, as an intervention to raise clients' concentration, applies the concepts and practices of Right Mindfulness (*samma-sati*), Right Concentration (*samma-samādhi*), and Right Effort (*samma-vāyāma*) of the Noble Eightfold path. In any Buddhist-derived intervention, raising awareness is always the first intervention (Lee et al., 2017). Often, suffering is a product of a client's unwholesome habitual pattern of action and narrow focusing on a particular phenomenon to quench their thirst for permanence. The Note phase of treatment aims to help clients deconstruct their experiences into different conditions so that they can start seeing conditions for what they are: ephemeral and impermanent. In this stage, Buddhist counselors aim to guide clients' minds by focusing on particular conditions that arise at any moment in order to cultivate their ability to direct and sustain their attention on conditioned phenomena and objects that they previously ignored. Through constant practice during and outside therapeutic sessions, clients should develop a heightened awareness of how different factors of their experience result in a subjective feeling of suffering. The Note phase also helps clients find an anchor for their attention in the present moment, allowing them to mentally step back from thoughts, images, or urges that lead to suffering. At this stage, the counselor's job is to train a client's mind to raise its awareness rather than providing solutions or probing the client to solve a problem.

The *Satipaṭṭhāna Sutta*, teaching that "the body is just the body," provides a highly effective entry point into this phase (Anālayo, 2003). When clients discuss emotionally difficult experiences, Buddhist counselors guide them to note their bodily sensations and gradually strengthen and expand their awareness of physical changes through dialogue and the teaching of mindfulness (e.g., asking the client to note and describe their sensations in the nostrils during their in-breaths and out-breaths, their bodily sensations while listening to sounds, their bodily movements, etc.). An uncultivated mind has a limited capacity to sustain and direct attention, hence many bodily sensations become misinterpreted, and even aggravated, through ruminations on thoughts and ideas beyond the actual bodily sensations. Training the mind to stay focused on physical sensations, pausing proliferating thoughts, and accurately noting the body's reactions to sensations can prevent additional physical and emotional suffering from arising.

Teaching clients to note helps them track their surrounding conditions and notice how different thoughts, feelings, and behaviors lead to different consequences. The noting stance manifests as a fully present state of awareness in which the mind does not pursue a thought or dwell on a particular feeling. This nonattached way of noting and seeing also includes directly turning towards sensations and feelings without distractions and making use of intentional relaxation mechanisms. When focusing on physical sensations without pursuing thoughts, one can mobilize the mental capacity to observe and understand how each thought leads to different physical, emotional, and behavioral consequences. There are two ways to achieve this goal.

## Re-Centering to the Present as Mindful Haven

The first step is to cultivate and sustain equanimity and pleasantness in the present moment, which is parallel to the idea of fostering the state of *samatha*, the tranquility of mind or peaceful abiding aimed for in Buddhist meditation. I call this peaceful, embracing, and present mind state a **mindful haven**, which is a product of meditation. There is a subtle and pleasant feeling in the present moment, but it takes persistent practice to notice it and sustain it. Our mind functions like a highly distractible monkey and quickly grasps onto thoughts, feelings, or other internal and external stimuli. When the monkey mind grasps onto things, it thinks, postulates, fantasizes, and proliferates them, thereby amplifying the intensity of thoughts and emotions. The pleasantness inherent in breathing usually gets masked by discomfort, pain, thoughts, or emotions. A part of mindfulness practice is to remove hindrances and distractions from this pleasantness and gradually flourish and sustain this pleasantness. Sustaining attention on this pleasantness can ground and establish the mind in a stable and clear state.

Moreover, this sense of pleasantness is also an indication of proper practice. Feedback to the mind through a specific sitting posture, paying attention, muscle contraction and relaxation, and bodily balance will help the mind to notice such pleasantness. When a teenage client is bored, such a practice can be an alternative to kneejerk electronic escapes such as VR and Instagram; when a sad client has had a bad day at work, it can be a haven to relax and focus on the beautiful scenery on his way back home; when a frustrated working mother is tired of her children, it can be like a spiritual oasis during her coffee break. Such practice is readily accessible to breathing meditation and can be progressively refined through mindfulness.

## Developing Mental Distance from Thoughts and Emotions

An unskillful mind suffers because it is fully immersed in unskillful thoughts and emotions, resulting in losing control over itself. A skillful mind can cleverly and competently see how unskillful thoughts and emotions arise and cease so that it can mindfully consider views without clinging, disengage from suffering thoughts, and choose actions resulting in less suffering. The main difference between the two minds is the existence of mental distance. This mind space allows flexibility and possibilities, like a camera zooming out to see a wider angle, so that the mind can take different perspectives without clinging to a particular one. To note is to ground the mind in the present moment with clarity while also developing mental stability. For example, if you are rudely treated by a salesperson at a department store, anger-provoking and retaliating thoughts may emerge in your mind. Pursuing these thoughts will fuel the concept and experience of anger, leading to abrasive replies to the salesperson. However, if you have been breathing mindfully since the beginning and noticing the sensations of each in- and out-breath, you will see the inner voices and imagery with mental distance, as if they are in the background. You may still experience discomfort in the body, an increasing heart rate, and other unpleasant sensations. However, a mind grounded in the present process of breathing will anchor itself against the proliferation of negative thoughts. In this process, the anger-provoking thoughts will not disappear and they do not need to disappear because your relationship with them has become different: you are no longer entangled with them and you see these thoughts as just thoughts. This mind stance allows you to decide what to do with these anger-provoking thoughts, which involves a subtle but deliberative choice at every moment, and only you can notice the best choice points.

## TREATMENT GOAL OF NOTE

According to previous findings, researchers (e.g., Aguilar-Raab et al., 2018; Shonin et al., 2014) have shown that increasing clients' ability to pay and sustain attention helps reduce suffering. Practicing mindfulness by intentionally focusing on an object can teach clients to stay in the present moment and gain mental distance from negative thoughts and feelings. Aiding in the consistent presence of single-pointed mindfulness, regulated attention to breathing can expand feelings of relief and anchor the mind, allowing one to more clearly see the physical sensations that arise from triggers, such as unpleasant thoughts about a trauma. Ultimately, in the Choose phase, this awareness prepares one's mind to make a conscious decision not to focus on and expand upon unpleasant thoughts. The mind can also switch to focusing on more positive thoughts, such as reminders of physical safety in the present moment, compassion for the self, or associating the trauma with new meanings.

Note's overarching aim is to help clients gain more control over their minds by paying deliberate attention to different senses, each of which can be categorized into three major domains: Body, Breath, and Mind. In other words, the treatment goal of Note is to *increase awareness of body, breath, and mind*. Various techniques may achieve the same goal. For example, Buddhist counselors can guide clients to practice mindful breathing, calligraphy, painting, tea drinking, or other activities. If the client is Buddhist, he or she could be encouraged to recite a meaningful Buddhist chant or mantra, read Buddhist scriptures, or do Nianfo (reciting the names of the Buddha or other Bodhisattvas). Once clients start to quieten their minds, Buddhist counselors can help them to deepen their awareness by noticing and observing their bodily sensations, thought processes, and emotions to understand how their minds work. Since, again, the purpose of Buddhist counseling is to help clients master their minds, it is not important whether a client can practice certain techniques flawlessly; instead, it is about whether the methods advance their ability to control their mental clinging.

In particular, counselors will learn to use the Note interventions to achieve the following objectives: (1) *Recentering*: re-center clients' attention on the present moment by guiding them to focus on body, breath, and mind to create a mindful haven; (2) *Sustaining*: strengthen their ability to sustain attention through consistent practices in daily life; and (3) *Observing*: foster mental distance to observe the mechanisms and nature of the mind's activities, thereby deepening one's understanding of their interpretation of sense contacts. Buddhist counselors can use each of the interventions to help the client re-center their mind to the present moment and foster an initial experience of a mindful haven and then gradually foster sustaining attention in the observing of changes in body and mind. This is a continual process of cultivation for clients, with the long-term goal of developing concentration.

## Beginning Note: Re-centering Attention to Soothe and Notice

To start the Note phase, psychoeducation and a mindful breathing exercise are practiced. Psychoeducation means educating the client about the counseling process and how it relates to a reduction in suffering. It can help some clients understand their causes of suffering, how their actions may increase or reduce their suffering, and ways to generalize insights gained in counseling to their daily life. Psychoeducation can actually be a continuous process throughout treatment, with increasing depth and breadth to address the client's concerns. For Note, the process usually starts with breathing and noticing bodily sensations. In particular, it is good to educate the client about the relationship between breathing and emotional distress. The following dialogue illustrates a conversation between a Buddhist counselor and Sam, a client suffering from intense anxiety:

COUNSELOR: We're going to discuss breathing today. How we breathe actually has a direct impact on our emotions. For example, our rhythm, depth, and length of a breath, whether intentional breathing or naturalistic breathing, all play a role. As you mentioned about how you became anxious at work, did you notice how you were breathing at that time?

SAM: Kind of ... I ... I ... have been a very, very anxious person for a long time. As long as I can remember ... I think I breathe quicker than usual when I get anxious.

COUNSELOR: Yes! So, intentionally breathing slower tends to soothe our body and mood. It's really important to be aware of our breath and to practice breathing mindfully so that it becomes a soothing ground for you when you become anxious. Would you like to try a mindful breathing exercise together?

SAM: Okay.

According to the *Satipaṭṭhāna Sutta*, mindfulness of the body is the first foundation of mindfulness, an essential first step for clients to increase their body awareness through breathing. For this reason, the Note phase usually starts with teaching clients mindful breathing to increase their bodily awareness and awareness of their breath. This mindful exercise applies the foundational teaching of the *Satipaṭṭhāna Sutta*, which states:

... only with keen mindfulness, he breathes in, and only with keen mindfulness, he breathes out. Breathing in a long breath, he knows, 'I breathe in a long breath'; breathing out a long breath, he knows, 'I breathe out a long breath'; breathing in a short breath, he knows, 'I breathe in a short breath'; breathing out a short breath, he knows, 'I breathe out a short breath.'

(Jotika & Dhamminda, 1986, p. 8)

This teaching guides Buddhist counselors to help clients note their breathing patterns and gradually become aware of the whole body in the processing of breathing. Through the repeated practice of noticing the changes in breath and body, this awareness will lead to a calming effect. This can be seen in the following dialogue:

COUNSELOR: Great. If you were to rate your anxiety level, 1 being the most relaxed you can be and 10 being the most intense and stressed state you can ever imagine, where are you from 1 to 10 at this moment?

SAM: I think ... it's about a 5.

COUNSELOR: A 5, alright. Let's see how it may change after this mindful breathing exercise. Let's gently get yourself in to what feels like a stable and alert posture in order to feel relaxed. There is a balance between being alert and relaxed. This balance is an important issue. Now close your eyes. Please remember that the most basic thing we're doing is simply noting and noticing what is happening in the present moment. It is as simple as it sounds. Before you have any ideas about getting concentrated or being peaceful or making something happen—just take note. So you might take a moment now to just notice how you are, what's going on for you, what your own imagined experience is—your lived experience—here and now.

So first, you are breathing in deeply, and, second, you are breathing normally and just scanning the body (and mentally softening whatever body parts you can). Next, see if you can get a global awareness of your body. Don't try too hard, just whatever broad awareness of your body that you can establish, letting your attention wander around your body, kind of from the inside, feeling it, sensing it.... Feeling the contact of your body against your chair or cushion.... Then, within your body, as part of your bodily experience, become aware of how your body experiences breathing. How does your body know that you are breathing or feel that you are breathing? What happens in your body as you breathe? What moves, what changes, what shifts? Some people can feel the movement of their belly going up and down, rising and falling, or their chest rising and falling, the rib cage expanding and contracting. Some people can feel the air coming in and out of the nostrils. If you have trouble finding your breath or connecting to the experience of breathing, you can put your hand on your diaphragm or belly ... perhaps feel the movement there.... So, wherever you feel your breathing most predominantly in your body, let that be your home base. You're going to try and cultivate your ability to stay in the present moment for the experience of breathing in that place.... Now, there might be various hurdles that might make it difficult for you to stay continuously with your breathing, like being distracted by your thoughts. Be relaxed about that. The idea is to just know what is happening. Know "I'm easily distracted. I'm easily concerned about other things." Just know that. The mind so easily just wanders off in thought. Then gently, smilingly, the moment you notice that happens, bring your attention back to your breathing. Take your awareness and attention and enter the experience of breathing as if it's something you can deeply trust. It's a good place to be.... Try to notice, be alert enough to notice, when you wander off in your thoughts, then relax yourself and come back to your breathing. When you connect to the breathing again, stay with it, do it with some sense of determination to hang in there with the breathing, so you can hang in there with the rhythm of many in-breaths and out-breaths in a row.... You might notice you have various concerns or issues that are vying for attention. See if you can let them be in the background. In the foreground, you are just tuning in to the breath. Being with the breath. Being with the rhythm of breathing in and out. Being with the physical experience of breathing. Perhaps as you do that, just being with it starts to be calming or settling. Some people find it helpful to label the in-breath "in," the out-breath "out".... Just a very quiet whisper in the mind that encourages you to hang in there, stay present, instead of getting distracted.... Gently sit for two more minutes and continue to note the in-breath and out-breath.... In these last couple of minutes, see if you can stay connected to the breath and to the breathing."

*After two minutes*

COUNSELOR:  How do you feel now?

SAM:  Seems like ... I'm a little more relaxed.

COUNSELOR:  Where in the body do you notice changes?

SAM:  ... I think my shoulders became less tight ... and I no longer feel the headache in the back of my head.

COUNSELOR:  Good! Then from 1 to 10, how anxious do you feel now?

SAM:  It's like a 2–3 now.

COUNSELOR:  One does become more relaxed with practice, and it would be very useful if you can try to do this mindful breathing daily for 5–10 minutes. Do you think you can try at home?

SAM:  Okay, I think I can try in the mornings.

In this dialogue, the Buddhist counselor was able to soothe the client's anxiety and help the client note bodily sensations with the arising and ceasing of subjective anxiety. Teaching clients to note helps them track their conditions and notice how different thoughts, feelings, and behaviors lead to different consequences. The noting stance manifests as a fully aware and present mind state that does not pursue a thought or dwell in a particular feeling. It also involves directly turning towards sensations and feelings without distractions, intentional relaxation, or other controls; it is a non-attached way of noting and seeing. When focusing on physical sensations without pursuing thoughts, one can mobilize the mental capacity to observe and know how each thought leads to different physical, emotional, and behavioral consequences (Kornfield, 2009). It is essential for all Buddhist counselors to be familiar with teaching this introductory mindful breathing technique. Applying one's knowledge and experiences in practicing and teaching mindfulness skills, good Buddhist counselors should be prepared to answer clients' questions regarding mindfulness practice and tailor their guidance to fit different clients' needs.

Moreover, there are many different forms of mindful breathing to help the client concentrate. All the following techniques serve the same purpose: to help clients consolidate attention onto their breath as a single object of focus. However, different methods resonate with different individuals, so it helps for Buddhist counselors to be familiar with a few more breathing methods.

### Belly (Diaphragmatic) Breathing

Previous studies have pointed out that diaphragmatic breathing is effective in relaxation and anxiety reduction (Chen et al., 2017), as well as being a more conducive breathing method for meditation than chest breathing. However, many clients may not know how to breathe using their bellies. One way to prompt clients is to start by putting their hands on the belly and noticing the rising and falling of the diaphragm along with in-breaths and out-breaths. It is useful to let clients experiment with their bodies by expanding their belly along with the in-breath and vice versa. Buddhist counselors will remind the client to notice the sensations of each in- and out-breath and ask them to simply notice what is occurring instead of changing anything.

### Counting Breaths

A Buddhist counselor may guide clients who are easily distracted by their thoughts to try counting their in- and out-breaths as a way to synchronize the mind and body by teaching the client to count "one" before an in-breath, then "two" for the next breath, up to ten, then starting over again after ten. Like other methods, the Buddhist counselor can gently remind the client to notice when the mind wanders and start counting to acknowledge how the mind wandered off.

### Finger Breathing

The sensation of breathing through the nostrils may not be salient enough for some clients to notice. In this situation, Buddhist counselors may teach clients to put a finger under their noses for a while to see if they can feel the difference between in-breath and out-breath. Buddhist counselors can also raise clients' awareness by reminding them to observe each breath's temperature, rhythm, moisture, sensations, and duration.

### Alternate Nostril Breathing

Another method to strengthen sensations of the in- and out-breaths is to experiment with alternate nostril breathing. Buddhist counselors can consider using the following steps:

1 Exhale completely, and then use the right thumb to close the right nostril.
2 Inhale through the left nostril and then close the left nostril with your fingers.
3 Open the right nostril and exhale through this side.
4 Inhale through the right nostril and then close this nostril.
5 Open the left nostril and exhale through the left side.
6 Repeat the cycle.

After clients start to realize the sensations of in- and out-breath, Buddhist counselors can guide a client to resume and consolidate regular mindful breathing to develop sustained attention on the breathing process.

### Rapid Belly Breathing

It may be more difficult for clients with heightened emotionality, such as anger and anxiety, to calm the body and mind through regular mindful breathing. One very useful breathing method is rapid belly breathing, in which a Buddhist counselor instructs clients to use belly breathing at a fast pace for about 30 seconds to 1 minute. Different from other mindful breathing approaches, this intentionally speeded-up breathing helps the client to release certain emotional distress. Clients can be a little tired afterwards, so Buddhist counselors can lead clients back to regular mindful breathing.

Again, all these breathing methods serve the same goal: to help the client train the mind's capacity for concentration and increase their awareness to note experiences in the body and mind.

## Other Note Techniques

While mindful breathing is a fundamental practice, various techniques help the client re-center attention to the present moment and raise awareness of different internal and external conditions. This section will introduce a few common Buddhist counseling Note techniques.

### Grounding Technique

Besides using breathing experiences to re-center the client's attention, Buddhist counselors can invite attention from different senses for the same purpose. Some clients may present with strong emotional reactivity, which makes it difficult for them to self-soothe by breathing, so mobilizing other senses can be more useful. According to Buddhist psychology, every person has six senses: sight, hearing, smell, touch, taste, and mind. The rationale of the grounding technique is to guide the client to focus intentionally on each sensual experience to bring the mind back to the present target of focus:

1  Grounding of the body
   - Put your feet on the floor.
   - Notice the feeling of your feet/shoes on the floor.
   - Push your feet into the floor and feel your leg muscles flexing.
   - Now relax and sit back in your chair.
   - Notice your body on the chair and the feeling of gravity pulling you onto the chair.
   - Notice the feeling of your feet on the floor.
   - Notice the position of your arms and legs.
   - Feel your trousers around your lower body and describe the sensation.
   - Stomp hard on the ground.

2  Grounding the ears
   - Now zoom out and listen to the sounds around you.
   - Try to identify three different sounds.
   - Come back to your body in the chair, noticing the feeling of gravity again.

3  Grounding the tongue
   - Taste your mouth and swallow some saliva.
   - What can you taste?

4   Grounding the nose
   • Take three slow deep breaths.
   • What can you smell?

5   Grounding the eyes
   • Name all the colors you can see around you and say them out loud.
   • Name all the shapes you see around you and say them out loud.
   • Name all the objects you see around you and say them out loud.

6   Grounding of the mind
   • Name as many kinds of food as possible.
   • Name as many countries as possible.
   • Tell me your favorite thing to do in life.
   • Tell me one thing you are happy about.
   • Tell me one thing you like about yourself.


### Chanting Technique

As mentioned in Chapter 2, religious chanting can be an effective coping strategy to allevi-ate the fear response. In Buddhism, chanting is a religious practice as well as a meditative training of the mind, the objects of chanting usually being Buddhist scriptures, the names of Buddhas and Bodhisattvas, and mantras (e.g., *Om mani padme hum*). Chanting involves either reciting statements in a repetitive manner or making melodic sounds with the voice. Buddhist counselors can also develop secular statements with non-religious clients as chanting material.

In Buddhist counseling for Buddhist clients, the previously mentioned objects of chant-ing are usually associated with compassion, peace, and other positive qualities in order to develop and consolidate a mindful haven to fend off or hold strong emotional disturbances. There are multiple ways to implement such chanting, although initially several considera-tions are necessary. First, it is important to refrain from imposing the counselor's religious beliefs on the client. Even for Buddhist clients, Buddhist counselors should get to know the extent of their clients' backgrounds in Buddhism and get their permission to use chanting as a coping technique. Second, it is usually more beneficial to use chanting within the client's religious context. Some clients may have had some positive experiences with chanting, although it may not have been a consistent practice. Buddhist counselors can try to practice with the client in the session and then process the experience with them. Third, there are many different styles, levels, and complexities of chanting in various Buddhist traditions. For counseling, maintaining simplicity is critical because learning a simple way to chant is more feasible for clients to remember and use during times of emotional distress. For that reason, a monophonic way of repeating a statement or a phrase is good enough. In summary, five steps are required when planning on the use of chanting:

1   Explore the client's experiences with chanting and get the client's permission to use this religious technique.
2   Foster the client's understanding of the object(s) of chanting.
3   Practice chanting with the client to help them learn it.

4  Process the experience with the client and adjust if needed.
5  Encourage the client to develop a regular chanting practice and review that with the client during the next session.

Here is a sample dialogue with a Chinese Buddhist client, "Audrey," who has been going to a Buddhist temple for five years and has some experience of chanting:

COUNSELOR:  As you have been a Buddhist for a couple of years, what is your experience of chanting?
AUDREY:  I do chanting when I attend ceremonies at my temple.
COUNSELOR:  How was it for you?
AUDREY:  I kind of like it. Chanting in the temple gives me a calm feeling, but I rarely chant when I do not attend such services.
COUNSELOR:  Would you like to try using chanting as a way to cope with your stress?
AUDREY:  Sure, if it helps.
COUNSELOR:  Is there any particular Buddha figure or Bodhisattva who resonates with you?
AUDREY:  (Pondering for a while) … I like Guanyin (Avalokiteshvara) the most!
COUNSELOR:  What makes you like Guanyin so much?
AUDREY:  My grandma used to teach me to chant the name of Guanyin when I was scared, a practice which she also does for herself. When I think about Guanyin or see her statue, I can feel some calmness, as Guanyin is so compassionate and accepting. It's almost like when she is here, everything will be fine.
COUNSELOR:  Great! So Guanyin brings you a sense of compassion and safety. We can actually use her name for chanting. Would you like to join me in chanting her name together?
AUDREY:  Alright.
COUNSELOR:  You can follow me to chant together … (*counselor chants slowly and client joins with the chanting*) Namo Guan Shi Yin Pusa (Chinese: 南無觀世音菩薩), Namo Guan Shi Yin Pusa, Namo Guan Shi Yin Pusa …
*After three minutes of chanting*
COUNSELOR:  How did that chanting feel for you?
AUDREY:  At first, it was a little hard to focus, but once I found my rhythm, it became more soothing. I I feel more relaxed now.
COUNSELOR:  So, focusing your mind in chanting can give rise to a feeling of peace. You can actually develop a daily practice of chanting, such as designating a time for chanting or even chanting quietly while waiting for a bus or lining up at a check out with your groceries. Even further, if something triggers your negative emotions, you can also try to chant in your heart to come back to this mindful haven, as we have discussed.
AUDREY:  Okay, I will give it a try!

Here are some sample chanting resources to help Buddhist counselors get familiar with chanting:

1  Early Theravāda Buddhism Chanting of the Karaniya Metta Sutta in English and Pali by Dr. Gil Fronsdal (www.audiodharma.org/series/184/talk/6017/);

2   Chinese Buddhism Namo Guan Shi Yin Bodhisattva chanting in Chinese at Dharma
    Drum Mountain (www.youtube.com/watch?v=wie77P88wZ8);
3   Chanting of Namo Avalokiteshvara in Vietnamese at Plum Village (www.youtube.com/
    watch?v=ntBfYFFlbV8).

Moreover, some clients find listening to chanting a soothing experience providing relief,
which Buddhist counselors can consider a related Note technique.

For non-religious chanting, Buddhist counselors can collaborate with the client to
develop a chant with a wholesome meaning. It is usually helpful for clients to develop statements of compassion such as "May I accept myself the way I am," "May I be peaceful and
happy," "I unconditionally love and accept myself," or "I care about myself, and I know that
I am good enough." Especially for highly critical clients, Buddhist counselors can review
these self-compassion statements with them to find or develop one that resonates. Similar
to Buddhist chanting, a Buddhist counselor will:

1   Identify or design the statement with the client according to the client's concern(s).
2   Chant with the client together.
3   Process the feeling with the client and make adjustments as needed.
4   Encourage the client to develop a regular chanting practice and review it with the client
    during the next session.

### Singing Bowl Technique

In Buddhist psychology, any one of the six senses can be a medium to foster concentration.
Again, the six faculties include eye, ear, nose, tongue, body, and mind. The first five senses
process physical objects, while the mind processes mental objects. Among all the senses,
the auditory medium is usually the strongest and most receptive for most of us. Using the
auditory sense as the main sense contact, listening to a singing bowl can instantly assist a
wandering mind to focus and pay attention to the present moment. When paying attention
to the singing bowl, the realization of the sound gradually deepens, such as the length of
each bell sound and changes in volume throughout the duration of the sound, including the
vibrant oscillations and rhythms. Each new realization results from increased concentration,
which is the main reason why many clients return to a state of calm by listening to the
singing bowl. To use the singing bowl as Note technique, Buddhist counselors can prepare
a singing bowl as a counselling tool and proceed as follows:

1   Start by guiding the client to become settled, sitting straight in a relaxed posture.
2   Hold the singing bowl in the palm of one hand at heart level and take three gentle breaths.
3   Invite the client to listen to the singing bowl three times, focusing completely on each
    in- and out-breath, along with the sound.
4   Invite the client to listen to the singing bowl mindfully three more times.
5   Process the client's experience and ask whether they noted any changes in the sound.
    Reflect on observations of the client's changes in affect and body (if any) and enquire
    about any changes in the client's feelings before and after listening to the singing bowl.
6   (*Alternatives*) Teach the client to count the breaths between each singing bowl sound.

If a Buddhist counselor or client does not have a singing bowl, it is possible to use smartphone apps, such as "Mindfulness Bell" or "InsightTimer," although an actual singing bowl is usually more penetrating of a client's auditory sense. It is also crucial for Buddhist counselors to be well-practiced in using the singing bowl before using it with a client.

### Buddhist Art Technique

In psychotherapy, art therapy techniques are standard counselling tools to activate cognitive and sensorimotor functions, raise self-esteem and self-awareness, promote insight, cope with conflicts and distress, and promote other positive changes in clients. Buddhist counselling acknowledges the effectiveness of art therapy techniques and primarily employs such tools to foster concentration and raise awareness in clients for the development of a mindful haven. Moreover, some Buddhist art techniques are used to discover and nurture feelings of compassion. The next section introduces several simple Buddhist art techniques.

#### Mindful Drawing

Drawing easily lends itself to meditative and mindfulness exercises, with minimal materials needed, such as paper or pencils. Brushes and paints provide more tactile and visceral opportunities for reflection. The goal is to practice mindfulness through the medium rather than clinging to the medium itself. In particular, slowing down the pace, experiencing the present body and mind, maintaining mindful breathing, and contemplating compassion, gratitude, or other mental states are key. By applying the Buddhist counselors' creativity and experiences, many art forms can become meditative exercises. Here is an example of mindful drawing using circles:

1  Getting ready
   a  Feel the pen and notice how your hand is holding it.
   b  Draw in the air to experience the motion and magnitude of one's movements.
   c  Breathe and anchor the mind in the present moment.

2  Drawing circles
   a  Make one uninhibited brushstroke to draw a circle of togetherness.
   b  Focus on and note the experience of the interaction between pen and paper.
   c  Note any changes in the drawing of the lines.
   d  Breathe mindfully and notice your bodily sensations.
   e  If distracting thoughts arise, return to the present moment of drawing.
   f  (*After at least five minutes*) You may stop any time if you think you are done.

3  Appreciation
   a  Appreciate the beauty of the circles.
   b  Accept their imperfection and try to appreciate the beauty of that.
   c  Experience the peacefulness and quietness of this moment.
   d  Reflect on the circles and think of a meaningful word, phrase, or mantra that can capture its essence.

4 Reflection
  a Use a new paper and draw one last circle.
  b Write a word or phrase that comes to your mind in the middle of the circle.
  c Share your experience with your mind, body, the ink, the paper, and the circle.

It is a good idea to try using a paper, a brush, and water for this exercise to experience the impermanence of circles and then to contemplate on that.

*Mindful Haven Drawing*

Making mindful haven art can concretize a visualization of safety and promote feelings of peace and centeredness. Buddhist and Buddhism-inspired counselors can consider using the following steps using three pieces of paper:

1 **Externalizing a Concern:**
  a After learning about the client's reported concern, invite the client to draw out the concern (e.g., depression, anxiety, fear, etc.) on a piece of paper.
  b Process both the client's bodily and psychological feelings when drawing out the concern.

2 **Generating an Image of Mindful Haven:**
  a Now ask the client to think about anything, including their environment, experiences, persons, or anything else that makes the client feel secure and relaxed.
  b On the second piece of paper, invite the client to draw that which gives them a pleasant and safe feeling.
  c Label this picture as the Mindful Haven and process the client's feelings in body and mind when drawing it.

3 **Embracing Concern in the Mindful Haven:**
  a On the third piece of paper, ask the client to draw the same concern in a small size and then draw the safe haven in a really large size on the same piece of paper.
  b Process the feelings in body and mind again and then reflect on the client's changes in body and mind from the first drawing to the last.
  c Invite the client to contemplate the last drawing while trying to sustain focus on the Mindful Haven, which is readily accessible to protect clients from distress and danger.

## Art of Compassion

After compassion or loving-kindness meditation (see Chapter 10 for more information), Buddhist counselors can invite clients to draw their visualization of compassion on a piece of paper in order to further cultivate a compassionate state of mind. For example, Buddhist counselors can:

1 Invite the client to visualize any compassionate person standing in front of them, experiencing the person's smile and energy.
2 Use a piece of paper to draw the person and the experience of him/her.
3 Be mindful of the client's body and mind during the creation of this drawing.
4 Process the experience with the client.

### Psychological Techniques

Some traditional psychological techniques may be useful for Buddhist counselors to help clients cope with overwhelming emotions and thereby develop a mindful haven. For example, progressive muscle relaxation, distraction techniques, and visual imagery could be useful techniques for this purpose. Buddhist counselors can refer to the Cognitive Behavioral Therapy techniques written by Leahy (2018) and Neenan and Dryden (2015) for more detailed descriptions.

## The Application of Note to Cindy

To illustrate the Note phase more thoroughly, this section modifies one of my previously published articles (Lee & Tang, 2020) to discuss the case example of Cindy. Cindy presented with a strong emotional disturbance of depression, which hindered her introspection about how her mental activities contributed to her suffering. The groundwork of the Note phase is to attentively listen as she communicates her understanding of her overwhelming emotional pain, which has arisen from her repeated failures to earn love and acknowledgment from her mother and the feeling that she is not finding a way out of this cycle. Taking mindful breathing as an example, a Buddhist counselor can guide Cindy to first sit in a position balanced between alertness and relaxation, identifying the sensation of breathing as the object of her meditation and sustaining attention on each in-breath and out-breath. After Cindy's positive experience with mindful breathing during the session, the counselor then assigns her 15 minutes of daily mindful breathing at home, along with the regular exercise of noticing how she breathes during different activities in her daily routine. After consistent practice of noticing and sustaining attention on the breath, the counselor introduces the idea that there is a subtle pleasantness in the present moment of breathing. The counselor then gradually guides Cindy to expand this positive feeling, which becomes a peaceful, pleasant, and restful target of her meditation (Anālayo, 2003). With guidance in the practices of mindfully scanning and relaxing the different parts of her body, returning attention to her breath, and investigating the sensations that arise in her nostrils, the counselor can facilitate Cindy's realization of an inherent pleasantness in breathing, placing her mind's attention peacefully and stably on this sensation; such concentration gradually fosters equanimity and sooths her depressed mood.

After Cindy begins to successfully sustain stable attention on her breathing, the Buddhist counselor guides her to revisit the most recent incident of being rejected by her mother and direct her mind to recollect and examine the actual sense contacts (e.g., her mother's facial expressions, tone of voice, and exact wording used), her bodily sensations, her mental labels for the previously mentioned sensual inputs, and her thoughts and intentions at that moment. The counselor goes at a slow pace, inquiring into each aspect of Cindy's experience and encouraging her to reveal her bodily and mental experiences. By mindfully anchoring to her breathing as she revisits the incident, Cindy starts to detach from the overwhelming frustration and begins to note discomfort in her chest, her pounding heart, her clenched fists, her perception of her mother's gesture as "pushing her away," her inner voices telling her to need her mother, her intention to change her mother's thoughts, and her strong feeling of irritability:

COUNSELOR: When you talked to your mother about your agency's decision of not renewing your contract, what happened?

CINDY: She was just rude! She never really listens to me, and I am so tired of her!

COUNSELOR: Let's try to slow down and take a more detailed look at the interaction. What was her wording?

CINDY: She said ... something like, 'Of course they would save money to hire someone better' and 'I told you to get married when you were much younger ... no man would want you now.'

COUNSELOR: How does it make your body feel talking about this incident?

CINDY: I sense a strong discomfort in my chest, almost like something heavy is pressing down on me.

COUNSELOR: When you focus on this strong sensation on your chest and listen to it now, what does it say to you?

CINDY: It keeps on saying things like 'Why don't you just listen to me,' 'I deserve more respect from you,' 'Isn't it reasonable for a mother to be a little more caring for her daughter,' and so on like that.

COUNSELOR: The voices sound like you really want her to be there for you and love you.

With more mental distance in observing and realizing her bodily sensations and inner voices, Cindy expresses surprise that she used to ruminate over these incidents and mentally blame her mother for not treating her more nicely. However, she could not see the associations between her bodily sensations and some of her inner voices. After this mental revisit, Cindy became aware of her frustration with her mother for rejecting her, and frustration with herself for longing so deeply for respect and care from her mother. She also notices a strong physical discomfort in her chest, which seems to be a "heavy burden" of muscle tightness. The next phase is to analyze this information from her body and mind to generate more knowledge of the causes of her suffering.

## CONCLUSION

To Note is to focus and become aware. Note directs the mind's attention purposefully to wholesome thoughts, interpretations, feelings, volitions, or other objects, thereby depriving unwholesome processes of attention. This process's repetitive practice gradually shapes the mind to be more "under control": when you tell your mind not to think negatively, it can really stop. It sounds easy, but *practice* is the key. To motivate clients to practice Note, it is important for Buddhist counselors to help them reach a moment of equanimity using Note techniques during the session. The first moment of equanimity will become a strong reinforcement for the client to try this practice, as many suffering individuals have not had a single moment of peace for a long time. Furthermore, it is crucial for counselors to experience the techniques themselves before implementing them with clients.

## Contemplative Questions for Buddhist Counselors

A key component of Note is to find and develop a mindful haven, thereby creating a safe mental ground and container to disengage from emotional reactivity and mental proliferations. Before we can effectively help a client develop a mindful haven, Buddhist counselors should be the first to experience and benefit from such a safe zone. I wouldn't trust any salesman who has never tried the product. Similarly, our interventions will be much more "convincing" if we can directly benefit from them.

Let's start with our mindful breathing ritual. Gently attend to your body, breath, and mind at this moment and observe how they interact. Observe how you are sitting and slowly adjust your posture and muscles to reach a balanced position with your back upright and muscles relaxed. Let go of any intention to think, memorize, or predict. Let your mind rest in the present moment. Next, attend to your breath without judgment. Start with saying a simple verse to yourself:

*Breathing in, I know I am breathing in.*
*Breathing out, I know I am breathing out.*

Note how you breathe in and out in each moment. With your eyes closed, follow your breath for a few minutes.

Attend to the following questions with openness and curiosity, slowly and mindfully reading them one-by-one and jotting down any reflections. Know that your answers may vary according to the time, context, or state of mind at this moment, although you just need to be open to all experiences coming through:

- "Where is the safest physical or spiritual place for you to let down your guard and just rest?"

_____

- "Is there a person who makes you feel secure and contained?"

_____

- "What activities give you a sustainable sense of ease, security, and focus?"

_____

- "When you are upset, what activities can effectively soothe you?"

_____

- "Which practice of mindfulness or meditation gives you the most equanimity and joy?"

_____

In answering the questions, you are likely to identify one to two potential activities to practice a mindful haven. It is important that the activity used to create a mindful haven is also employed as a regular practice as well as an immediate skill to soothe a disturbing mind state. Perhaps the simplest example is mindful breathing, which can be a 20-minute daily practice as well as a five-second exercise to re-center attention to bodily experiences.

Once you are able to identify such an activity, use the following reminders to deepen the immersion in such an experience:

- Notice how you feel in the body and mind before the activity.
- Focus and re-focus on an object of meditation, such as the sensation in your nostrils when breathing, or your belly movements. Use this focus as an anchor to the present moment.
- With this anchor, note your bodily sensations during the activity. Should there be unpleasant or even painful sensations, try to openly observe it and see how it arises, changes, and ceases.
- Note the feeling tone arising from your sense contacts by attending to any pleasant, unpleasant, or neutral feelings throughout your body.
- Note the chatter in your mind and try to disengage from the inner voices by observing them.
- Follow your breath without changing or controlling it. Just follow and observe it as it is.
- Allow yourself to rest and fully immerse in the activity.
- Note any joy and pleasant feelings arising and let yourself enjoy the moment.
- Reflect on any changes in your body and mind after the activity.
- Contemplate how to incorporate this practice or experience to cope with your suffering in daily life.

The development of a mindful haven can be a very private process as every person has their own unique way to resonate with different mindful activities to reach a calm and focused state. Therefore, both counselors and clients may need to explore different activities and sustain regular practice in order to foster the stability of a mindful haven. Remember, the key is to let your mind fully arrive and rest.

# REFERENCES

Aguilar-Raab, C., Jarczok, M. N., Warth, M., Stoffel, M., Winter, F., Tieck, M., Berg, J., Negi, L. T., Harrison, T., Pace, T. W. W., & Ditzen, B. (2018). Enhancing Social Interaction in Depression (SIDE study): Protocol of a Randomised Controlled Trial on the Effects of a Cognitively Based Compassion Training (CBCT) for Couples. *British Medical Journal Open, 8*(9), Article e020448. https://doi.org/10.1136/bmjopen-2017-020448

Anālayo, B. (2003). *Satipatthāna: The Direct Path to Realization*. Birmingham, UK: Windhorse Publications.

Chen, Y. F., Huang, X. Y., Chien, C. H., & Cheng, J. F. (2017). The Effectiveness of Diaphragmatic Breathing Relaxation Training for Reducing Anxiety. *Perspectives in Psychiatric Care, 53*(4), 329–336. https://doi.org/10.1111/ppc.12184

Jotika, S. U., & Dhamminda, U. (1986). *Maha Satipatthana Sutta the Greater Discourse on Steadfast Mindfulness*. Maymyo, Burma: Buddha Dharma Education Association, Inc.

Kornfield, J. (2009). *The Wise Heart: A Guide to the Universal Teachings of Buddhist Psychology*. New York: Bantam Books.

Leahy, R. L. (2018). *Cognitive Therapy Techniques: A Practitioner's Guide* (2nd ed.). Guilford Press.

Lee, K. C., & Tang, J. (2020). Note, Know, Choose: A Psychospiritual Treatment Model based on Early Buddhist Teachings. *Spirituality in Clinical Practice.* Advanced online publication. https://doi.org/10.1037/scp0000220

Lee, K. C., Oh, A., Zhao, Q., Wu, F., Chen, S., Diaz, T., & Ong, C. K. (2017). Buddhist Counseling: Implications for Mental Health Professionals. *Spirituality In Clinical Practice*, 4(2), 113–128. doi:10.1037/scp0000124

Neenan, M., & Dryden, W. (2015). *100 Key Points and Techniques. Cognitive Behaviour Therapy: 100 Key Points and Techniques* (2nd ed.). Routledge/Taylor & Francis Group.

Shonin, E., Van Gordon, W., & Griffiths, M. D. (2014). Current Trends in Mindfulness and Mental Health. *International Journal of Mental Health and Addiction*, 12, 806–823. https://doi.org/10.1007/s11469-014-9513-2

CHAPTER 9

# Intervention and Techniques

## *Know*

Personal suffering so easily triggers an instinctual response of blaming a person, an event, or certain external factors for causing such suffering. For example, during a painful breakup, it is tempting to attribute problems to the other person ("She's not the right one," "He cheated," "She never respects what I do") instead of reflecting on how we played into the dysfunctional dynamic and contributed to the suffering in the relationship. However, the Buddhist remedy to suffering comes from within. We cannot change external reality, but we do not need to because many times problems arise from our view of events instead of the events themselves. In the Noble Eightfold Path, Right View means seeing things as they are, without distortion, fabrication, or inference based on what we want or do not want (Karunadasa, 2013). This realistic view results in the least suffering. One aspect of it is knowing how our thoughts, volitions, and choices contribute to our suffering. The moment we know them is also the moment we start to be unbounded by them.

## RATIONALE OF KNOW

To know is to gain insight which refers to gaining a correct and deep understanding of someone or something. Insight is not usually a sudden experience of enlightenment in which a person instantly becomes awakened and liberated from all suffering; instead, it is a gradual deepening process to cultivate a capacity to know the true nature of things. It is like peeling off the layers of an onion until we eventually see the empty nature at its core (Figure 9.1).

In the Note, Know, Choose model of Buddhist counseling, insight has been categorized into various interdependent and interrelated levels. Usually, clients reach out for help because of their initial awareness of specific *symptoms*. The symptoms are usually (1) external behavioral problems, such as a gambling addiction, relational problems, or parenting, (2) internal experiential symptoms, such as depressed mood, anxiety, or loss of meaning in life, or (3) a combination of both. The baseline is that they know something is not right and hope to do something about it. The second level of awareness and insight is a *relational pattern*. Most individuals tend to look for psychological and physical satisfaction from relationships.

Moreover, the nature of relationships is imprinted in our minds as somewhat stable and rigid frameworks, with each person becoming drawn to a particular type of relationship to get their needs met. Although we engage in relationships, we may not be aware of the inner

DOI: 10.4324/9781003025450-9

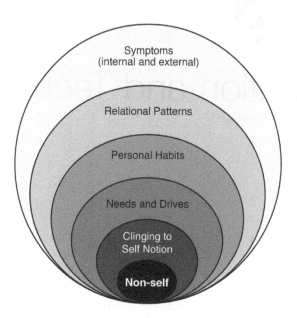

**FIGURE 9.1** Levels of Insights in Buddhist Counseling

needs and desires that fuel our pursuit of them. For example, a girl may grow up having a conflictual relationship with her extremely critical and arrogant father from whom she never received approval. In this relationship, the girl may have learned that a love relationship is signified by criticism and requires diligence to earn recognition. When she grows up, she may subconsciously decide to date men who are self-absorbed, dominant, and competent and try hard to win their acknowledgment and approval. This relational pattern may represent her deeper needs, almost like a missing part, to be loved and accepted by her highly critical father.

Beneath this relational pattern is a *personal habit*. In Buddhism a habit refers to a mental tendency and a potent force fueled by kammic moment-by-moment choices (Karunadasa, 2010). In other words, a person's volition, verbal choices, and behavioral decisions actively perpetuate a certain habit of mind, which then perpetuates the same psychological and physical choices, reinforcing existing habits in a feedback loop. As a result, the mind will be charged and narrowed by the habit, automatically repeating itself without discernment. For example, a person who feels hurt reacts with angry outbursts, which grants a sense of power and control. Regardless of the suffering that arises with the anger, the person dwells on the temporary pleasant feeling by pursuing anger-provoking thoughts and sensations. The next time the person perceives offense, they become quicker in angry reactions, further watering the seeds of anger. Several iterations of this vicious cycle will perpetuate the habit of an angry response and limit the person from noting and knowing alternative feelings, thoughts, and reactions. As personal habits are a product of numerous and persistent practices, it can be challenging to discover our habits. Moreover, personal habits drive our relational patterns and are fueled by our deeper needs and drives.

In the world of saṃsāra, every individual must have innermost desires, needs, and yearnings (Karunadasa, 2010). These needs and drives can be roughly divided into (1) existential needs—a sense of identity, control, competence, and meaning, (2) emotional needs—love, respect, acceptance, acknowledgment, and emotional security, and (3) biological needs—sensual pleasure and physical safety. In simplified terms, Buddhism believes in non-self (we are only a provisional existence supported by causes and conditions), but our minds cling to an assumed ultimate self-existence. In other words, the mind needs to identify and personalize different things in the world to self-convince of its existence in a process known as *clinging to the self-notion*. For example, yearning for love, grasping onto an identity as a competent and caring person, holding onto relationships to find a sense of importance, possessing material goods, or pursuing personal achievements over others are all common ways to prove a fabricated existence.

The deepest level is the non-self, a nature of emptiness. Insight at this level can be considered as the ultimate level of realization in Buddhism as it is the contemplative, experiential, and transformative enlightenment of one's true nature (Anālayo, 2003). It is a product of the perfection of moral discipline, concentration, and wisdom, leading to the highest psychological state constituting true happiness. However, it takes highly committed practice and intense devotion to reach this surpassing level of insight. From a mundane and secular perspective, many needs, such as the need for love, acknowledgment, acceptance, and the need for a self-notion, can be considered healthy. However, the Buddhist counseling model for everyday use may not need to aim for complete detachment from the self-notion, as many clients may not be dedicated to the entire Buddhist path. For this reason, the current Buddhist counseling model uses the non-self as the ultimate direction even though it may not be the actual treatment goal. This mundane application of Buddhist counseling aims to help clients increase their insights by gradually knowing the non-self nature, thereby reducing suffering.

In this sense, Buddhist counseling aims to learn to live harmoniously with the self, become more flexibly attached to it, and eventually liberate from it. Should there be any distressing moments when "my" needs are not met, "I" am disappointed, or "I" cannot become whom "I" wish to be, a more skillful attitude is to take a step back and to acknowledge: "Ah! I am holding too tight onto 'me' which hurts quite a bit. Let's take a breath, come back to the present moment, and know that I don't have to be this and that to be happy." With this more nonattached mindset, one can free up mental space to think about the most skillful decision at the moment, and this mental space can foster the sensitivity to appreciate different joyful and peaceful experiences in each moment of life.

## TREATMENT GOAL OF KNOW

The *Know* phase of treatment is parallel to the concept of wisdom (Pāli: *paññā*) in Buddhism. To cultivate wisdom, Buddhist counselors use Know techniques to achieve one main goal: to understand what, how, and why one's mind is clinging (Lee & Tang, 2021). This phase offers to help clients gain a more profound knowledge of their suffering through the mind-analysis technique. The nature of this knowledge is highly experiential and contemplative because clients exercise their heightened awareness from the Note phase to introspect and scrutinize the multiple factors supporting the phenomenon that causes their suffering.

All psychological experiences, including various forms of suffering, are considered conditioned or constructed phenomena in the Buddhist paradigm; hence, they are divisible into interrelated components. One significant result of the analysis conducted in the *Know* phase is to deconstruct a previously solidified experience and to then release the mind from the labels attached to it, thereby granting clients a sense of relief and tranquility, as well as to see the interdependence of phenomenon that we all experience. For example, a client has always labeled himself as a "highly anxious person" and tends to ruminate over the worries that he experiences in response to others' expectations of him to perform a task well. As he has habitually paid close attention to his worrying thoughts and tried to control them by rumination, his mind has developed an inclination to ignore his physical discomfort. He also overlooks his triggers, the sequential ways his thoughts arise, the desire running beneath those thoughts, his active pursuit of the thoughts that fuel those desires, and other conditions that build up to his state of "anxiety." This unskillful habit tends to gradually crystallize the construct of "anxiety" and reinforces his labeling of himself as a "highly anxious person." For such a client, to *Know* is to deconstruct this experience of anxiety into body and mind components in the present moment, thereby liberating them from bondage to the reifying concept of "anxiety."

A Buddhist counselor aims to cultivate clients' capacity to see what, how, and why they are clinging onto, thereby guiding them to realize the causes of their suffering (Lee & Tang,2021 ). Through teaching clients to reflect on and process introspective knowledge, the counselor guides them to notice the impermanence of their notions of suffering. For example, in the Note phase, the counselor guides the anxious client to note the sensation of tightness in their stomach, their accelerating heartbeat, the increasing muscle tension in their chest, the discomfort in their shoulders, their thoughts and images associated with being laughed at, and their mind grasping onto ideas about the need to prove themself to others. Gaining awareness of these operating components of their thought processes, the client will detach their mind from conceptual proliferations—i.e., their crystallized anxiety—and observe the activities of their body and mind from a perspective anchored in the present moment.

With a stabilized consciousness, the client, in collaboration with the counselor, can explore how their expectations and clinging are supporting their anxiety. For example, a patient with anxiety has formulated and continuously clung to the identity of a "perfect person" to feed their craving for existence. In this notion of self, the meaning of existence is to expect and receive acknowledgment and acceptance from others, making them highly sensitive and resistant to challenges and criticism. Instead of pausing and reviewing what image they are trying to sustain and whether it is necessary to sustain this image, they have formed strong habits to meet their self-demands.

By attuning with their clients, counselors can help them to reflect on their craving and clinging, process the cause-effect relationship between their desire and suffering, and gradually lead them to realize how their clinging influences them. To truly know requires a radical acceptance of unpleasant past experiences, life dissatisfactions, and undesirable characteristics of the self. For example, clients may mourn and lament never being loved by a mother, feeling useless and incompetent, feeling resentful towards a loved person, being selfish and manipulative with others, and many other disheartening and challenging experiences. An effective Buddhist counselor should role model acceptance of these negative sides of a client and compassionately accept and contain their suffering without judgment or rejection. With counselors helping them anchor their attention while offering unconditional acceptance and forging a solid therapeutic relationship, clients can develop radical acceptance for themselves and learn to see their attachment and clinging with mental distance. Such mental distance then fosters their flexibility and the possibility of making different decisions.

For these reasons, the overarching treatment goal of Know is to help the client gain insights into *how* and *why* different mind acts contribute to suffering and clinging (Lee & Tang, 2021 ). To achieve this goal, Buddhist counselors will learn to use the Know interventions to achieve the following objectives: (1) *Deconstruction*: Through repeated observations, gain insight into how the different causes and conditions shape an experience (e.g., external condition of lack of sunshine contributes to depression and internal condition of caffeine intake contributes to anxiety); (2) *Detachment*: Through the practice of Note techniques, ground one's mind in the present moment to observe itself with mental distance (e.g., sustaining attention to the in- and out-breath while attending to the experience of anxiety); and (3) *Discernment*: Through analysis and contemplation, gain insights into how different internal conditions, such as clinging to self-notion, yearnings, unfulfilled past experiences, or other views, contribute to suffering (e.g., that previous emotional trauma in relationships contaminated any perception or thoughts about love and romance).

## KNOW TECHNIQUES

Know techniques are perhaps the most difficult to describe in the Note, Know, Choose model. Helping clients gain progressive knowledge of their clinging to self-notion requires counselors to have patience, compassion, and direct experience of mental cultivation. To learn and practice the following techniques, Buddhist counselors should try to experience the techniques themselves through roleplaying and self-contemplation, helping clients develop more mental stability and clarity in the Note phase, and building a secure and trusting therapeutic relationship with the client as a prerequisite. With that said, if a client has not developed a robust mindful haven during the Note phase, it may not be appropriate for the counselor to proceed to Know.

### Know Technique for Deconstruction

#### Revealing Multiple Conditions

Buddhist counselors explore existing conditions with clients to understand how multiple conditions contribute to the phenomenon of suffering. In the counselor's mind, he or she analyzes and contemplates linkages between conditions and the client's current suffering to guide the flow of questioning and responding. To raise the client's awareness, the counselor constantly paraphrases, reflects, summarizes, and reveals relevant conditions by asking such questions as: "When you see all these stressors (*multiple conditions*) contributing to your feelings, what do you think and how do you feel?" and "What if your frustration is not just about your wife but is a reaction to all these things you are dealing with? What do you think?" Here is a sample dialogue between a Buddhist counselor and a 34-year-old male client, Vincent, who presents with intense anger and distress about his marital relationship:

VINCENT: My wife is such a pain in the ass! She basically forced me into buying this place, which is actually 10% higher than the market price. And if I don't do it, she will just keep nagging every night! She is so annoying! (*Anger increases*).

COUNSELOR: You also mentioned that you are having some financial difficulties. Is it related to buying this new place? (*Assessing different conditions*).

VINCENT: Yes! You know, I have to use up most of my savings and even lied to my mother about the high rate of return of this apartment, which is totally not true. The monthly mortgage now makes me have to quit my happy hour with friends! I have not really seen them for almost two months! (*Anger arises from the client's succumbing to anger-provoking views*).

COUNSELOR: You have to pay a monthly mortgage for a new home that you did not want to buy (*financial condition*); you do not like how your wife keeps spending money on luxurious things, but you cannot make her stop (*marital relationship*); you lied to your mother to borrow money from her so that you could afford your new home, although you never lied to her before (*family relationship*); you try to work extra hard to keep your job (*work environment*): and you have no one to talk to (*social relationship*). Of course you feel frustrated and depressed! (*Reflection of the multiple external conditions to client's awareness*).

VINCENT: ... (*pondering for a second*) When you put it this way, I guess I have a better sense of why I'm so stressed recently.

As suffering sometimes comes from our inability to understand and control the current problems, getting to know how multiple factors pile up into the present distress gives clients an immediate sense of relief. Knowing why usually provides a sense of agency and empowerment to face adversity. This technique is linked to the initial assessment, during which the counselor will have collected information on the client's external and internal conditions. Reflecting them all to the client will also demonstrate the counselor's attentiveness and understanding of the client's suffering.

### Labeling Mind State

Labeling the mind state (e.g., anxious mind, conceited mind, greedy mind, etc.) is a technique originating from a story in Chinese Buddhism: our three poisons are like thieves who sneak into our house to steal or destroy our property on dark nights. Wisdom involves turning on the light and allowing us to see these thieves. When the thieves are seen, they no longer have the capacity to do anything in the dark. Similarly, whenever we become aware of our poisons, defilements, or hindrances, we can know how they work and become unbounded by them. Therefore, labelling a mind state involves calling it out to guard against it, creating a mental distance from it, knowing it is a fabricated and dependently arising experience, and understanding its impermanent nature. It is a two-level technique that Buddhist counselors help clients with as follows: (1) *Analysis*: explore and deconstruct a solid experience into its components such as bodily sensations, feelings, perceptions, and thoughts; and (2) *Synthesis*:

label the mind state using mindfulness and discernment. After deconstructing the experience and observing how it changes when turning towards it, Buddhist counselors teach clients to use the mind label daily to identify and discern the experience and cultivate mental distance from it. It is important to note that the labeling should be a collaborative effort between the Buddhist counselor and client to select an appropriate way to call out a disturbing and unskillful mind state. The mind experience is highly idiosyncratic, and hence every label is unique. It is also crucial to know that labels are just labels so that neither the counselor nor the client clings to them. The following is an example with Jenny, a 21-year-old female university student suffering from generalized anxiety disorder:

COUNSELOR: I see how anxiety has been a disturbing problem for you. So let's try to understand more about the nature of this anxiety. How does it make your body feel? (*Exploring bodily sensations for deconstruction*).

JENNY: (*Takes a deep breath and gauges her feeling*). Usually, it involves rigidity on my shoulders, some tension in the neck … and some headaches at the back of my head.

COUNSELOR: There are intense sensations on the shoulders, neck, and head. How do these feelings come across to you? Would it be some sort of discomfort, or is it just neutral? (*Exploring bodily feelings for deconstruction*).

JENNY: I would say they are pretty uncomfortable and sometimes very annoying!

COUNSELOR: So what happens after you realize these sensations and discomfort? (*Exploring perceptions for deconstruction*).

CLIENT: I would think, 'Oh, Shoot! Here is my ANXIETY again! I don't want it, what should I do? I can't take care of my daughter, but my family needs me now, oh no! …' Something goes on and on like that.

COUNSELOR: That seems to be a very intense experience! So what you have described was like this—your anxiety has several different components, including muscle rigidity on your shoulders and neck, pain at the back of your head, physical discomfort, a recognition of 'anxiety,' and then many thoughts popping up to resist this experience as well as strong fear about your role as a father. What I would like you to try is to label this state or situation of mind as an 'anxious mind.' Whenever you are aware of its signs, such as headache or muscle tension, just call it out to yourself, like, 'Oh, it's the anxious mind again' or 'OK, it seems like the anxious mind is coming back.' Label it, turn towards it, observe it, and see how it changes. (*Teaching client to label the mind state*).

In this example, the client starts to catch the signs of the anxious mind to practice mindful breathing before the anxious mind escalates and dominates. It is important to note that a Buddhist counselor works with a client to use labels flexibly and creatively as reminders to know their states of mind. One caution is to refrain from consolidating the label and seeing it as having a stable existence. The rationale is similar to a traditional Buddhist metaphor in which the Dhamma is like a raft: useful for crossing over the river but not for holding on to. To avoid holding on to mind labels, Buddhist counselors help the client understand different components of the mental state. They remind the client to catch the unpleasant state early and meticulously observe its arising, changing, and ceasing in order to understand its impermanent nature.

## Know Technique for Detachment

### *Detachment Visualization*

Detachment visualization is a mental representation of an object or event based on realistic conditions to elicit mind acts for observation and analysis. The mind needs to be grounded in the present moment, the content of visualization needs to have realistic support, and the direction needs to aim for a more flexible perspective on the phenomenon. Typical usage includes visualizing voices or pictures of a bodily sensation and seeing oneself from the outside. Counselors can also use expressive art, music, or another medium to help clients externalize an experience to cultivate mental distance. Here is an example of Valerie, a married woman who is constantly blamed by her family for her irritability and being ill-tempered:

COUNSELOR: I'm describing the situation and perhaps a more objective observation of the so-called 'ill temper' while you said, 'No, no, no. That's not true. I am just ill-tempered.' (*Differentiating objective reality and objective examination of perception*)

VALERIE: I'm trying to understand if you're right or not. It's hard to look at myself from a distance, and then what you explained to me … I'm like, 'Am I what you said?' I really don't know because I'm too close to myself. It's hard to get a distance and get an objective observation of who I am.

COUNSELOR: It almost is a split mind in this lived experience. On the one hand, you feel that 'I'm angry,' right? On the other hand, if we step back and imagine there is a fly on the wall watching this show going on and asking, 'Is it reasonable for that person to be angry?' (*Prompting client to contemplate from a perspective of detached visualization*)

VALERIE: When I look back now after the phone call … it was like after lunch and after the walk here and then being the fly looking back at the situation that happened an hour ago, I was like, 'They keep talking to me like this,' 'How come these people are kind of harsh to this girl....'

COUNSELOR: If I try to think back to previous situations about the hair (*mother criticizing her hair*), what your mother said this time, your brother calling you (*the brother's wife was angry about the client, blaming her and labeling her as ill-tempered, but the client handled it calmly*), and then what you described to me about what your mother said about your grandparents' picture (*the mother told the client that it's her fault for not being able to find a positive image of the late grandparents*), what is common in all three of these incidents is a statement that either implied or pretty blatantly says you're at fault. (*Pointing out the pattern across critical incidents*).

VALERIE: Yes, I don't think it's fair! They blamed me every time and that's why I was irritated.

In this example, the Buddhist counselor was trying to help the client detach from her label. When the Buddhist counselor invited the client to visualize herself as a fly on the wall, this suggestion led the client to temporarily disengage from her existing emotions and thoughts and visualize her mind from another perspective. As a result, the client gradually realized how her family actually treated her unfairly which irritated her and she eventually held onto her self-label of being "ill-tempered." With this entry point to gain detachment, the Buddhist counselor pointed out to the client such patterns in similar incidents. Observing how the family habitually labeled the client as the problem finally helped the client see one perspective of reality outside of her self-concept: her family was unfair to her, and it was reasonable for her to be angry.

### Detachment Art Technique: Drawing Out the Self-Notion

Many art therapy techniques can be used as Buddhist counseling techniques. For example, drawing, storytelling, dance, music, drama, poetry, movement, calligraphy, photography, and other mediums can be effective interventions for clients to raise awareness of clinging and to experience momentary detachment from such clinging. However, there is one Know art technique—*Drawing Out the Self-Notion*—that has been useful to help clients increase their understanding of their self-concepts and experience detachment from them.

To prepare, Buddhist counselors can take an A4 piece of paper and some coloring pencils to facilitate the expression of emotions and needs. To start with, instruct the client to fold the A4 paper into a door base or a single gatefold style. Place the A4 paper in a horizontal position. Next, fold the two outside panels towards the middle—you will then have a card-like paper with two "doors."

There will be three parts to the drawing instructions:

1  First, use the "front door" of the paper and invite the client to draw in response to the question: "How do people see you?" (See Figure 9.2.)

    Figure 9.2 gives an example of the drawing "How do people see you?" by a pseudo client. She described how people see her as a "shining star" in the workplace and at school. This outer self-notion represents a sense of responsibility, competency, and pride.

2  Turn to the back of the paper and invite the client to draw in response to the question: "How do you wish to be seen by people?" (See Figure 9.3.)

    In Figure 9.3 the same client showed the drawing of heavy books, representing both her diligence in preparing for herself behind people's back, but imposing a huge amount of stress on her at the same time, causing her deep depression, while always trying to show a smiley face' so that her family and friends would not worry about her. This signifies the client's effort to sustain a certain self-notion to satisfy certain egoistic needs.

3  Finally, ask the client to open the "door" and use the inside of the paper to draw "How you really are" (see Figure 9.4).

    Figure 9.4 reveals the pseudo client's response. In the inner part of self-notion, the client hopes to enjoy life by traveling to different European countries and just relaxing. If she does not have to fulfill expectations of self and others, she will paint, drink coffee, ski, and experience different cultures. This symbolizes an inner self-notion with a yearning to be peaceful, joyful, and relaxed.

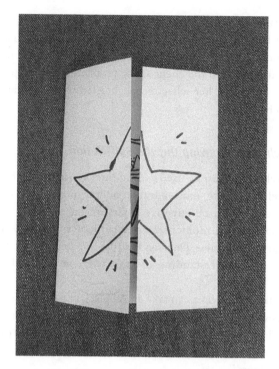

**FIGURE 9.2** Detachment Art Technique I: "How do people see you?"

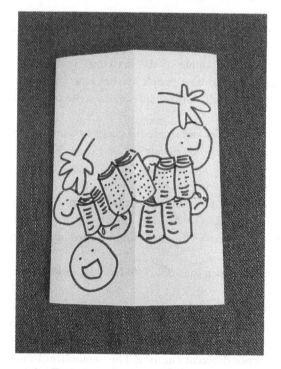

**FIGURE 9.3** Detachment Art Technique II: "How do you wish to be seen by people?"

**FIGURE 9.4** Detachment Art Technique III: "How you really are"

During the process, counselors need to attend to the client's nonverbal expressions and mindfully accompany them throughout the therapeutic journey. In addition, after the client finishes the drawing, there are some questions to consider and process:

- How did you feel doing this exercise?
- Can you describe to me each picture and their meanings?
- How does it feel to see the three different pictures?
- Do you notice any sensations in your body during this exercise?
- So, by reviewing these three drawings, who is _____ (client's name)?

The last step of the exercise begins with inviting the client to let the Buddhist counselor hold the art piece. He or she will then aim to foster detachment by narrating about this person on paper to the client as if introducing the client to a new friend. For example, the counselor can say, "I want you to imagine you have never met this person before and you are meeting this new friend for the first time. As you do not know anything about this person, you may be curious about their inner world, so I will introduce him/her to you ... 'Hi there, you have not met _____ (client's name), so I will tell you more about this person. _____ (client's name) is ...'"

It is imperative that the Buddhist counselor genuinely and objectively describes the client in the drawings without judgment or distortions. In particular, a Buddhist counselor can draw out the characteristic self-notion and the deeper needs and desires of the third picture. When doing so, observe the client's emotional expressions and process the client's experiences of knowing this person from a detached perspective. Here is an example with a 29-year-old Korean female client, Sooyoun, who has been struggling to be loved by her father:

COUNSELOR: … Hi there, you have not met Sooyoun, so I will tell you more about this person. Sooyoun is a 29-year-old girl who has worked hard in life. Her friends and colleagues tend to see her as a peaceful and helpful person who is always willing to support others. They also think she works extremely hard, although sometimes she does some silly things. How people see her is somewhat like how she wants to be seen, except that Sooyoun also hopes to be a tough and dependable person who can take leadership roles. She wants to make people feel that if she is there, everything will be fine. However, deep inside, Sooyoun is exhausted in her role as a competent and supportive person. She knows that she works so hard to prove herself to others or please others, especially her father. While it is important, she wishes to be lazy, relaxed, and not care about all that. She just wants to lie on the bed doing nothing, appreciating the blue sky with a silly smile, and probably taking a nap.

Sooyoun started crying after listening to the narration.

COUNSELOR: You feel touched. What brings tears to your eyes?

SOOYOUN: Sooyoun is just a girl … I mean, I always thought I am abnormal, and I keep doubting why I am so weird … but now, listening to how you described me, perhaps I am just a regular girl with some common needs. There is nothing strange about it!

This exercise fosters Sooyoun's knowledge and acceptance for her self-notion and needs, which became a building block to more skillful choices later.

## Know Technique for Discernment

### Analytical Dialogue on Clinging to a Self-Notion

For a mundane approach to counseling, Buddhist counselors only try to inspire insight into clinging to self-notion as an overall direction while adjusting the depth of counseling according to the client's readiness and needs. With that said, helping clients to raise awareness of their habits and deeper needs and desires is already a desirable therapeutic outcome. These habits and needs are some of the manifestations of clinging to a self-notion. Moreover, this process of Knowing must occur in a safe and trusting therapeutic relationship.

In the definition of this model, to discern is to clearly understand and judge how and why a mental act is wholesome or unwholesome. Discernment is a quality cultivated by contemplation and reflection. As part of the follow up, there are three reference statements for Buddhist counselors to contemplate with the client:

- To Know there are many reasons and factors for whatever happens, and "I" cannot see a complete picture by holding onto just one reason.
- To Know my innermost desires and what "I" have been doing to satisfy them.
- Knowing my rigid grasping onto these desires brings me a lot more suffering than what "I" have to go through.

In the technique of knowing and becoming aware of clinging to a self-notion, Buddhist counselors may have these contemplative statements in mind in the exploration process with the client. Often, the innermost desires and needs are related to unfulfilling past experiences. While Buddhist counseling is a present-focused approach that does not dwell into the past, an unskillful mind may not have the ability to ground itself in the present. It may keep dwelling on the past or future as an attempt to gain illusory control over events. In such an unskillful mind, the past and future are not time periods but mental events occurring in the present. In fact, time is determined by events, and if there is no event, there is basically no time. For example, a person who keeps recollecting physical abuse and harsh criticism by parents may transfer this previously learned relational pattern to present authority figures, thereby expecting their teachers and supervisors to be harsh and aggressive. To avoid potential threats, the person chooses to satisfy their expectations as much as possible, even while the person cannot see the kindness and care of the current authority figures. For this person, the past is present.

To help the client start knowing about their clinging to self-notion, Buddhist counselors can process the impact of past events and childhood experiences on the client's present mental state. After learning more about the client's background, Buddhist counselors should contemplate whether the client's current disturbance is associated with his or her clinging to previous events. Every attempt at clinging attempts to satisfy particular needs, and it is the Buddhist counselor's task to collaborate with clients to reveal these desires and needs. To illustrate this, the following dialogue took place between a Buddhist counselor and Chris, a 41-year-old male client, who became depressed after being rejected for an important job appointment:

COUNSELOR: What was the most upsetting part of this incident for you?

CHRIS: I guess ... it may be about my supervisor.

COUNSELOR: How so?

CHRIS: When I shared with my supervisor how I was rejected for a promotion because of my university degree, he was so mean! It was totally frustrating because he could have shown more respect.

COUNSELOR: How exactly did he say it? (*Assessing sense contact*).

CHRIS: He said something like, 'Why would you go to a school like this?' He also said it in a belittling tone!

COUNSELOR: When you heard what he said, what was the first thing that went through your mind? (*Assessing perception*).

CHRIS: I was like ... he should have supported me! He is the one who should know I am good enough for the position!

COUNSELOR: Do you mean you feel somehow rejected or disrespected by him? (*Clarifying perception*).

CHRIS: Hmmm ... I think it was more like rejection. Yes, a blunt rejection.

COUNSELOR: Then what makes you expect him to have an obligation to accept you? (*Assessing desires and needs*).

CHRIS: ... I don't know ... I think he has always been like a father, so ...

COUNSELOR: I can see that he cares about you, but what do you really want from him? (*Exploring desires and needs*).

CHRIS: ... Love? No ... attention? ... I don't know ...

COUNSELOR: OK, let's explore this. Attend to what your mind is saying ... what is it that you want so much from him? So you said, 'love,' 'attention,' and then what else?

CHRIS: Love ... attention ... acknowledgment ... acceptance! Yes, I really hate that feeling of rejection, and I want acceptance. I think as he knows me and cares about me, he should actually accept me and not judge me in this unreasonable way!

COUNSELOR: Let me ask you this question. Even for a father, a parent, or a close mentor who really cares about you, what makes you believe that they have an obligation to accept you as you are? (*Bringing up clinging to a perceived reality*).

CHRIS: (*A few seconds of pondering*) ... I guess you are right. They actually don't, but that's what I have always wanted.

After the client realizes that although he desires acceptance from the supervisor and other important people in his life, they do not have a responsibility to understand and accept him, he has a moment of relief. In this process, the Buddhist counselor knows that the client has been trying hard to prove himself to his parents and other authority figures, so the counsellor used it as a reference in mind to process the client's deeper desires and needs behind his depressed mood. Out of the counsellor's expectation, the client presented as depressed when discussing the failed appointment, while he became irritated when the dialogue shifted to his supervisor. This trigger of different emotions was indicative of deeper unmet needs. To reveal such needs, the Buddhist counselor prompted the client to contemplate the nature of the relationship and encouraged him to continue revealing his deeper needs. Finally, the Buddhist counselor used a somewhat confrontational technique to ask the client what made him have such expectations, which is not fulfilled in reality. It is crucial to note that this kind of confrontational technique requires a positive rapport between counselor and client and that the client is ready to contemplate without defense. In this situation, the client could then reach a deeper insight into his needs and reality. In that regard, when he knew that grasping onto being accepted is painful, he spontaneously eased the grasping at the moment of being aware of it.

### The Two Arrows Exercise

As pointed out previously, the two arrows represent two types of suffering: the first arrow refers to uncontrollable aspects of suffering such as birth, ageing, illness, and death, while the second arrow refers to the controllable aspects of suffering such as the resistance and hatred towards birth, ageing, illness, and death. In light of this metaphor, a significant part of suffering is rooted in at least three unskillful mind acts: (1) mistakenly seeing uncontrollable events (First Arrow) as controllable, (2) ignorantly neglecting the controllable conditions (Second Arrow), and (3) attaching an additional layer of emotional suffering by fabricating, proliferating, and resisting the original level of suffering of the First Arrow (Subsequent Second Arrows). If one can see and accept the First Arrow as it is, one can be instantly relieved from the numerous Second Arrows of suffering. The Two Arrows Exercise applies this concept to cultivate a client's capacity to accept what cannot be changed, to change what can be changed, and discern the difference between the two. Together with

**TABLE 9.1** The Two Arrows Exercise with Sample

| Please fill in the suffering at this moment in each box provided | Internal conditions (e.g., thoughts and emotions) | External conditions (e.g., environment) |
|---|---|---|
| 1st arrow: Uncontrollable Events | • Anger<br>• Pop-up thought of "he intended to make fun of me in front of everyone!" | • Deadline at work<br>• Heavy workload<br>• Difficult project<br>• Horrible boss |
| 2nd arrow: Controllable Events | • Ruminating on how he shamed me in the middle of the night<br>• Blaming myself for not working harder | • Whether to change a job<br>• The way of talking to my boss<br>• Taking break from work |

the concept of internal and external conditions, counselors can work with a client to write down or describe the conditions and have a dialogue on whether they are controllable or not (see Table 9.1).

In this example, the client originally suffers from lots of stress at work, including a highly critical boss, unfriendly colleagues, and an unreasonable workload. Being a perfectionist, the client clings onto a highly competent notion of self and often feels a strong urge to outperform others at work in order to gain recognition and respect. The lack of acknowledgement from his boss and colleagues made him extremely angry. He copes with the anger by forcing himself to work more diligently which resulted in significant physical and emotional disturbances. Discussions between a client and counselor can foster understanding of how certain things cannot be changed. In using the Two Arrows Exercise, the Buddhist counselor was able to help the client differentiate between controllable events and uncontrollable events using questions, dialogues, and reflections. More importantly, the counselor focused on what the choices are for the client (internal conditions) and in the environment (external conditions). This exploration empowered the client to detach from certain anger-provoking thoughts and then help him decide what he can do to take better care of himself.

### Stories and Metaphors

Stories and metaphors are powerful tools for helping clients gain insights into Buddhist practice and psychology. In fact, the Buddha and his disciples used many metaphors and stories in their teachings, such as using a monkey to describe the nature of the mind and a chariot to bring out the idea of dependent co-arising. In Buddhist counseling, telling Buddhist stories that resonate with clients' suffering facilitates their detachment from clinging to a point of view, thereby creating opportunities for new insights. Furthermore, a major step is to process the client's thoughts and reactions to the story and discuss its relevance to the client's concerns. Here is an example of a 26-year-old Sri Lankan client who presents with low self-esteem as he holds onto a view that he is not good enough for his girlfriend. The Buddhist counselor begins first:

> What you said reminded me of an old Buddhist story. There was an old scavenger named Niti in an ancient city where the Buddha usually went for alms with his disciples. One day, seeing the Buddha approaching from a distance, this old man decided to hide himself, thinking, "I am a scavenger from a very low class, and my hands are covered in mud and dirt. The Buddha comes from such a high class, so I shouldn't come close to him in order not to offend his purity." However, the Buddha saw him and walked directly over to him. Then the old man begged the Buddha to stop, saying, "Oh Buddha, please let go of me … I am dirty." The Buddha smiled and said, "My friend, we should not look down upon ourselves. One does not become distinguished by one's birth but by one's behavior. You clear the dirt from people's homes; I clear the dirt from people's hearts. Hence, you and I are the same."

After telling the story, the Buddhist counselor guides the client to reflect on the story's meaning as well as the emotions and sensations coming up while listening to it. This story is culturally congruent with the client's background and affiliation with Buddhism makes it effective. The client realized that there is another angle to evaluate his worth, and he gained the insight that he can at least get to know his girlfriend's father better before forming a judgment. Here is another metaphor to help clients gain insights into how thoughts and emotions arise and cease:

> Observing thoughts is like being a security guard of an apartment building. When you are sitting at your booth, tens of residents show up to use the escalator, pass by your desk making a comment to you, and gradually walk away to the escalator. Some residents are nice enough to give you a warm greeting, while some residents can be angry, mean, sad, or even intimidating. The common ground is, regardless of whether they are pleasant or unpleasant, each of one of them will come and leave. As long as you sit back and just observe them, you will realize that no one will stay long at your booth. This is how our thoughts work.

There are many Buddhist and Buddhism-related stories and metaphors applicable to counseling. For example, in *Kisa Gotami and the Mustard Seed*, Kisa realizes that everyone in the world inevitably loses family members to death. There is also the story of an old Zen monk carrying a woman across a river that exemplifies the art of letting go, and the metaphor of how Buddha describes being non-reactive to insults is like returning parcels to senders. Some books I remember include Zen Buddhist stories in Paul Reps' *Zen Flesh, Zen Bones: A Collection of Zen and Pre-Zen Writings*, metaphors in Buddhist scriptures such as Soonil Hwang's *Metaphor and Literalism in Buddhism the Doctrinal History of Nirvana*, and a fresh and visual presentation of Buddhist teachings in Rodney Alan Greenblat's *Dharma Delight: A Visionary Post Pop Comic Guide to Buddhism and Zen*. I suggest that Buddhist counselors review and contemplate such Buddhist stories and metaphors to equip themselves with this effective tool.

### Reflections on Buddhist Writing

In addition to stories and metaphors, Buddhist counselors can choose Buddhist writings as reflective materials pertinent to a client's suffering. To do so, Buddhist counselors need to understand the client's background and suffering, think about the Buddhist concept that the client can benefit from, and select a relevant sutta, commentary, poem, or other related writing to foster new insights. In the sessions, the counselor can read the selected passage with the client or assign it to them as homework and then discuss it during an upcoming session. For example, when Buddhist counselors hope to help clients acquire the concept of impermanence, several types of writing may help. For clients who have a strong affiliation with Buddhism, such as monastic members, excerpted Buddhist scriptures may be useful. For example:

> Monks, form is impermanent. What's impermanent is suffering. What's suffering is not-self. And what's not-self should be truly seen with right understanding, like this: "This is not mine, I am not this, this is not my self." Seeing truly with right understanding like this, the mind becomes dispassionate and freed from defilements by not grasping
>
> (SN 22.59)

For clients who are interested in Buddhism but who may not be attracted to Buddhist scriptures, many commentaries and writings from contemporary Buddhist masters can be helpful:

> It is not impermanence that makes us suffer.... One day, when you're strong enough and determined enough, you'll let go of the afflictions that make you suffer.
>
> (Thich, n.d.)

> When life is good, do not take it for granted as it will pass. Be mindful, be compassionate, and nurture the circumstances that find you in this good time so it will last longer. When life falls apart, always remember that this too will pass. Life will have its unexpected turns.
>
> (Brahm, n.d.)

After reading with the client, Buddhist counselors can process the material in many different ways, such as asking, "What do you think about this?," "How do you understand what it says?," "What bodily sensations/emotions/thoughts come up when reading it?," "How does it relate to your problem?," and "How would you apply this wisdom to your life?" If the writings resonate with the clients' suffering, they will likely gain new insights through the Buddhist counselor's contemplative dialogue.

### Insight Meditation

Insight, or *vipassanā* in Pāli, means to see things as they are. In particular, it is an ability to see and discern how mental and physical phenomena arise, change, and cease, thereby understanding the dependent co-arising nature of the world. During Insight meditation, the practitioner applies the concentration nurtured in mindfulness practice to contemplate the mechanisms of the body and mind to gain insight into the nature of suffering. That is, insight meditation is a skillful means to know the "self" through observations, analysis, and contemplation, thereby realizing the insubstantiality or emptiness of phenomena. In this model of Buddhist counseling, insight meditation can become a tool for Buddhist counselors to help the client know about their clinging and needs. After the client has enhanced their clarity and stability of mind, Buddhist counselors can use prompts during insight meditation to explore and analyze at a more in-depth level. There are usually four steps: (1) Soothing and stabilizing the client's mind, (2) Turning towards the mind, (3) Contemplation, and (4) Returning to the present moment. After this practice, Buddhist counselors need to process the experience with the client and integrate the insights. Here is an illustration with a client who has been struggling with depressed mood:

**Step 1: Soothing and stabilizing the client's mind.**

COUNSELOR: Let's start this exercise with mindful breathing. This time, just try to follow your breath as it is. There's no need to control, alter, or judge it. Simply observe each breath and experience it for its full duration. Notice the sensations of each in- and out- breath. Follow your own pace ... Observe the rhythm. Know whether it is a long breath ... or a short breath. Notice the gap between each breath. Just simply observe. (*Pause for 30 seconds*).

**Step 2: Turning towards the mind.**

COUNSELOR: Now, experience yourself in this sitting position. Know that your mind and thought processes are within this physical body. Let's gradually attend to your mind. Follow your mind. Should there be any unpleasant sensations, try to turn towards it. Stay with it. (*Pause for 30 seconds*). I see your mouth being drawn downwards, and your body is shivering slightly. What are you experiencing right now?
CLIENT: I feel that there is some discomfort in me ... somewhere in my chest ... I don't know what it is ...
COUNSELOR: Continue to follow your breath while attending to the chest area. Just observe. Know that it is a safe place here and know that you are capable of seeing through it. Keep on turning towards it ... observing it ... knowing it.

**Step 3: Contemplation.**

CLIENT: I feel that I am going into something.
COUNSELOR: What do you see?
CLIENT: Darkness ... everywhere is so dark ... I feel like being in a dark hole ...
COUNSELOR: What thoughts or emotions are you experiencing right now?
CLIENT: Nothing really ... it's just darkness here ... almost like I am falling down in an endless dark hole. Maybe a little scared ...

COUNSELOR: I am here in the darkness with you. I am accompanying you to see the nature of this darkness. Let's stay there and observe what it is.

(*Pause for 20 seconds*). Client starts crying.

COUNSELOR: I can see tears coming ... what are those tears saying to you right now?

CLIENT: A past memory came up ... I was in my grandmother's home by myself. I think I was about 5 years old. I woke up from a nap and there was just me. I could not find any adult and I was scared. Not just scared, but angry! How come no one is around? How come no one is there for me when I have a temper tantrum? How come no one understands me? ... I feel so lonely ... Yes! Loneliness! There is a sense of loneliness here!

COUNSELOR: Loneliness. It seems like you have experienced a deep emotion in you.

Client continued to cry and said, "Yes ... yes ... I am indeed a lonely person. I feel depressed when I don't feel understood and accepted because it is really lonely ..."

After containing the client's emotions and letting him cry, the counselor continues: "Knowing that loneliness is a deep emotion and that being understood and accepted are some deep yearnings, let's contemplate some questions: (1) Can I accept myself the way I always wanted to be accepted by others? (*Pause for five seconds*) (2) Can I understand myself the way I always wanted to be understood by others? (*Pause for five seconds*) (3) Can I let go of my suffering in the past and live fully in the present moment and be capable of loving and holding this lonely and scared 5-year-old boy? (*Pause for five seconds*) (4) If I truly love this boy, what could I say to him now? Please say out loud what you want to say to him."

(*Pause for five seconds*).

CLIENT: I want to tell him ... I know it sucks when no one understands you. I know it is sad and scary when you have to be by yourself. But I am here with you and I will try my best to listen to you and protect you.

COUNSELOR: Good. For the final part, let's try to shift our perspective. We can try to see this boy and his suffering of loneliness as a product of many causes and conditions. The experience with your grandparents, experience with your parents, your memories, your body, your mind, your self, and all other people and all other things. Every one of these conditions is changing moment by moment and nothing really lasts forever. It's just like carrying a big bag of heavy stones all the way, but when you stop and decide to open the bag, you find nothing inside ... we have labeled this wounded child and his loneliness skillfully, but it's time to also know they are both impermanent. They are just the experiences of mind. As long as you are willing to let go of them, they are free to disappear. We always want to be something, but in fact, we don't have to be anything. We can be nothing. By being nothing, you are everything.

**Step 4: Returning to the present moment.**

COUNSELOR: Now let's come back to the bodily sensations. Gently feel your breath. How is it now? Is it slow or fast? Is it strong or gentle? Let's take some deep breaths in and out ... mindfully breathe in and out again. Experience the in- and out-breaths through your nostrils and the sensations of each breath. (*Pause for five seconds*). When you are ready, you can come back to the room and gently open your eyes.

As seen earlier, Buddhist counselors may personalize step 3 to help clients contemplate various aspects and experiences related to their suffering. They can also tailor the length and depth of the exercises according to the client's presenting problems and readiness. Most importantly, Buddhist counselors should process the experience with the client, consolidate the insights gained, and provide compassionate listening to the client's emotions.

## Application of Know to Cindy

To cultivate wisdom for Cindy, the Buddhist counselor reflects on her pattern of failed attempts to change her mother, her expectation of what her mother should be like, and her need for her mother to provide unconditional love. By examining the discrepancy between her reality and her expectations, Cindy gains more knowledge of how she has denied reality by attempting to alter her mother's perception of her. Although it is difficult to accept this reality, Cindy comes to the insight that perhaps her cause of suffering is not just how her mother behaves but how she expects her mother to be. She also begins to turn towards her deep resistance against the reality that her mother never loved her the way she wanted. At this point, Cindy experiences more relief as she develops a deeper understanding of what has contributed to her frustration and depression.

COUNSELOR: It seems to me that you have tried very hard to convince your mother to love you even though you are a daughter, not a son, but it has not been successful.

CINDY: Yes, I don't even know why I just keep on trying.

COUNSELOR: What if your mother is incapable of loving and accepting you because of how she is?

CINDY: (*Ponders for a while and starts tearing up.*) I think part of me knew it, but I just don't want to believe it. It is very sad to believe that my mother does not love me, and I don't know what else to do except keep trying harder. I am just frustrated by how stupid I am to keep on craving love from a stone-cold person!

To Know is to radically and compassionately accept who we are, regardless of how scary, ugly, or aversive the recognition of our clinging can be. Knowing is a detached view that allows us to see how we suffer from our clinging and understand our clinging motivations without judgment or rejection. To accomplish this, the Buddhist counselor uses a visualization exercise to help Cindy generate self-compassion:

COUNSELOR: Yes, it is truly saddening to know one's mother does not love and accept her own child, and it is frustrating to get rejected every time, no matter how hard you tried. However, it is not stupid at all.

CINDY: How is it not stupid?

COUNSELOR: Imagine a little girl being born and raised in a family with strong favoritism for boys. She has always been treated as a 'less than,' and her mother never really saw her. She believed that she would get all the love and respect she ever wanted so long as she worked hard enough. However, no matter how hard she tried, her mother still failed to grant this little girl what she wanted. In fact, what she wants is very simple:

just a warm hug, a caring smile, and praise from her mother so that she can finally feel loved. Would you blame this little girl for trying to get something she needs?

CINDY: When you put it this way, I think I have much more compassion for this poor little girl …

## CONCLUSION

To Know is to deepen one's understanding of the causes of suffering, and these causes can be many: rigid attachment to who we are and how others should treat us, a need for validation and acceptance, a severe illness in our body, stressors in the environment, and any other factors you may have experienced. The job of Buddhist counselors is to deeply listen to clients and their conditions, reflect those conditions to them, and collaboratively reveal and realize their causes. For new counselors, it is common to find this idea very abstract and then feeling unsure of what to do. There are times when new students will take the list of questions, ask them one-by-one during roleplays, believe that the session was finished, but then not know what to do next. These students could not genuinely connect to the suffering of their peers and be curious to learn about their views and thought processes. One thing that takes time and experience to develop is our so-called *clinical sense*, which is the acumen to intuitively know and discern the cause, nature, and solutions around a clinical problem. Even when I was a student, I would also ask myself, "How come my supervisor just saw something that I could not see?" Years after, my students would ask me the same question. Two conditions that account for this difference are the direct experiences of embodying and contemplating knowledge to benefit myself and then applying that knowledge in practice through dialogue to understand every person I encounter. In short, to know suffering in others one should start with knowing the suffering in ourselves. To stimulate such an awareness, contemplate the following questions.

### Contemplative Questions for Buddhist Counselors

As we know suffering is a result of clinging to a self-notion, the key to reducing suffering is to ease our rigid grasping onto this constructed identity. This process of detachment, or realization of non-self, is the key concept to Know as well as a highly experiential process which needs to go beyond cognitive learning. To help Buddhist counselors gain direct experience of non-self, the following exercise is designed as an insight meditation for counselors to reflect and contemplate. As with all other exercises, we will start with mindful breathing to re-center our minds as a mindful haven.

Experience your body, breath, and mind at this moment. Gently and gradually relax them one by one. Observe how you are sitting and slowly adjust your posture and muscles until you reach a balance of uprightness and relaxation. Attend to your breath and relax all intention to control or change it. Simply make a note in your mind: "From these sensations, I know I am breathing in; from those sensations, I know I am breathing out." Follow your breath for a few minutes.

When you are ready for contemplation, slowly and mindfully read each of the following questions, taking a ten-second break in between each question to reflect:

- When I observe my mind at this moment, what is it like?
- Are there inner voices, imagery, or ideas?
- If I just sit back and observe my mental activities, like watching a movie, what are they trying to say?
- Where am "I" in this mind movie?
- Am "I" the main character in this movie?
- If I am, do "I" have to play this role?
- What are the causes and conditions of this role?
- Is it a permanent role or has it been changing?
- Is there a part of me wishing to hold onto this role?
- What would happen if I just let go of this role?
- Let's sit back again to observe my mind: What thoughts are going on in my mind right now?
- How do the thoughts arise?
- How do the thoughts change?
- How do the thoughts cease?
- If thoughts are impermanent, am I also impermanent?

Take a few deep breaths and relax. Write down your thoughts, feelings, and insights for further reflection. Also, notice your feelings, sensations, and suffering at this moment. Come back to this very present moment with your body and mind. Contemplate each of these questions one-by-one:

- In scanning my body, have my bodily sensations changed in this process?
- While observing thoughts, inner voices, and imagery in my mind, has my mind changed in any way at all?
- Have my feelings of suffering changed?
- Have my feelings of happiness changed?
- If there are so many changes, am I still the same person as 15 minutes ago?
- If I am not the same person, who am "I"?
- Is this "Who am I?" question even an important question?
- Can I love and accept all the possibilities of me as well as all the possibilities of non-me?
- Can I be fully settled and contented in this grounded moment of awareness?

The self is not an intrinsic and ultimate existence, although we certainly wish it to be. One easy way to understand non-self is: we are just our mind activities. In these activities, we keep defining and re-defining ourselves and holding onto these definitions to try and confirm some sense of a continuous existence. However, it can be draining and painful because reality usually clashes with our desirable definitions. But if we know how our rigidity gives us suffering, we can have flexibility and creativity to define who we are. This openness to *flow* is the essence of detachment as well as the window for compassionate acceptance.

# REFERENCES

Anālayo, B. (2003). *Satipaṭṭhāna – The Direct Path to Realization*. London, UK: Windhorse Publications.

Brahm, A. (n.d.). *Quotable Quote*. goodreads. Retrieved from www.goodreads.com/quotes/989532-when-life-is-good-do-not-take-it-for-granted.

Karunadasa, Y. (2010). *The Theravada Abhidhamma: Its Inquiry Into the Nature of Conditioned Reality*. Hong Kong: Centre for Buddhist Studies, Hong Kong University.

Karunadasa, Y. (2013). *Early Buddhist Teachings: The Middle Position in Theory and Practice*. Hong Kong: Centre of Buddhist Studies, The University of Hong Kong.

Lee, K. C., & Tang, J. (2021). Note, Know, Choose: A Psychospiritual Treatment Model based on Early Buddhist Teachings *Spirituality in Clinical Practice*. Advanced online publication. https://doi.org/10.1037/scp0000220

SN 22.59. Anatta-lakkhana Sutta: The Discourse on the Not-self Characteristic, translated by Mendis, N. K. G. (2007). *Access to Insight (BCBS Edition)*. Retrieved from www.accesstoinsight.org/tipitaka/sn/sn22/sn22.059.mend.html

Thich, N. H. (n.d.). *The Pocket Thich Nhat Hanh Quotes*. goodreads. Retrieved from www.goodreads.com/work/quotes/18538015-the-pocket-thich-nhat-hanh#:~:text=%E2%80%9CIt%20is%20not%20impermanence%20that,take%20good%20care%20of%20ourselves.

# CHAPTER 10

# Intervention and Techniques
## *Choose*

How many choices do you usually make in a day? Whether it is choosing clothes to wear in the mornings, the type of transportation to take to work or school, food to eat for lunch and dinner, or what TV channel or Netflix movie to watch at night, most people will say that we make 30–50 decisions at most. However, we make A LOT more choices than that. In a conversation with professor Jean Kristeller, a prominent expert in mindful eating, I have learned that we make more than 500 choices just about eating every day: beginning with the choices to look at on the menu, scanning through each item, visualizing the food items, deciding "No, I don't want that" or "Sure, let's get some pasta," asking for our order to be taken, using a particular wording and tone as you order, and so on. In the stream of consciousness, each of our thoughts and behaviors is connected by our moment-to-moment choices. The question is, how capable are we of making good choices?

Life is full of choices. In Buddhism, the standard translation of *kamma* is "action," but some scholars prefer to translate *kamma* as decision or choice. The latter translation emphasizes the idea that the mind controls what we do and that each choice will have consequences. While many kammic consequences are unpredictable, the most direct impact of each choice is in the immediate experience of the chooser. For example, choosing to say compassionate words brings peace and compassion to the speaker, while choosing to insult others agitates the speaker's mind with hatred and ill-will. Good choices protect and nurture the mind of the chooser. In this final phase of the Note, Know, Choose model, we will discuss how to cultivate clients' minds to develop the capacity for making more beneficial choices for themselves and others.

## THEORETICAL RATIONALE OF CHOOSE

In psychology, choice is commonly referred to as a behavioral decision. For example, Dialectical Behavioral Therapy helps the client learn how to develop a wise mind balanced between emotionality and rationality that can then choose more functional ways to cope with stress, communicate, and avoid self-injurious behaviors. In Buddhism, a behavioral decision is one of three types of action. In the *Maha Kammavibhanga Sutta, Kayagata-sati Sutta,* and other discourses, the Buddha explained kamma as volitional actions in the forms of body, mind, and speech. The core element of these volitional actions comes from a mental

DOI: 10.4324/9781003025450-10

process involving a subtle cognitive decision. In other words, the core of choice is making the effort to pay attention.

The mind functions as a stream of consciousness flooded with a kammic rush of habitual decision making. It constantly lands on physical and mental objects, thereby generating thoughts and imagery. Driven by our previously formed habits, not all mental experiences are volitional. When these mental experiences trigger the latent ego-consciousness, the ego arises in pursuit, resistance, or fabrication of them according to the person's previous habits. The background rationale of Choose serves to mindfully slow down the series of habitual decisions so that one can become more informed and thoughtful in making wiser decisions.

For example, when a man who loves French fries sees the McDonald's logo, a visual image of French fries appears, and he starts to pursue the mental images and fantasize about the satisfaction offered by the crispy, salty, and greasy flavor. He then decides to go to McDonald's to buy a bag of supersized fries to satiate his craving. From the Early Buddhist perspective, his decisional process started from his motivation to enjoy fries arising as a visual image, not with the purchasing behavior. His cognitive act of dwelling on the visualized sensual pleasure of fries gradually crystallized into a state of craving that fueled his decision to walk into the fast-food shop. This temporary satisfaction of his craving also reinforced his habit of clinging to fries as a source of satisfaction. The Choose phase helps clients establish a clearer and more stable mental state from which to deliberatively select physical, mental, and behavioral actions that result in less suffering.

If the man in the previous example was to mindfully observe the cognitive acts that arise in response to the McDonald's sign and discern his craving for fries, he would find many possible entry points to change the course of his habitual patterns. For example, when he notices the suffering of craving for fries and chooses to visualize possible aversive consequences of giving in to his craving, such as gaining weight, increasing his risk for heart attack, or getting a sore throat, he is more likely to choose to walk past the McDonald's. In the Buddhist understanding of the mind, mental activities occur in a flash, and an external stimulus can morph into an alarming emotional reaction in a millisecond. However, embedded in every individual's mental activities are numerous decisions that the mind has made before the escalated emotion results. With an enhanced ability to note and know, one can put these mental activities into slow motion to identify various choice points that can begin to lead to a negative thought, feeling, or behavior.

## TREATMENT GOAL OF CHOOSE

Kamma is volitional action that leads to responsive consequences in a positive feedback loop. For this reason, a significant factor contributing to suffering is unskillful habits and inclinations of thoughts and behaviors rooted in previous courses of action. But with a clear and calm mind developed through the noting and knowing practices, counselors can guide clients to slow down their habitual patterns of pursuit or resistance and examine each cognitive act. *Choose* is the practice of wise attention (*Yonisomanasikāra*) which is to attend, think, and reflect on the interdependent and impermanent nature of phenomenon, thereby volitionally making decisions resulting in less suffering. Choices are evident in each moment if one pays heedful attention and then makes use of the will to reduce suffering. Unfortunately, even when choice points become clear, some clients are still driven by powerful emotionality to make unskillful decisions, especially those who have been traumatized or who have lived with difficult relationships. In such situations, the counselor can consider using techniques to help the client cultivate radical acceptance, forgiveness, and compassion towards self and others.

In summary, the overarching treatment goal of Choose is to foster the client's capacity to reflect on causes and conditions at the moment, make wholesome choices and reduce unwholesome choices (Lee & Tang, 2020). To achieve this goal, Buddhist counselors will learn to use the Choose interventions to achieve the following objectives: (1) *Identification of choice points*: With an enhanced ability to note and know, Buddhist counselors collaborate with the client to put mental activities into slow motion in order to identify various choice points in mind, behaviors, and speech, thereby revealing to clients potential alternatives; (2) *Check-in with realistic conditions*: with the choice points identified, Buddhist counselors can dialogue with the client to examine the different perspectives, causes, and conditions of the event, possible choices, and the benefit and harm of different choices; (3) *Skillful decisions*: Buddhist counselors help clients to nurture various wholesome mind, speech, and behavioral choices in order to foster new and more wholesome habits.

## CHOOSE TECHNIQUES

The Note, Know, Choose model includes an overarching Choose technique based on the Early Buddhism model of cognition called Mind Moment Analysis (MMA). This technique integrates the Note and Know phases to enhance a client's concentration and ability to analyze the mind's action moment-by-moment. Three objectives—identification of choice points, check-in with realistic conditions, and skillful decisions—are all embedded in this intervention.

### Mind Moment Analysis

Based on an article published on MMA (Lee, 2021), this section provides an update on an overall framework that aims to release the mind from overwhelming conceptual proliferations. One way to cease suffering is to practice not taking delight in the welcoming and holding onto conceptual proliferations, thereby gradually diminishing unwholesome states of mind (Karunadasa, 2013). MMA initiates this process by identifying a disturbing incident in which the client is assailed with and dominated by conceptual proliferations. These incidents and the client's responses to them are sources of data. By examining them, the client iteratively and gradually notes the body-mind components of an unwholesome state, analyses their root causes (especially the underlying craving), and identifies choice points at which they can extricate themselves. Thus, MMA cultivates awareness of how and why mental activities contribute to suffering and how suffering arises, changes, and ceases with different cognitive and behavioral choices. The Buddhist counselor introduces this meditative practice through active listening, dialogues, questioning, and sharing insights to help the client cultivate the flexibility needed to withdraw attention from conceptual proliferations and become grounded in the present moment. An MMA involves nine steps: (a) mind education,

(b) identifying a critically disturbing incident, (c) locating sensory contacts, (d) expanding awareness of bodily sensations and feelings, (e) noting cognitions, (f) understanding conceptual proliferations, (g) identifying choice points, (h) checking in with realistic conditions, and (i) making skillful decisions (see Table 10.1).

**TABLE 10.1** The Nine Steps Mind Moment Analysis

| Step | Description |
|---|---|
| 1. Mind education | Mind education is a technique for understanding the nature of the mind from the perspective of dependent arising. The therapist explains to the client the nature of the mind to highlight the mental space that exists between the present moment and subsequent conceptual proliferations. |
| 2. Identifying a critical incident of disturbance | Identifying a critical incident is to collaborate with the client in pinpointing a recent experience of suffering. The goal is to recollect the incident and its details to raise the client's awareness of multiple environmental, bodily, and mental factors contributing to the suffering. |
| 3. Locating sensory contacts | Locating sensory contacts, the therapist guides clients' attention to mindfully examine various visual, auditory, tactile, gustatory, olfactory, and mental inputs during the identified incident and then to notice the unpleasant sensations that result. Thus, the therapist aims to foster the client's heedfulness of the multiple sensory inputs contributing to a phenomenon of suffering, thereby deconstructing the totality of experience into its components. |
| 4. Expanding awareness of bodily sensations and feelings | Expanding awareness of bodily sensations and feelings allows the therapist to use dialogue, questions, and reflections to enhance clients' awareness of physical sensations and use such bodily sensations as a present-moment anchor to ground the client's mind. The goal is to further deconstruct a phenomenon by seeing the bodily and sensual components supporting a phenomenon of suffering. |
| 5. Noting cognitions | Noting cognitions is to help the client use a focused mind grounded at the present moment to observe, examine, and analyze mind activities from a mental distance. In particular, this step aims to help the client see how one's mind initiates wishful relationships with events and persons. |
| 6. Knowing conceptual proliferations | Knowing conceptual proliferations allows the Buddhist counselor and client to collaboratively examine and analyze conceptual proliferations to gain knowledge of root causes and effects, such as yearnings and cravings. The goal is to help the client know how one's intention to satisfy his or her craving actually causes suffering. |
| 7. Identifying choice points | Identifying choice points is to help clients see realistic conditions beyond their mental proliferations, examine the stream of cognitive processes and therefore to discover entry points leading to alternative mind acts, and assigning homework to foster mindfulness in response to future incidents. |
| 8. Check-in with realistic conditions | While focusing the client's mind on the choice points, Buddhist counselors reflect the understanding of realistic conditions to the client's growing awareness. In this way, the client has the opportunity to become nonattached from their needs and desires and gain the flexibility to see other possible perspectives of the same event. |
| 9. Skillful decisions | In this step, Buddhist counselors work with their clients to practice different skillful choices regarding mind, behavior, and speech. Once the client can acquire new and more wholesome skills, it is crucial to encourage the client to apply them in daily life, thereby consolidating new and more wholesome patterns of mind activities. |

The following hypothetical case vignette illustrates the practicality of MMA.

**Case Vignette:** "Jimmy" is a 53-year-old Malaysian male from a lower socioeconomic background working as a registered electrician. He lives in a small apartment with his wife (aged 50) and his son (aged 13). He was diagnosed with generalized anxiety disorder and has had panic attacks for which he was prescribed a low dosage of an SSRI (Lexapro) by a psychiatrist. During his sessions with you, he displays worries about parenting issues, reports poor relationships with family members, and claims to have had anxiety problems for more than ten years. He says he tends to "overworry," which has been "harming my relationship with my son."

Jimmy is preoccupied with his son's academic work and expects his son to study every minute. When asked about his childhood, he described his father as "neglectful' and "very harsh." His mother died from cancer when he was age two, with no subsequent memories of her. His aunt (his mother's younger sister) was his primary caregiver who took good care of him after his mother died. Out of love for him, his auntie initially put him in a good school, but his father vehemently refused, thinking it would be a waste of money. Instead, he put his son in a lower-tier school in which there were gangs, drugs, and bullies. The client described the school as "dangerous" because there were gangsters everywhere, and his classmate even offered him some "drug pills." Jimmy did not complete high school and started working as a construction worker. He described the first working experience as "scary" because he was bullied and laughed at and often got hurt at work. Finally, he realized that studying was his only way out of adversity, so he strove to gain vocational certification as an electrician, bringing him a more stable income and a safer working environment. As a result of this effort he was able to work at a major electric company and raise a family. His conflict with his son arose when his son started secondary school. His son goes to a middle-tier secondary school, but he does not like to study. Jimmy personalizes the responsibility and believes his son's resistance results from his failure as a parent. He then related a situation in which he once broke his son's phone to "scare" him in an attempt to force him to study. Jimmy showed lots of regret about his impulsive behavior, claiming that it was his first time breaking his son's belongings, and that it was due to anxiety over his son's academic performance.

## Mind Education

Many clients suffering from severe emotional disturbances are unaware that their experiences are due to multiple conditions that have built up in the mind. As a result, these clients tend to interpret these emotional phenomena as actual events and actively pursue or resist them, which only aggravates the emotional suffering. Mind education is a technique for understanding the nature of the mind from the perspective of dependent arising, which introduces a mental space between the present moment and conceptual proliferations.

JIMMY: I guess my son's schoolwork makes me anxious ... If he doesn't study hard enough, he will not get into good schools, and his life will be ruined! But he just doesn't see my point ... I am just stressed out. Then my health gets worse too.

COUNSELOR: I hear you talk a lot about how this anxiety is truly disturbing. One thing we can do is to work collaboratively and understand what is inside this so-called 'anxiety.' By analyzing and dissecting it together it will be less haunting and scary.

JIMMY: What do you mean?

COUNSELOR: The term 'anxiety' seems to be a scary word in your mind, but do you know that 'anxiety' is actually a compound noun? It is not a solid entity. It can be broken down into components, and then it loses its power. Let's try an example. You have seen candlelight, right?

JIMMY: Sure.

COUNSELOR: What are the different things that make up candlelight?

JIMMY: ... Like wax?

COUNSELOR: Yes! What else? Tell me all you can think of.

JIMMY: Hmm ... wax, candlewick ... oxygen, and high temperature?

COUNSELOR: Very good! What would happen if one of these conditions were taken away?

JIMMY: Well, we probably couldn't light the candle.

COUNSELOR: That's right. Anxiety is the same: just like when you take out a supporting piece from the Jenga game and the whole thing collapses.

JIMMY: So you mean if we change something about my anxiety, it will collapse somehow?

COUNSELOR: Yes. Would you like to give it a try?

### Identifying a Critical Incident

The starting point of such mind training is to identify the most recent incident during which the client experienced suffering. It is crucial to identify an incident recent enough so that the client has fresh memories of the details. The counselor then facilitates the client's recollection of different components of the event. In Jimmy's case, a recent strong emotional disturbance occurred when he broke his son's phone.

COUNSELOR: When was the last time that you were really anxious?

JIMMY: It was last week when I had a conflict with my son.

COUNSELOR: Can you tell me more about this conflict?

JIMMY: Well ... I saw my son playing his online game on this phone, and I got worried that he would fail his final exam. So I tried to ask him to study, but he ignored me. Then I got really mad, and I took his phone and threw it to the ground. You know, this is the first time for me to really break things ... He still hasn't talked to me since.

COUNSELOR: You seem to be very upset about how you broke his phone, and then your son stopped talking to you. However, it happened within seconds, and it seems a lot was happening in your mind from when you walked into his room to when you threw his phone. Let's slow it all down and go through the details step-by-step.

### Locating Sense Contacts

In Buddhist psychology, sense contact refers to the meeting point of the sense object, the sense organ, and consciousness, which signifies the beginning of the cognitive process (Karunadasa, 2010). A classic example is the coming together of a visible object, the eyes, and attentive sight, which gives rise to visual information. Buddhism identifies six senses: sight, hearing, smell, touch, taste, and mind. The mind is capable of cognizing all these senses and of generating mental objects such as images, inner voices, or thoughts. Suffering arises from misinterpretations and fabrications of sense objects through the mind's inclination to conceptually proliferate, which results in a distortion or rejection of the original sensual input. The task of a Buddhist counselor is to direct Jimmy's attention to various visual, auditory, tactile, taste, smell, and subjective inputs during the identified incident and noticing the unpleasant sensations that result. Breaking down an overwhelming incident into its various components is the first step in the deconstruction of such challenging life experiences.

COUNSELOR: What was the first thing you saw when you walked into your son's room?

JIMMY: My son … using his phone, playing on his phone!

COUNSELOR: How was his facial expression?

JIMMY: He was kind of smiling and seemed to be very excited.

COUNSELOR: What else did you notice?

JIMMY: I also saw his books on his desk.

COUNSELOR: You mean textbooks?

JIMMY: Yes, textbooks and homework books, not even opened.

COUNSELOR: Did you hear anything?

JIMMY: Yes! The sound of the gaming. It was pretty loud!

COUNSELOR: When you walked in, saw him on his phone, leaving his books unopened on the desk, and hearing the gaming music, which of these experiences started to trigger your anxiety?

JIMMY: I initially thought it was my son's face as he was so excited, almost like he is addicted to video games. But when I thought about it again, I actually didn't feel upset until I saw the books unopened on his desk.

By investigating his sensual inputs, the client starts to discern the nature of his mental activity in response to different sensual data and then reach a correct understanding of his clinging. For example, the client was initially bothered by the unopened books instead of the gaming. This guidance helped him to identify the sense contacts that triggered his unpleasant feelings. With a clearer understanding of their triggers, and by starting to see the supporting factors as well as the impermanence of an experience, clients are less likely to make inferences or postulations that misinterpret incidents.

### Expanding Awareness of Bodily Sensations and Feelings

According to the *Satipaṭṭhāna Sutta*, becoming mindful of various parts of the body and their functions leads to a correct understanding of the body and the arising and ceasing of physical experiences (Anālayo, 2003). Thus, focusing on bodily sensations by attending to the present and momentary awareness of the physical dimension of one's reality is a practical first step in re-collecting and focusing a scattered and distracted mind. Applying this concept to Buddhist counseling, mindfulness of the body during an anxious state is a crucial step in penetrating the conceptualized power of anxiety. This process is exemplified in the following dialogue:

COUNSELOR: Okay, let's talk more about the different components of this 'anxiety.' Did you notice any bodily sensations that arose in you when you saw the unopened books?

JIMMY: Let me see ... I think there was a feeling of heat in me, around the chest area. I think my fists also tightened.

COUNSELOR: Let's focus on the chest area for a moment. As we are recollecting the moment of conflict with your son, how does it feel?

JIMMY: I sense some heat there, too.

COUNSELOR: Can you describe this sensation more?

JIMMY: I wouldn't say painful ... but uncomfortable. It's like something pressing on my chest.

COUNSELOR: Heat, something pressing on the chest, and discomfort. Let's continue your in-breath and out-breath and mindfully watch it for a moment. How does it change?

JIMMY: (*after a few seconds*) ... The heat seems to fade out a bit. It's become less uncomfortable.

COUNSELOR: So, after turning towards an uncomfortable bodily sensation and just observing it, it somehow makes it less intense?

JIMMY: Yes, that's interesting.

In this example, the Buddhist counselor used questioning to deepen the client's awareness of bodily sensations and then showed him the arising and ceasing of a sensory experience. Strengthening the breadth and depth of awareness is vital to mindfulness training. By guiding clients to focus on various parts of the body and investigate their sensations, Buddhist counselors teach them a new way to pay attention that increases the mental space between physical experiences and conceptual proliferations.

### Noting Cognitions

In MMA, cognition is a generic term that illustrates the cognitive processes of perception involving both initial thoughts and sustained thoughts as driven by an individual's previous experiences. As each individual has a unique system of conceptualization and knowledge, the same sensory inputs can generate quite different cognitions, not all of which are reflective of an object in reality. Cognitions usually manifest as inner voices, an internal monologue, or some kind of "self-talk," such as a subtle and neutral voice when recognizing a person, or a loud and unpleasant inner voice when disliking another person. While the cognitive contents can vary based on multiple conditions, the process of cognition is the first step in the awakening of ego consciousness, so such voices usually take as their subject the "I" and then fabricate a relationship with an object. Moreover, there can be many voices, with one driving another, but an uncultivated mind can usually only become aware of the loudest or most pressing voices. This step of noting cognition then aims to raise clients' awareness of their sequence of cognitions and their initial thoughts, reflecting how the mind wishes to relate to external objects or events, thereby gaining first-hand knowledge of the habitual mechanisms of the mind and their effects. This process is seen in the following dialogue:

COUNSELOR: When you noticed the heat in your chest and then saw the unopened books, can you remember what was the first thought that came into your mind?

JIMMY: ... Yes. I thought to myself: 'He should be studying, or else he will fail his final exam, which will be such a disaster. He may even be kicked out of school.'

COUNSELOR: Jimmy, let's try to go back to what might have initiated this line of thinking that ended up increasing your anxiety. It seems that 'he should be studying' would be a later thought, as there is usually something happening to lead you to conclude what he should do. If you think about how you just walked in and saw your son playing on his phone, what thoughts popped up in your mind?

JIMMY: (*After thinking for several seconds*) I think it's something like 'Oh, no!'

COUNSELOR: 'Oh, no!' Anything else?

JIMMY: ... 'He can't be like this! Stop!'

COUNSELOR: What would be the 'this' you were referring to?

JIMMY: He ... He can't be like ... like me.

COUNSELOR: It sounds like something about seeing your son playing on his phone reminded you of something in yourself.

### Knowing Conceptual Proliferations

In this step, the Buddhist counselor and client collaboratively examine and analyze conceptual proliferations to understand the root causes and their effects. This investigation aims to facilitate clients' deconstruction of phenomenal, experiential, and conceptual proliferations and discern the volitions that fuel those proliferations. The Buddhist counselor usually listens to clients' proliferations and draws out the main themes, examines the client's expectations and needs that support those mental acts, and helps clients realize the craving embedded in their meanings and values. Through this reflective, dialectical process, the Buddhist counselor applies his or her understanding of reality to examine clients' fabrications of conceptual proliferations to help them gain insight into the discrepancy between their expectations and reality.

COUNSELOR: What might your son remind you of?

JIMMY: You know, education is so important nowadays. If my son does not study now, he will end up where I was. It was miserable. I was bullied, and no one was there to protect me, and the only thing that made my life better was education!

COUNSELOR: Your shoulders seem to be tight, and your voice becomes louder when you talk about how difficult it was when you were young. You also sound stressed and agitated because you are afraid that your son will grow up into what you are and go through the same misery.

JIMMY: Exactly! Education is the only way out of this!

COUNSELOR: And there seems to be an intense fear behind this.

JIMMY: ... I am really afraid that he will have to live a harsh life like me.

COUNSELOR: Let me see if I get what you said. When you saw your son playing smartphone games and not studying, you were reminded of how you didn't receive enough education, and you believe that is why you went through many overwhelming challenges like fear, bullying, and struggling to sustain a living. It sounds like you didn't like how you were, and you don't want your son to become like you.

JIMMY: Yes! My life is miserable. Even now, I can't really control my anxiety.

COUNSELOR: Let's go back for a moment to hear more about what's in your mind. When you saw your son playing on the phone, and you became anxious, what was your thought right before you took your son's phone?

JIMMY: … It was something like, 'I have got to stop him!'

COUNSELOR: So, stopping him was a strong thought. To prevent your son from walking the same path, you really wanted to stop him because it is so scary to imagine him suffering like you do. However, he didn't listen, so you escalated your action by breaking his phone. Is that right?

JIMMY: That's probably why. I know it's wrong, but I just didn't know what to do.

In this dialogue, the Buddhist counselor reflected upon the client's thoughts and actions to understand what drove the client's conceptual proliferations and his response to them (breaking his son's phone). The client can articulate the event's meaning through exploration: he disliked his past, so he tried very hard to stop his son from becoming like himself. He is not a violent person, but he chose a violent means, and his disproportional reaction might be based on fear and resistance. In Buddhist psychology, this strong volition to aggressively prevent his son from turning into someone like himself emanates from the poison of aversion, or even ill-will, towards himself. In the client's childhood, he did not have the experience of being protected by a positive and influential parental figure, contributing to his sense of vulnerability and weakness. His rejection and experience of bullying reinforced this notion, but he does not believe his son can do the same and protect himself. This notion of vulnerability and weakness may make the client highly anxious in his daily encounters. He has a strong resistance to this identity and a craving for a distinguished self. Since education was his only means of security that protected him from physical and emotional danger, he has fantasized about education as a remedy to vulnerability. However, his son's resistance to studying reminded the client of his past adverse experiences and triggered his craving for non-existence. Charged by conceptual proliferations of fear and insecurity, the client acted aggressively to stop his son from turning into him. Unfortunately, and ironically, doing so ended up pushing his son further away.

### Identifying Choice Points

In this step, the Buddhist counselor helps clients to review the stream of cognitive acts and locate entry points for making alternative decisions. By recollecting an incident in detail, Buddhist counselors can use a slower pace and a more reflective approach to help clients notice possible choice points. Moreover, Buddhist counselors can reflect on salient thoughts, emotions, or bodily sensations as signs of proliferations. Detecting the signals early, clients will learn to make alternative choices before negative thoughts and feelings escalate. The following dialogue can illustrate this process.

COUNSELOR: We have discussed the incident from how it arises to how it ends. Now, I hope to go back to the incident again, but we will slow down to look at different decisions you may have made this time.

JIMMY: Alright.

COUNSELOR: Going back to the moment when you saw your son playing an online game on his phone, you were worried, and you thought about how playing video games will make him fail his exams. This worry quickly escalated into breaking his phone, which you regretted doing. So if we look at it again, the sequence started from a strong sense of worry, is that right?

JIMMY: Yes, it sounds like it. Sometimes worries and anxiety make me lose control.

COUNSELOR: Let's imagine something. Before you decide to ask him to stop, what might you do with this worry?

JIMMY: Well ... breathing to calm down? Like what we have practiced before?

COUNSELOR: Very good! So you see, that point is already a moment of choice, and breathing certainly helps to calm you down. Now, say that you decided to talk to him. From that moment of just talking to him to the moment of throwing his phone, can you see any intermediate point when you can pause so that you don't end up the same way?

JIMMY: I am not sure ...

COUNSELOR: OK, let's start with your body. Do you remember the bodily sensations when you felt worried?

JIMMY: You mean the uncomfortable feeling in my chest I told you about?

COUNSELOR: Yes. Do you remember when this feeling became more obvious?

JIMMY: Yes, when I saw the unopened books ... And I remember you said a chest feeling is a sign of anxiety, so you mean I can choose to soothe it once I notice it?

COUNSELOR: You've got it! The moment that you noticed the discomfort in the chest is another choice point. You can choose to continue to let it grow into anger ...

JIMMY: I want to try that.

COUNSELOR: ... or you can choose to de-escalate and self-soothe.

JIMMY: That I can try.

In this dialogue, the Buddhist counselor suggested entry points as alternative possibilities, providing room for the client to reflect on hypothetical choice points. Both techniques—of entry points and choice points—are essential to facilitating the client's capacity to realize how he may notice and pause at a bodily sensation, thought, or emotion, thereby preventing the unwholesome sequence of choices from arising. Moreover, this line of exploration empowers the client to recognize his ability to make different choices, a significant ability to support the client's confidence in regulating his mind, speech, and behaviors.

### Check-in with Realistic Conditions

This step helps the client to see realistic conditions that differentiate his son from him so that he can detach from the concept that his son represents to him. This differentiation can be accomplished using counter questioning, which was one of the Buddha's skillful ways to help individuals gain insight (Bodhi, 1995). Let us now portray this process in another dialogue.

COUNSELOR: Now you know some choice points to make different choices, I want to explore the reasons behind the choices. Once we know the reasons better, we will see if the reasons are realistic, an awareness which can lead to better decision making.

JIMMY: Okay.

COUNSELOR: Coming back to your thoughts about your son, what makes you think your son will grow up exactly like you?

JIMMY: You know, education is so important nowadays. If my son does not study now, he will end up where I was. It was miserable. I was bullied. No one was there to protect me, and the only thing that made my life better was education.

COUNSELOR: Besides education, parents play an important role in child-rearing. Do you think there are any similarities between you and your father?

JIMMY: No, I think I care a lot more about my son than what he did about me.

COUNSELOR: Friends and schools are also important. Does your son go to a similar school to the one you did?

JIMMY: No, his school is much better. At least there are no gangsters to threaten him.

COUNSELOR: Let's pause and look at it from another perspective. Experiences of growing up are very important factors, too. Did your son have any similar experiences to what you had?

JIMMY: No! He is much happier and healthier! He is almost my height now.

COUNSELOR: Then what makes you think your son will grow up exactly like you?

JIMMY: So, what you mean is, my son and I grew up in very different backgrounds, so we may turn out differently?

COUNSELOR: What do you think?

JIMMY: … I guess it makes sense.

In this example, the client starts to see the actual conditions according to a dependent arising perspective of an event. In this way, the client learns to see how multiple conditions contribute to a person's development, so his fear starts to ease.

### Skillful Decisions

The last step is to help the client acquire skillful choices. In each moment, an individual continuously selects what thoughts to pursue or resist, what behaviors to act out, and what concepts to speak about. However, most individuals are unaware of their subtle mental decisions or the volitions driving their body, thoughts, and speech. Because of this, the Buddhist counselor consolidates the client's insight in the sessions and helps him build mindful practices for use in daily encounters, as follows.

COUNSELOR: Let's return to the moment where you were anxious and threw your son's phone. You now realized your inner voice of 'He is like me' and 'I have got to stop him.' How do these thoughts sound to you now?

JIMMY: I think I am more aware of how these voices make me anxious and force me to stop my son immediately.

COUNSELOR: That's a great awareness! So, when you go home from this session and see your son not studying again, what do you think you will do?

JIMMY: … I didn't think about that. But of course, I will not break anything this time.

COUNSELOR: I would like you to try what we have practiced just now. When you see your son not studying, take a pause and breathe slowly. Pay attention to your body to notice sensations and note what your mind says to you. After you calm your mind, think about what your options are.

JIMMY: Alright. I think I can do it.

In the coming two sessions, the Buddhist counselor uses MMA to help the client investigate his mind acts and discern potentially positive alternative actions. Finally, in the fourth session, the client returned with a more alleviated affect.

COUNSELOR: So, how did it go this time?

JIMMY: It went better. When I saw my son playing on his phone and not doing his homework, I felt my heart beating, my palms sweating, and my shoulders were tight. I know I was nervous, and I heard my mind saying, 'You can't turn into me!' I took a deep breath and calmed down, and I tried to look into his face again. He was actually a little scared, and I felt bad. I took another deep breath to calm down, and then another thought came to my mind. Maybe I should get to know him.

COUNSELOR: That's an amazing turning point. So what did you decide to do?

JIMMY: I sat down and asked him what he was playing. I think we are getting closer again.

In a mind state laden and charged with conceptual proliferations, attention is dispersed towards proliferated thoughts, limiting potential choices and decisions. However, once the mind is soothed and re-centered to the present moment, new and wholesome mental resources will arise. Buddhist counselors using MMA play the role of collaborators who facilitate the client's relinquishment of conceptual proliferations and help them learn to return to the present moment as a solid ground for making mindful choices.

To summarize, MMA is mind training to help clients gradually develop the skill to soothe a disturbed mental state, investigate mind activities, realize differences between thoughts and reality, and choose healthier mind acts. Therefore, MMA is usually an iterative process that helps clients foster first-hand knowledge of bodily and mental activities through a cyclical process of mind exploration. However, some clients may not yet know enough skillful means to make skillful decisions. For this reason, the next section will discuss three categories of skillful choices that can be used as techniques for Buddhist counselors.

## SKILLFUL DECISION TECHNIQUES

Using the concept of the three kammas as a foundation, this section discusses three counseling techniques. To supplement the use of MMA, Buddhist counselors can help clients learn and practice these techniques to address clients' conceptual proliferations and substitute unhealthy choices with wholesome ones. The general rules for practicing these choices are to (1) foster wholesome choices, such as choices that nurture compassion, loving-kindness, and equanimity, and (2) reduce unwholesome choices, such as those leading to hatred, ill-will, and conceit. Following this simple direction will gradually shape the client's mind into a more conducive and peaceful state, thereby making it easier to make wholesome choices during states of heightened emotions. Moreover, Choice techniques are interdependent with Note and Know techniques. In other words, Buddhist counselors can flexibly use Note and Know techniques to help clients engage in skillful choices.

## Mind Choice

A mind choice is a deliberative cognitive act, such as thinking, refraining from thinking, accepting, rejecting, or letting go of mental objects. Among all three choices, mind choice is at the core because the mind is the engine for speech and behavior. Mind Choice develops from the idea of Right View and Right Intention according to the Noble Eightfold Path. Applying this framework, making wholesome mind choices should always be incorporated as an effective technique for clients to practice. Therefore, any technique that Buddhist counselors use should enhance a client's capacity to pursue thinking in a wholesome direction and thereby disengage from thinking in an unwholesome direction. This section suggests several mind choice techniques.

### Thought Substitution

According to the *Vitakkasanthana Sutta*, thought substitution is one of the ways to remove distracting thoughts and is a regular reflection practice to guard the mind. According to the sutta, in the face of distracting or evil thoughts related to desire and craving, a practitioner should reflect on a different object that is wholesome. With this rationale, the Thought Substitution technique aims to help clients replace unwholesome mind states with wholesome ones. There are several wholesome mind states in Buddhism, such as equanimity of mind, faith, mindfulness, diligence, decorum, the shame of wrongdoings, compassion, or non-attachment. In the current model of Buddhist counseling, the central wholesome mind states to develop are equanimity, compassion, and non-attachment.

First, it is helpful to assist a client to cultivate a wholesome mind state that employs the Note technique by developing a *Mindful Haven*. Second, in the thought substitution technique, Buddhist counselors can use guided visualizations to help clients experience a non-attachment stance to the arising and ceasing of distracting thoughts.

First, to help a client develop an equanimous mind state, a Buddhist counselor can start by contemplating this question: "What makes you feel peaceful?" The answer can be a person, a place, an experience, or an object. Then, using dialogue, artwork, or other means, the Buddhist counselor collaborates with clients to consolidate this peaceful mental object. For example, a client can discuss how his or her grandmother always had a peaceful presence, draw images of Buddhas or Bodhisattvas, or show pictures of natural scenery. Upon consolidating the wholesome object, Buddhist counselors can start a visualization to foster a mindful haven by sustaining and expanding attention to this mental object. Inviting clients to close their eyes while sitting in a balanced position and attending to their breath, Buddhist counselors can guide them to think of a wholesome mental object in detail.

For example, for a client who feels peaceful whenever she sees the Buddhist temple on her way home, the Buddhist counselor can say:

> Visualize yourself seeing this temple that gives you a sense of peace, a sense of equanimity. Take a closer look at the features and characteristics of the temple. What do you see? (*pause for three seconds*). What do you hear? (*pause for three seconds*). How does it feel in your body? (*pause for three seconds*). How does it feel in your mind? (*pause for three seconds*). Let's walk closer to the temple. Gently walk inside and take a look at its interior. Appreciate the statues and settings of the temple. Let your mind rest and immerse yourself in this moment of peace (*pause for three seconds*). Should any distracting thoughts arise, gently acknowledge them and choose to let them go and cease. Mindfully come back to this experience, this temple, and enjoy this very moment of peace.

Competent Buddhist counselors should always process the experience with clients and address any questions or concerns. Buddhist counselors can invite clients to describe their experiences of the process and whether there is any experiential difference after the practice. Moreover, it is crucial to explore clients' bodily sensations and/or reflect the counselor's observations of clients' somatic sensations to raise their awareness of their changes in body and mind.

For situations when a client starts to have painful or disturbing imagery, the counselor must stop the visualization and help them re-center their attention on the present moment through deep breathing, mindful bodily movements, or other techniques. Using the mindful haven idea, Buddhist counselors can use mindful breathing, chanting, compassion meditation, or other means to help clients choose to engage in a whole mind state during daily life. The primary purpose is to help clients see through choice points in everyday life and access their ability to engage in thought substitution. For example, as mentioned earlier, a Buddhist counselor can practice thought substitution with a client to find the *mindful haven* of a temple that he or she often passes by. With this insight, the counselor can work with the client to recognize situations where they become too stressed and then mindfully choose to take a mental break by visualizing the peaceful temple for five minutes. It is important to note that a mindful haven is different from spiritual bypassing or dissociation in at least two ways. First, the overarching goal of a mindful haven is never to hide from or avoid an experience; instead, it is to cultivate a peaceful abiding state of mind (*samatha*) which comes with a comprehensive awareness of the experiences of body and mind. Second, this tranquility of the mind aims to support the inquiry into more painful or stressful issues with mental distance so that one can analyze and contemplate to gain insights.

### The Four Immeasurables Recollection

The Four Immeasurables (*brahmavihārās*) are four important and boundless Buddhist virtues used for meditative cultivation. The virtues include: (1) Loving kindness: a wish for the welfare and happiness of others, (2) Compassion: an understanding of suffering in another person and motivation to remove such suffering, (3) Joy: an attitude of rejoicing in the happiness of self and others, and (4) Equanimity: a state of inner equipoise. This technique aims to help clients recollect any experience of the Four Immeasurables regularly in order to foster awareness of the experiences of the immeasurables as well as reinforce choices to practice the immeasurables in daily life.

Buddhist counseling can explain the Four Immeasurables with a client and implement three steps: Recollection, Reflection, and Action. In recollection, a Buddhist counselor can guide clients to think about how any of the Four Immeasurables were practiced that day by using prompts. Examples might be the client's acts of loving kindness towards others, others trying to listen to the client's suffering, their sharing of food with colleagues which contributed to a feeling of mutual joy, or an experience of equanimity while walking slowly in a park. If a client has a problem with it, Buddhist counselors may provide examples to clients, such as: "You might recollect how you chose to accept praise for yourself, helped your colleague with something, or see how people offered food to the poor when you passed by. Any such kinds of observation that bring you any one of The Four Immeasurables would be good."

The counselor can help the client write down occurrences of the Four Immeasurables from their daily life (see Table 10.2). In making such notes, it is important to remind and ask the clients: (1) to be specific (when did it happen, what was the client doing, and what did the other person do?); (2) how did the events occur (i.e., causes and conditions); and (3) to be mindful of what thoughts went on in their minds and how the event made them feel.

Once the experience is concretized and drawn out, Buddhist counselors can move towards a reflective process on each immeasurable and then discuss clients' experiences

**TABLE 10.2** The Four Immeasurables Recollection Exercise

| Four Immeasurables | What happened? *Specific details of the event* | How did it happen? *Conditions contributing to the event* | How did you feel? *Experiences of the event* |
|---|---|---|---|
| **Loving Kindness** *Recollect a situation when you offered or received loving kindness.* | | | |
| **Compassion** *Recollect a situation when you were accompanied in your suffering, or you accompanied a person in their suffering.* | | | |
| **Joy** *Recollect a situation when you experienced joy for yourself or others.* | | | |
| **Equanimity** *Recollect a situation when you felt peaceful and calm.* | | | |

of them. There are different questions to contemplate with the client, including why the compassionate act occurred, what caused the moment of equanimity, what inner resources and external factors contributed to the moment of joy, and how the client can use these experiences to foster future loving kindness towards self and others. It is good to be patient, curious, and reflective of the client's answers and process. Moreover, the counselor can reflect on the client's verbal and nonverbal expressions to raise the client's awareness of how fostering the Four Immeasurables in the mind induces positive changes. If the client cannot think of any of the Four Immeasurables, the Buddhist counselor can discuss with the client how to cultivate them in daily life.

In order to practice, Buddhist counselors can consider assigning this technique as homework. The counselor can then check in during the next session to discuss the experience and how it might create positive changes.

## Speech Choice

Speech choice is the verbal kamma that manifests as interpersonal communication in everyday life. One of the ways that the Buddha described Right Speech is with four considerations, including right timing, being factual, speaking with goodwill, and presenting content that benefits the recipient. Using this framework, skillful speech choice aims to communicate in order to benefit others, being genuine and compassionate, and skillfully speaking at the right time. Furthermore, as interconnectedness is a major assumption in Buddhism, skillful communication tends to promote positive relationships. This next section will introduce two speech choice techniques.

### What I Really Wanted to Say is ...

Speech is an important kamma and a causal factor for many relational problems. Primarily, clinging, defilements, dukkha, or other impurities hinder our compassion towards our significant others, thereby masking and discoloring our goodwill with unskillful communication patterns. This technique is meant to help clients nurture compassion for the important people in their lives, particularly during their direct communication. The *What I really wanted to say is ...* technique has four steps: Recollection, Processing, Reframing, and Action.

Starting with recollection, the counselor prompts the client to reflect on the client's regular communication with significant others—parents, children, partners—and identify one person with whom he or she has difficulties. Next, the counselor guides the client to reflect on whether there are any negative statements that he or she often says to this person. For instance, the Buddhist counselor can say to the client, "Think of one statement that you say all the time to your important ones, especially when you are upset." Some examples include, "Stop nagging me, Mom," "Not again my dear!" and "Why can't you cut down your gaming time and do all your homework?"

During processing, a Buddhist counselor can ask the client to write down the statement in its original form and try to say it in his or her usual tone. Processing this experience with the client can raise the client's awareness of their communication habits. The Buddhist counselor then explores the meaning of the statement with the client, including contemplating what the client really wants from this person, what the client hopes this person will get to know, and, importantly, what love is embedded in the client's statement.

In reframing by using the client's insights about their love and care for this other person, the Buddhist counselor invites the client to rewrite the statement into a completely wholesome, positive, and pure statement. One must remind the client to avoid criticism, complaints, or resentments in the statement. The statement will take this form: "What I said was _____ (essence of previous statement), but what I really wanted to say is _____ (rewritten statement)." For example, a client worrying about his son's gaming expressed a previous statement of: "How come you never work hard at school? Why do you keep playing computer games all the time?" After the reframing process, the new statement becomes: "I know I nag you all the time asking you to study, but what I really wanted to say is, I worry about you because you are so important to me. As I think academic achievement can bring a better fortune, I want you to study so that you can live a good life. I don't want you to suffer like what I had to go through."

In the action step, the counselor invites the client to practice saying the statement with a kind and calm tone to the counselor, as if the counselor is the target person. The counselor then processes the experience with the client in terms of bodily sensations, emotions, and thoughts and invites the client to use the new statement in the next communication with his or her loved one.

### Non-I Statement

As suffering originates from clinging to the self, most of our communications use "I" as a central reference point. This egoistic style of communication is ripe for the experience of dissatisfaction, resulting too often in conflict and discord. The Non-I statement employs a dependent co-arising framework to restructure our "I" statements to disengage the focus from selfhood to causes and conditions. By purposefully not using "I," "me,"

---

**Non-I Statement 1**

Using a recent discord or conflict as source information, please complete the following statement to review the incident from a dependently co-arising perspective:

A  **Non-I expression** (*please do not use "I," "my," "myself," or other references to the self*):

"When seeing/hearing _____ (what client experienced at the moment), a sense of _____ (bodily feeling) arises, _____ (emotion) comes up, a thought of _____ (thought) comes to be, and the resulting action was _____ (client's behavior)."

B  **Reconciliation Invitation:**

"I want you to know that I desire for _____ (client's need) and that's what I did _____ (speech or behavioral choices). But now, I hope to listen to you and listen to how I have made you suffer. I am willing to take your side and listen to you."

---

**FIGURE 10.1** Non-I Statement 1

---

Non-I Statement 2

Using a recent discord or conflict as source information, please complete the following statement to review the incident from a dependently co-arising perspective:

A **Non-I Expression:**

"When seeing <u>the unopened textbooks</u> (what client experienced at the moment), a sense of <u>heat in the body</u> (bodily feeling) arises, <u>anxiety</u> (emotion) comes up, a thought of <u>urging my son to study</u> (thought) comes to be, and the resulting action was to <u>yell at him</u> (client's behavior)."

B **Reconciliation Invitation:**

"I want you to know that I desire for <u>your happiness</u> (client's need) and raised my voice to <u>you all the time, hoping you can follow my way to become happy</u> (speech or behavioral choices). But now, I hope to listen to you and listen to how I have made you suffer. I am willing to take your side and listen to you."

---

**FIGURE 10.2** Non-I Statement 2

or "myself" in the expression, and only expressing internal processes, the client may see and articulate experiences in a less attached manner. The second part is a reconciliation invitation in which the counselor can direct the client to revisit the conflict and try to see the suffering endured by the other party. The invitation is a humble and compassionate gesture which requires a strong willingness to detach from one's mindset and take on the other person's perspective. The sentence structure itself is more comprehensive than usual statements (Figure 10.1).

Now, using Jimmy's example, the Buddhist counselor can apply this technique to help him articulate the internal conditions that contribute to the unwanted behaviors towards his son using the Non-I Expression (see Figure 10.2) and then practice using this way to describe his experiences to the Buddhist counselor. The counselor can then explore Jimmy's understanding of his son's perspective and invite him to experience the reconciliation exercise (see Figure 10.2). It can be helpful for a counselor to practice with a client individually before offering this invitation. This can provide a safe and containing environment for the client to experience this invitation and their vulnerability safely. Again, it is important to offer support and acknowledgement of a client's courage to reconcile a conflict and to reflect on their loving kindness for the other person.

## Behavioral Choice

In the Noble Eightfold Path, Right action and Right livelihood signify the essence of wholesome behavioral choices. From a Buddhist perspective, promoting an ethical life will contribute to a conducive environment resulting in less suffering. Although clients attending Buddhist counseling may not be devoted Buddhists and may therefore not be ready to follow all of the five precepts, Buddhist counselors can use Choose techniques to increase the client's skillful behaviors for aligning with the Buddhist teachings. The following are some examples:

### Exploration of Change

To sustain a cycle of suffering, one needs to continually make unskillful decisions and engage in harmful activities, misbelieving that such activities provide more pleasure than pain. For these activities, most of us and our clients may hyper-focus or fabricate the short-term pleasure while being ignorant of the long-term aversive effect. To foster skillful choices, Buddhist counselors can try the technique *Exploration of Change*. This technique involves three steps: identifying unskillful behavior, contemplating the negatives, and finding skillful substitutions. First, a Buddhist counselor collaborates with the client to identify an unskillful behavior. Here is an example with Frankie, a 45-year-old male who failed many times in trying to quit smoking:

FRANKIE: I have been smoking for almost 25 years. It's soothing for me to smoke during breaks at work. I kind of got used to it already. I usually smoke when I am agitated or stressed at work.
COUNSELOR: Is it a good way of coping or a not-so-good way of coping for you?
FRANKIE: I am not sure. That's why I want to bring it up with you.

Clients often doubt their unskillful behaviors, and so sometimes they are undecided about what to do. Having doubts is actually a good beginning for a client to explore the potential for change. The next step is to contemplate the negatives, as we can see in the following dialogue.

COUNSELOR: Besides seeing smoking as a way to soothe your agitation, how else does smoking help you?
FRANKIE: I think it's also about taking a break. Smoking is an excuse to take a break from work.
COUNSELOR: That's a good insight. Smoking is not just the cigarette itself, but it's a way to create a physical and mental space to rest. Anything else?
FRANKIE: Yes … usually, I smoke with colleagues, which usually leads to fun conversations.
COUNSELOR: I see, so smoking is also an opportunity for a social gathering.
FRANKIE: Right.
COUNSELOR: Let's talk about the negatives. What do you see are the problems with smoking?
FRANKIE: I guess cancer would be a big one.
COUNSELOR: Yeah, that would definitely be one.
FRANKIE: Ah … there is some craving when I don't smoke. It's even worse than it sounds. Sometimes I feel like if there were only water and cigarettes left in a desert, I would pick the cigarettes.
COUNSELOR: It sounds like an intense craving that brings quite a lot of suffering! When you think about the two sides, what is a better choice for you?
FRANKIE: I guess quitting. Although I like the social part of it, I don't want to feel so restricted.

After the client develops the motivation to try a more skillful behavior, the Buddhist counselor will explore possible alternatives or potential skillful ways to stop an unskillful behavior by using Note techniques.

COUNSELOR: Do you remember the chanting we practiced before?

FRANKIE: Of course, I chant a couple of times per week.

COUNSELOR: Good. What if we try an experiment? The next time you feel agitated, can you try chanting quietly for one minute before you reach out for a cigarette?

FRANKIE: Okay … so what if I still want to smoke after that?

COUNSELOR: It's okay, but the goal is to extend the gap between your intention to smoke and your actual smoking behavior. Let's see whether you feel differently.

After the session, the client tried to chant before he smoked, and he then found himself smoking less. In the next session, the Buddhist counselor processes the incident with the client:

FRANKIE: There were several times that I did some chanting before I smoked, and a couple of times when I just did not feel like smoking anymore. I don't know why.

COUNSELOR: So what thoughts or feelings come to mind after you chant?

FRANKIE: I feel a little calmer, and then I think, 'Maybe I don't need to smoke right now'.

COUNSELOR: So you become more mindful about your intention and behavior of smoking. How does it make your body feel?

FRANKIE: Ironically, I feel calmer by smoking less.

COUNSELOR: What you realize is that cigarettes actually make you more agitated, which is very different from what you thought.

FRANKIE: Yes. Perhaps it is not a very productive way to cope with agitation.

### Basic Self-Care

It may sound straightforward, but one of the most critical choices to make in life is to commit to self-care. From my experience, Buddhist masters, psychologists, and psychiatrists have given very similar answers on how to have good psychological health: sleep right, eat right, and move right. First of all, sleeping should be a crucial part of a regular self-care routine. Allowing oneself to gain enough hours of sleep (6–8 hours), sleeping early and waking up early, avoiding stimulants at night, and minimizing or avoiding artificial light (e.g., smartphones) for two hours before bed are essential ways to foster better sleep. Second, knowing what food is good for oneself and choosing to engage in this diet is highly important. It can be helpful to use superfoods or recommended healthy foods, but it would be most beneficial for clients to become mindful of their reactions to different types of food to find out their optimal diet.

Finally, moving right is about exercising and getting in touch with nature. Enjoying warm sunshine, hiking, breathing fresh air, and having regular cardio exercises are likely to contribute to good health. Should clients present with any physical conditions, Buddhist counselors can encourage clients or refer clients for medical check-ups and to discuss any worries and fears hindering the healing process. Although such knowledge is commonly accepted by most clients, the Buddhist counselors' compassion and credibility is likely to foster a client's mindfulness of the need to improve their self-care. In Buddhist counseling, these are valuable conventional truths that may be introduced to clients to help them build a healthy self-care lifestyle.

## Good Kamma List

According to Buddhist teachings, certain behaviors are likely to contribute to good kamma, such as helping others, practicing mindfulness, or chanting. A *Good Kamma List* is an inventory of activities to discuss with clients that reminds them of these wholesome activities (see Figure 10.3). Many of these activities can provide efficient self-care, promote social engagements, and facilitate concentration. When working on skillful decisions, the counselor can provide the Good Kamma List and review it with the client. Clients can then be instructed

### Activities for Good Kamma

*Please go through the list, circle those that will make you happy by doing them, and commit to doing one each day. Please feel free to add any activities that work for you.*

| Good Thoughts | Good Speech | Good Behaviors | Good Connections |
|---|---|---|---|
| Think of three good things before I sleep | Genuinely praise one thing about myself | Chanting | Volunteering |
| Recollect experiences of compassion | Genuinely praise one thing about others | Meditation | Visit an old friend |
| In my heart give blessings to anyone I see | Show a person gratitude | Calligraphy | Offer to help people I see |
| Pray | Speak to myself in the mirror, "You are good enough" | Take a walk in nature | Listen to a person deeply |
| Think about the good qualities of myself | Say, "Please" and "Thank you" often | Exercise (e.g., Yoga, workout, running, etc.) | Share or make offers to help people in need |
| Think about the good qualities of others | Keep a calm silence | Copy Buddhist scriptures | Refrain from killing animals (e.g., avoid ordering food that requires killing) |
| Embrace your feelings | Read an enlightening quote | Listen to music | Feed animals |
| Think about how to love oneself with compassion | Try not to say "I" but say "We" | Artwork | Play with a pet |
| Be patient with oneself | Apologize with humility | Clean up | Listen to a Dhamma Talk |
|  |  |  |  |

**FIGURE 10.3** Good Kamma List

to circle all the activities that can bring them pleasant feelings, which is a crucial reinforcer for engaging in wholesome activities. Buddhist counselors can then ask clients to commit to the practice at least once each day and then check in with them in the coming session. Moreover, it is possible to select skillful choices for clients in response to their chief concerns.

### Other Behavioral Techniques

Behavioral techniques from Cognitive Behavioral Therapy (CBT) and Dialectical Behavioral Therapy (DBT) can also be helpful options for making skillful decisions. Most importantly, Buddhist counselors should review and practice these techniques with themselves before using them with clients. The application of psychological techniques should also aim to reduce the client's clinging to a self, aiming instead to train the client's concentration and foster their wisdom. The following examples are some CBT/DBT techniques that Buddhist counselors can try:

- Activity Scheduling
- Controlled Breathing
- Communication skills training
- Journaling
- Progressive Muscles Relaxation
- Problem-solving skills training
- Roleplays
- Thought stopping
- Systematic desensitization.

Some of these techniques are described in the resources packet for Buddhist counselors. For other methods, I suggest *Cognitive Behavior Therapy: Basics and Beyond* (3rd ed.) by Judith S. Beck (2020), *Cognitive Behaviour Therapy 100 Key Points and Techniques* (2nd ed.) by Michael Neenan and Windy Dryden (2014), and *Doing Dialectical Behavior Therapy: A Practical Guide* by Kelly Koerner (2011).

## Application of Choose to Cindy

To foster positive future kamma, Buddhist counselors use Choose techniques that help clients discern different decision points to mindfully make decisions that result in less suffering. With a mind of clarity and calmness cultivated through the noting and knowing practices, they are able to guide clients to slow down their habitual patterns of pursuit or resistance and then collaboratively adopt a microscopic view through which they can examine each cognitive act. When one knows that each moment is discrete and unique, alternative choices are embedded in each moment, as long as one pays heedful attention and has a will to reduce suffering.

As we read earlier, Cindy has been suffering from enormous pain due to her desire to have a good mother, and she has never questioned the possibility of relinquishing this desire. Cindy's mind has habitually made numerous choices designed to change her mother by proving her worth and competency. However, she was not aware of her mind choices at each moment. The Buddhist counselor then helped her to recognize the disappointing reality, her strong desire, and the different options available to her, as seen in the following dialogue.

COUNSELOR: Now you know how she cannot love you the way you want, you see how hard you tried to earn love and acceptance from her, and you have experienced the devastating pain of all the past failures. At some point, you will need to decide how to go about it.

CINDY: What decision should I make?

COUNSELOR: Based on what you have learned about yourself, what do you think?

CINDY: Perhaps finding others to substitute for my mother?

COUNSELOR: Yes, as far as I can see, you can purposefully give in to your desire for her love and keep on trying, or you can find alternatives such as seeking approval from others, or you can let go of the desired mother in your mind and try to see her the way she is.

CINDY: (*Smiles with relief.*) What you said makes me think I can psychologically abandon her just like she has abandoned me?

COUNSELOR: (*Smile back.*) You certainly can.

CINDY: I am not sure if I can do it, but I do want to try.

The Buddhist counselor guided Cindy by practicing the NKC technique in daily life by noting her mind's clinging to the hope of love from her mother, knowing and accepting this strong desire, and choosing whether she wants to give in to or let go of the desire. This model is also a continuous practice undertaken in daily encounters that trains the mind's ability to notice, reflect, and make new choices. For example, after several NKC sessions, Cindy comes in reporting that she chose to talk back to her mother and asked her to "stop being so mean." To Cindy's surprise, her mother stopped criticizing her after she set her boundaries. Although her mother did not acknowledge or love her the way she wanted, Cindy reported a reduction of her depressed moods and frustration as well as feelings of relief.

In effect, this is a highly dynamic process in which both the counselor and the client go back and forth across healing phases when appropriate. For example, the process of noting, knowing, and choosing can occur in a glimpse of the moment or develop over some time. To introduce the NKC model to a client in a reader-friendly manner, each phase was linearly presented in this descriptive essay to highlight its key features.

## CONCLUSION

The Buddha taught two kinds of happiness in the world. One is the temporary happiness of satisfying each of our senses, while the other kind is the more sustainable happiness of detachment and renunciation. The term renunciation is not necessarily a denial or rejection of life experiences; instead, it is a letting go of clinging and desire in order to free one's mental capacity so that one can peacefully and fully enjoy immediate experiences. Thus, there is a continual choice between pursuing sensual pleasure or practising sustainable happiness via renunciation. Buddhist counseling helps clients see through the alluring nature of unskillful choices and gradually moves towards skillful choices moment-by-moment.

## Contemplative Questions for Buddhist Counselors

In order to help our clients make good choices, our own direct experience of such—especially choices of attention—is a necessary component in the fostering of a sound clinical sense. With established meditation practices, Buddhist counselors can become aware of how we choose to attend to or disengage from different mental events moment-by-moment. Building on such attention is fundamental to our thinking, conceptualization, proliferations, and eventually speech and behavior. All these subsequent actions are rooted in initial choices in one's mind, while contemplative practice will reflect back on our volitional choices as a form of awareness training. We will now use the Five Choices exercise to reflect on choices we have made as well as potential choices still available in the present moment. In every encounter, there are five choices we usually make in an attempt to satisfy our egocentric needs:

| Choice | Description |
| --- | --- |
| Pursue | To fight for, change, or negotiate in order to get our needs met. |
| Resist | To flee, reject, or deny in order to avoid not satisfying our needs. |
| Let be | To allow and foster a non-reactive stance for observing our needs (*First level of skillful choice*). |
| Embrace | To understand and radically embrace things as they are, including our needs and reality. Compassion usually ensues (*Second level of skillful choice*). |
| Let go | Detach from and gradually dissolve our needs to see things from a perspective of emptiness. Free of yearnings to make the best decision for self and others in the present moment (*Highest level of skillful choice*). |

To start with, review the list and descriptions. Then relax your body, breath, and mind and enter into the meditation. Adjust your sitting position and find the balance between uprightness and relaxation. Try to let go of any tension in your muscles while straightening your back to support your body. Gently focus on each breath. When you breathe in, know that you are breathing in. When you breathe out, know that you are breathing out. Breathe in this way and relax for a few minutes.

Re-center your attention to this moment and recollect a recent even that dissatisfied or disappointed you. Try to slow down and think about what happened, your emotional reactivity, your bodily sensations, and your perception of the event. Using the previous list, please reflect and identify choice(s) that you made in that event.

With your choices identified, contemplate the following questions:

- During the moment of suffering, what was my first immediate response and choice?

- How did my suffering change with my choice?
- Instead of that choice, what five other choices can I make?
- Do I have a pattern of making unskillful choices to pursue or resist certain situations?
- What would making the more skillful and wholesome choices feel like at the moment of suffering?
- Should the same trigger of suffering arise again, how can I make one of the more skillful choices on the list?
- What would happen if I choose to let the moment of suffering just "be"?
- What would happen if I choose to embrace the moment of suffering?
- What would happen if I choose to let go during a moment of suffering?

Please write down your thoughts, feelings, and insights. Also notice your feelings, sensations, and suffering at this moment. Especially pay attention to whether visualizing a more skillful choice makes you feel better about the same source of suffering. This can be an iterative exercise to revisit our habitual choices in order to raise awareness of choice points and explore possibilities for making better choices. If you benefit from this exercise, it can become a powerful took for you to use with your client. Similar to other tools, you can personalize this technique and integrate it into your Buddhist counseling approach.

**If you can note, you get to know;**
**If you can know, you get to choose.**

# REFERENCES

Anālayo, B. (2003). *Satipaṭṭhāna – The Direct Path to Realization*. London, UK: Windhorse Publications.

Bodhi, B. (1995). *The Middle Length Discourses of the Buddha: A Translation of the Majjhima Nikaya*. Somerville, MA: Wisdom Publication.

Karunadasa, Y. (2010). *The Theravada Abhidhamma: Its Inquiry Into the Nature of Conditioned Reality*. Hong Kong: Centre for Buddhist Studies, Hong Kong University.

Karunadasa, Y. (2013). *Early Buddhist Teachings: The Middle Position in Theory and Practice*. Hong Kong: Centre of Buddhist Studies, The University of Hong Kong.

Lee, K. C. (G.) (2021). Introduction to a Buddhist Counselling Technique Based on Early Buddhist Teachings: Mind Moment Analysis. *Contemporary Buddhism*. DOI: 10.1080/14639947.2021.1981062

Lee, K. C., & Tang, J. (2020). Note, Know, Choose: A Psychospiritual Treatment Model based on Early Buddhist Teachings *Spirituality in Clinical Practice*. Advanced online publication. https://doi.org/10.1037/scp0000220

# CHAPTER 11

# Termination

During the last days of the Buddha's life, the monastic community was immensely saddened to see their respected teacher leaving (Lopez, 2017). They also began to have worries and doubts about what to do without their teacher. When Venerable Ānanda, one of the Buddha's ten principal disciples, asked what they should do without a teacher, the Buddha responded by correcting Ānanda's view that the teaching ends with the teacher's life. Instead, the Buddha situated himself as a guide to the teaching, while the teaching itself should be the teacher. This dialogue has at least two important implications. First, the Buddha was the messenger to share realizations on how to liberate all beings from suffering, so he hoped his disciples would value the message instead of clinging to the messenger. Second, it is a way to say a good goodbye by assuring Venerable Ānanda that he has a clear path to walk, and he will be guided even though the teacher is gone. The end of this sutta describes the sadness, grief, and lamentations of all the disciples. At the same time, there were deep appreciations, recollections of the Buddha's teaching and insights, and peaceful funeral arrangements. Indeed, this sutta can be a good reference point for Buddhist counselors to consider the last stage of counseling: termination.

In order to foster a good termination, this chapter will discuss how to conduct a compassionate termination for both the Buddhist counselor and the client using several contemplative guidance questions.

## DEATH AND TERMINATION

A highly relevant concept in Buddhism regarding termination is the view concerning death, a verity that is also highly relevant to the psychotherapeutic concept of closure. For most people, death is a daunting and highly undesirable stage of life and is commonly handled with avoidance, rejection, refusal, or denial. Behind such understandable defenses against death lies a deep-rooted fear that we are annihilated and cease to exist. However, these manifestations of resistance tend to result in emotional suffering that is ironically more intense than the physical suffering of death. To remedy such anxiety, the Buddha taught several important contemplations on death which are also applicable to the process of termination in counseling. First, death is an inevitable experience in life. The *Kosala Sutta* pointed out that every sentient being living in this world is subject to death without exception (AN 5.49)

DOI: 10.4324/9781003025450-11

and hence the first step to cope with it is to fully and openly acknowledge its existence. Similarly, the beginning of a counseling relationship is also the first step towards its end. Knowing the fact that such a relationship is transient in nature, the counselor and client can be more prepared for its ending.

Second, by accepting the fact that death is uncontrollable and unavoidable, the Buddha taught that the mindfulness of death is a skillful attitude that encourages us to treasure every moment of life. The *Maranassati Sutta* also reminds practitioners about the urgency and inevitability of death, which serves as a strong motivation to value every precious moment as a chance for personal cultivation (AN 6.19). Death does not have to be an enemy, but it can be a friendly reminder to us to live life to its fullest every moment. Similarly, in a counseling relationship, the limited time together can be a good reminder to the counselor and client to treasure and value the therapeutic potential in each session.

Third, if we take a more detached perspective, life and death are nothing more than concepts. For instance, a counseling relationship was "born" from the agreement to start therapy and "died" in termination; however, the therapeutic changes are not bounded by this relationship. Similar to what the Buddha pointed out to Ānanda, the insights gained in counseling, the compassion radiating from the counselor to the client, the moments of deep attunement in accompanying someone in their suffering, and all other ingredients in a counseling relationship, will be experienced in the arising and ceasing of a relationship. A few of our clients will stay in our heart and we will continue to wish them well with our loving kindness all along. Similarly, a part of us as counselors and compassionate guardians will remain in the clients' hearts to support them during further challenges in life. The conditions within a counseling relationship are not exactly lost; instead, they are transformed into another form of existence. Death, or termination, could serve as a reminder to recollect and apply what has been learned, thereby sustaining and consolidating therapeutic gains.

In effect, such insights on the Buddhist perspective on death can shed some light on the process of termination.

## TERMINATION ISSUES FOR COUNSELORS

The first contemplation for a Buddhist counselor regarding termination is: "How do I feel about the ending of a relationship?" The process of termination is a mutual ending process for both counselor and client and can be difficult for both parties. Good Buddhist counselors should strive for a well-developed self-awareness, that is, starting the counseling process based on the cultivation of mind. Imagine it is the last time you see a particularly important friend. How would you feel? How do I usually say goodbye to loved ones? If there is a second chance to say goodbye to someone, what would I do differently? When a relationship with significant others ends, we can feel as devastated as the disciples did during the Buddha's last discourse.

Buddhist counseling, like the Buddha's relationship with his disciples, emphasizes rapport in the form of a trusting, secure, and comfortable environment. One criterion embedded in this assumption is the authenticity and genuineness of Buddhist counselors to treat clients as important spiritual friends, aiming to provide selfless and compassionate care. However, sometimes our clients, or even some of us, forget the fact that a therapeutic relationship is mutual and reciprocal, so it can be sad, unsettling, or challenging for counselors to say goodbye. For these reasons, one crucial lesson for Buddhist counselors is to acknowledge that we are all human beings with yearnings and emotions, and that it can be challenging to say goodbye. In counseling, we can get hurt by clients, and we can be sad about being dumped by our clients who unilaterally terminated without telling us. However, our humanity is what makes us compassionate.

Some of the most precious insights for clients come from the role modeling of counselors. During the termination process, counselors serve as positive role models to openly acknowledge, mindfully contain, and skillfully express whatever difficult emotions come up during this ending of the therapeutic relationship. If we do not want our clients to suppress or deny their feelings, we need to role model the courage and authenticity of facing these difficult and undesirable situations. What we can do is note our emotional reactivity and our vulnerability, know that it is a common human experience, and choose to nurture and mobilize our compassion to embrace ourselves and our clients. With this therapeutic stance, Buddhist counselors can examine the counselor–client relationship and decide when and how to terminate.

## TERMINATION ISSUES FOR CLIENTS

Termination is a professional term to describe the ending of a counseling relationship. A successful counseling relationship is a trusted, supportive, and collaborative alliance that helps a client overcome struggles and challenges. This relationship may have provided the client with their first experience in life of opening up to someone and becoming genuinely vulnerable. The ending of such a therapeutic relationship can be especially challenging for clients with experiences of abandonment and neglect. In certain situations, a premature or improperly handled termination can cause potential harm to clients, making them feel abandoned, or conveying a message that they are incapable of getting better, risks that Buddhist counselors must take the utmost care to avoid.

At the same time, a good termination is a therapeutic process. According to Buddhism, all relationships are phenomena that arise, change, and eventually cease. One critical practice then is to recognize this nature of events and let go of our clinging. A smooth termination can be a healing process by demonstrating the ending of a meaningful relationship with compassion, acceptance, and fruitful recollections. To achieve this goal, several criteria must be considered.

### Reasons to Terminate

In an ideal mundane world situation, termination occurs when clients have fully resolved their immediate suffering in the world, consolidated therapeutic gains with counselors, and taken the Note, Know, Choose techniques to continue cultivating their mind by themselves. However, terminations can occur in both expected and unexpected ways before reaching the treatment goals. According to Westmacott and Hunsley (2017), some common reasons or situations for termination are when:

- Clients have reached their counseling goals, or their problems have improved.
- Clients chose an alternative path to solve their problems.
- Clients did not like counselors, supervisors, or other staff involved in the counseling process.
- Clients do not find counseling useful, so they decide to stop coming.
- Clients can no longer afford the fees due to financial difficulties
- Environmental barriers such as transportation, childcare, changes in work, relocation, etc.
- Counselors see clients' presenting problems as beyond their scope of competence, thereby preparing for referral to a proper source.
- Counselors have to relocate for different reasons.
- Clients pass away (common situations for Buddhist counselors or chaplains working in palliative care and residential homes).

Some terminations are counselor-initiated, some are client-initiated, and some are uncontrollable or unpredictable (such as death). The grounds for termination can also differ according to the setting. For example, some Buddhist counselors working in institutions may only see patients one to three times, with termination as part of each session. Other counselors working in an office setting and providing longer-term services to clients have more planned and structured terminations. However, a second contemplation applies to all settings: What are the causes and conditions for termination at this time?

Buddhist counselors need to be open and honest to ourselves about our intentions and volitions for termination. The rule of thumb is to make the client's interests a priority so that, after counselling, they no longer need the counseling service. Counseling may also be terminated if it is not benefiting, or even harming, clients. Moreover, when the service may endanger the counselor, termination can become necessary to protect the counselor's safety. However, there are situations when counselors dislike the client and hope to refer out, but heedlessly fail to make reasonable arrangements to ensure that the client receives proper services, or does not allow enough time for the client to process the end of counseling. These would be unprofessional and potentially damaging actions.

The third contemplation is: Have I valued the therapeutic conditions as much as I could? Sometimes we have provided all the opportunities for healing and growth and treasured every moment as best as we can while the client still continues to suffer. Many counselors may self-criticize themselves as incompetent, doubting themselves for not trying harder, or blaming other things that they should have controlled. However, these thoughts may only serve to satisfy the counselors' egoistic needs to portray an illusion that things could be controlled and "I" could have controlled them. This attitude of conceit can bring great suffering to the counselor and it may also tempt us to think that we know better than our clients leading to getting irritated that clients did not follow what we said. If we hold on to these views, we are prevented from seeing the true nature of things and understanding the reasons of clients. From my experience, there are some situations when counseling was not able to effectively reduce the suffering of clients due to many causes and conditions, many of which are out of the counselor's or client's control. Compassion means accompanying clients in this helpless or even frustrating feeling and, as best as we can, to understand and accept reality as it is until the end of the counseling relationship.

## Ethical Considerations in Termination

There are several considerations when handling termination, as endings can be a sensitive topic for many clients. First, since Buddhist counseling aims to reduce suffering, the efficacy of counseling should be a top consideration. In other words, the third contemplative question for the Buddhist counselor and the client is: Has the client's suffering been reduced after participating in counseling? Sometimes, counseling is ineffective, the counselor and client are mismatched, or the client's counseling need goes beyond the counselor's scope of competency. These are good reasons to terminate counseling and make appropriate referrals.

If the counseling does not seem to be effective for the client, Buddhist counselors can make a professional referral. Based on the counselor's understanding of the client's needs and available resources, the counselor can recommend other qualified mental health professionals. In this process, good Buddhist counselors will try to make sure: (1) there is an open discussion on the referral process, including obtaining the client's written consent if the counselor needs to communicate with another professional on the client's issues, (2) the referral sources are available to take on your client, (3) the referral sources are competent in meeting clients' needs, and (4) there are various options (at least three) for clients.

When counseling has successfully helped a client reach goals so that it is no longer needed, termination can be a major step to continued growth. In the Early Buddhist framework, any phenomenon that arises will eventually change and cease. This idea applies of course to any relationship, including the counselor–client relationship. Regardless of how fruitful or insightful the counseling process may be, it will inevitably end, as our goal is to foster independence in clients so that they become confident and skillful in facing life challenges. It is normal for people to hold onto various "crutches" as it gives a sense of security in the growth process, especially in a process of recovery. However, counseling is like stabilizer wheels on a child's bicycle—it is no longer necessary once clients are ready to go forward on their own.

Second, the best termination involves a pre-set agreement between the counselor and client (Yalom & Crouch, 1990). This collaboration should be planned, thoughtful, and conducted to avoid harm, especially as termination can be a kind of loss. As mentioned earlier, improper handling of termination can lead to feelings of abandonment, negligence, or the triggering of earlier emotional injuries. A discussed expected end date allows both parties to process the loss openly, thereby fostering a therapeutic ending. Remember that termination can be a continual process instead of a one-time action. Some mental health professionals even believe that the process of termination starts with the beginning of counseling. Therefore, it is necessary for counselors to let the client know that counseling is a temporary process from the outset. Doing so allows the client to express emotions such as anger, sadness, appreciation, or even disappointment about counseling or the counselor. For example, it should be a regular check-in with the client to ask, "How has it been for you in counseling?" or "Has counseling worked for you?" Counselors can also regularly review clients' goals and progress towards their goals in counseling. These dialogues usually provide direction on where counseling should go and when to end it.

Third, what might happen after termination concerns many clients. Preparing clients for potential setbacks and plans to handle similar challenges can be crucial. It would be helpful to discuss with clients what to do if similar problems occur again. It can also be beneficial to identify support networks that clients can access for emotional support. For example, here is a conversation with a client initially suffering from an intense level of anxiety. The client has learned to regulate his body and breathe after several sessions and feels ready to terminate:

COUNSELOR: If your anxiety outbreak occurs again in four months after our termination, how will you respond?

CLIENT: I think I will be able to note my bodily sensations and use mindful breathing to regulate my emotions.

COUNSELLOR: What if these strategies do not work as well as now?

CLIENT: I think I would seek help much earlier than before, like talking to friends or coming back to see you. One thing I have learned is that I can actually turn towards my anxiety instead of just running away from it.

COUNSELOR: That's certainly a great insight. Like you said, if it's not working well, I do want you to call us so you can come in sooner.

## How to Terminate

If the counselor and client can have a pre-set termination date, there are usually several arrangements in the termination session or some sessions before that. This section introduces some skillful means.

### Saying Goodbye

The most skillful practice is to value, appreciate, and consolidate the gains so that Buddhist counselors become healthy role models of skillful means for their clients. With genuineness and compassion, Buddhist counselors give their best wishes to clients from the bottom of their hearts. Many times, specific exercises can be helpful:

#### Goodbye Cards

One way to honor the relationship, show appreciation, and consolidate gains is to write down affirmations and blessings on cards. The instruction is simple: (1) Prepare one card for the counselor and one card for the client, (2) The counselor and the client should write or draw any gains made on the therapeutic journey, their thoughts about termination, and the giving of blessings for each other on the card, (3) Exchange the cards and read them, and (4) Process the experience. It can be a simple but powerful experience to bring closure to the relationship. Moreover, some counselors write a letter to their clients that may describe the client's story from the counselor's perspective, describing any positive changes that occurred, and reminding the client of gains and memorable moments.

*"What I will take with me" exercise*

One processing question for termination is: "After all the hard work in counseling, what I will take with me is: _____." Counselors can write out this statement for the client to complete, ask this question for discussion, or invite the client to draw, or even use music or other media, to express a response. After listening to clients' sharing, counselors can reflect and summarize the gist to show they understand the client's internal processes and then summarize the client's gains.

*Beginning in an Ending*

In Buddhism, "beginning" and "ending" are labels that describe phenomena, and there is no inherently existing beginning or end. As a processing exercise to dissolve clients' existing concept of "ending," counselors can introduce the concept of *aloha* to clients and explain the multiple meanings. The Hawaiian word *aloha* can mean greeting, goodbye, compassion, and interconnected existence. In this word, every ending can be a new beginning with the blessings of love and compassion. Counselors can also develop this concept into an art activity to cut out, print out, or draw four-leaf clovers. Each leaf will have a bolded word of one of the four concepts: greeting, goodbye, compassion, and interconnected existence. The counselor then invites the client to draw or write on the paper using this prompt:

- Greeting: How was it for you when you first came to counseling?
- Goodbye: How do you feel at this moment?
- Compassion: How will you treat yourself with compassion?
- Interconnected existence: How will you use interconnectedness to benefit yourself and others?

*Therapeutic Gift*

Therapeutic gifts can be symbolic or physical. The goal is to provide a transitional object to remind clients of what has been accomplished as well as their strengths, provide compassionate blessings, and assure them that the insights or wisdom will stay with them. Commonly, I will buy inexpensive but meaningful Buddhist books as therapeutic gifts for clients. For example, for a client suffering from an eating disorder, I purchased the book, *How to Eat*, from Venerable Thich Nhat Hanh and wrote down the growth I observed in clients and my blessings on the first page as a therapeutic gift.

## Reviewing Gains

Buddhist counseling transforms and polishes clients' minds through encouraging and fostering their continuous, mindful, and contemplative efforts in daily life. As a result, clients have usually gained particular insights or attained certain transformations in the process of Buddhist counseling. One thing Buddhist counselors can do to consolidate these gains is to

| | Morning | Day | Night |
|---|---|---|---|
| **Weekday** | Daily Mindfulness Practice after waking up (10 mins). | Noticing what is going on around me throughout the day, e.g., breathing, voices, colors, bodily sensations, and seeing if I can relax one group of muscles. (3 mins × 3 times a day) | Undisturbed peaceful time for one activity, e.g., drawing, journaling, listening to music, etc. (15 mins) |
| **Weekend** | Wake up later for self-care on Saturday mornings. | Work for 3 hours/learn a new hobby. | Enjoy family time or time with friends. |

**FIGURE 11.1** Self-Cultivation Plan

summarize and reflect on clients' improvements during treatment. Some questions to help clients consolidate the gains are:

• What has been helpful about the sessions so far?
• What has not been helpful about the sessions so far?
• What changes do you see yourself making throughout the sessions?
• What changes would you still like to make?

### Ongoing Path of Self-Cultivation

The Buddhist understanding of suffering as a shared experience, and continuous practice as necessary to liberating oneself from it, is helpful to revisit as the counseling process ends. A counselor can prepare clients for post-counseling insights by setting up an ongoing plan for cultivation. For example, counselors can collaborate with clients to set up a routine for practice and discuss any potential barriers. Figure 11.1 gives a sample plan.

## Application to Cindy

After gaining insights into her clinging and deciding to let go of the desired mother image, Cindy gradually changes her expectations and attitude towards her mother. Cindy starts to understand and accept that her mother is incapable of loving her the way she always wanted. She begins to have more compassion for her mother and learns to love herself the way she wants to be loved. With this new and skillful intention, Cindy realizes she has become less self-critical, and her depressed mood slowly recovered. She thinks she can handle life again, and the counselor works with her on their last session.

COUNSELOR: How do you feel about ending counseling?
CINDY: I guess I have mixed feelings. On the one hand, I am really glad that I feel better. On the other hand, it is not easy to say goodbye. I would probably miss not having you to talk to every week.

COUNSELOR: You know what, I would miss that too. It has been a great pleasure working with you and accompanying you through this deep and vulnerable wound.

CINDY: Thank you. I still remember how miserable I was when I saw you the first time, and it feels good walking out from the zone of depression. Thank you for walking with me on this path.

COUNSELOR: Yes, and I hope you know that you are not alone. If anything happens, you can always call me again.

CINDY: (*with a smile*) Certainly.

COUNSELOR: If we were to summarize, what would you say have you gained from counseling?

CINDY: (*pondered for a while*) I have a choice … I mean, to face my mother, live my life, or decide whether to love myself more. There is always a choice, but sometimes I just don't see it. Now I know I have a choice, I guess I can try to make better choices for myself.

COUNSELOR: How might you manage life differently with these insights?

CINDY: (*with a smile*) Well, of course, like what you reminded me, to be more compassionate to myself.

COUNSELOR: Yes, that's probably one of the best remedies of all.

## CONCLUSION

In a conversation with a clinical psychologist about termination, she described how one job of mental health professionals is to accept that we are constantly "being dumped" in relationships. It makes me think of how clients perceive our professional image as counselors. Sometimes clients may forget the human side of us, imagining us as ideal individuals who will not be hurt or disappointed by ending a relationship with them. As successful counseling relies on authentic and genuine care in the counseling relationship, the connection between counselor and client involves mutual bonding, and many feelings are reciprocal. Therefore, good Buddhist counselors should become good at saying goodbye and taking every moment with their clients as precious gifts.

In every moment with each client, we need to genuinely care about them as if they are very important friends. Mobilizing our resources of compassion, we attend to and accompany their suffering and use our "self" as an agent to alleviate it. When the client is leaving, we are filled with blessings and loving-kindness as we wish them well. It is a process of learning for both parties to let go. It is also a process of embracing impermanence.

## Contemplative Questions for Buddhist Counselors

Termination is a loss. As human beings in *saṃsāra*, we are inclined to become possessive of love, security, support, and connection. That is why termination, or any kind of goodbye, is difficult. Moreover, it can be difficult for both Buddhist counselors and clients. However, attaching to the label of "loss" or "ending" may not be a skillful attitude to relationships. The most precious ingredients in any relationship are the mindful moments of connection. In Buddhist counseling, these mindful moments of attunement, containment, validation, and accompaniment are perhaps the most important therapeutic experiences for many clients. Termination should glorify, reminisce, and consolidate these moments so that they become skillful mental factors in clients' minds to guard them against suffering.

For this reason, we can contemplate several questions in preparing for a termination session:

- How do you say goodbye to important people in life?
- What is a good goodbye?
- If you were given a chance to say goodbye to an important person again, what would you say?
- If it is the last time in life you will see this client, what would be the best for this client, for you, and for this counseling relationship?

Remember to breathe and notice your breath. Then, take a moment to notice your bodily sensations, thoughts, images, and other experiences in your body and mind. Take note of any strong thoughts or feelings and be curious about what triggered such experiences in you. Contain and accept all experiences arising at this moment and please remember to get in touch with your inner and abundant resources of compassion.

When you are ready, think of a client that you are going through the process of termination with and slowly and mindfully read the following questions and statements:

- How do I feel about termination with this client?
- Does any part of me feel hurt or abandoned?
- From my understanding of this client, how would this client feel about termination?
- Would this client feel hurt or abandoned?
- In reflecting on this counseling process, what were the most memorable moments?
- What personal growth and strengths have I observed in this client?
- If I were to give this client a spiritual gift or blessing, what would it be?
- Thinking of this client with compassion, I wish this client: _____
- What would be the most wholesome thing I could do with this client in the last meeting?

Do not judge any feelings or thoughts. Note them and be curious about them as they arise, and observe how they change and cease. As a spiritual friend for your client, I believe you have worked hard to provide counseling based on your embodiment of Buddhist teachings. I hope you can take the last step to acknowledge all you did out of compassion and radiate compassion to yourself. And, last but not least, gently let yourself know that your counselling work has been good enough.

## REFERENCES

AN 5.49. Kosala Sutta: The Kosalan. Aṅguttara Nikāya, translated by Bhikkhu, T. (1997). *Access to Insight (BCBS Edition)*. Retrieved from www.accesstoinsight.org/tipitaka/an/an05/an05.049. than.html.

AN 6.19. Maranassati Sutta: Mindfulness of Death. Aṅguttara Nikāya, translated by Bhikkhu, T. (1997). *Access to Insight (BCBS Edition)*. Retrieved from www.accesstoinsight.org/tipitaka/an/an06/an06.019.than.html.

Lopez, D. S. Jr. (2017). *Hyecho's Journey: The World of Buddhism*. University of Chicago Press.

Westmacott, R., & Hunsley, J. (2017). Psychologists' Perspectives on Therapy Termination and the Use of Therapy Engagement/Retention Strategies. *Clinical Psychology and Psychotherapy*, 24(3), 687–696.

Yalom, I. D., & Crouch, E. C. (1990). The Theory and Practice of Group Psychotherapy. *British Journal of Psychiatry, 157*(2), 304–306.

CHAPTER **12**

# Ethical Considerations in Buddhist Counseling

The last chapter introduces a proposed set of ethical principles for professional Buddhist counselors as a reference point for individuals interested in learning Buddhist counseling. This chapter briefly introduces the background of Buddhist ethics, discusses the four ethical principles in Buddhist counseling, and makes some additional considerations on the role of the Buddhist counselor.

## BRIEF INTRODUCTION TO BUDDHIST ETHICS

In the threefold Buddhist training of wisdom, concentration, and discipline, the latter is crucial for beginning practitioners and is a safeguard for one's purity of mind throughout the journey on the Buddhist path. Unlike ethical values and guidelines designed for social harmony, Buddhist ethics has the primary goal of mental cultivation. It is a common misunderstanding that avoiding wrongdoings is mainly to prevent bad kamma, punishment by a higher power, or other deleterious consequences. While negative actions lead to negative kamma, the Early Buddhist emphasis on kamma is not about cosmic punitive implications or undesirable afterlife.

Karma (Pali: *kamma*) means "action." Actions mold the actor's consciousness and shape the person according to the nature of those actions. In every moment, the mind is conditioned and develops with each act of body, mind, and speech; in turn, morally wholesome acts lead to the purification of mind and liberation of suffering while morally unwholesome acts continue to cloud and delude the mind. Kammic actions run as an energy field to form habitual patterns to reinforce speech, behaviors, and thoughts of the same kind in future encounters. For example, a person inclined to lie and deceive people for personal gain will perpetrate a pattern of false speech that shapes one's mind to be greed-driven and continues to cause suffering. Therefore, the primary goal of Buddhist ethics is to counter these unwholesome tendencies and protect the spiritual wellbeing of the practitioner.

In the *Dhamma-Vinaya*, The Buddhist Monastic Code (Oldenberg, 1982), discipline was portrayed as an essential ingredient in the liberation from clinging:

Discipline is for the sake of restraint, restraint for the sake of freedom from remorse, freedom from remorse for the sake of joy, joy for the sake of rapture, rapture for the

DOI: 10.4324/9781003025450-12

sake of tranquility … release for the sake of knowledge and vision of release, knowledge, and vision of release for the sake of total unbinding through non-clinging.

(Pv.XII.2)

The monastic code discusses in detail how discipline progressively leads to liberation from clinging and suffering. One noteworthy point is understanding how discipline is a critical first step to the shaping of a conducive internal environment in one's mind, just like pruning the damaged, weak, and hazardous branches of a tree to let it grow in the right direction. In applying Buddhist ethics to Buddhist practice, there are some recommendations for householders in a social context. They include gaining awareness of how one's decisions may cause harm to oneself and others, fostering a life with basic sanity and stability, and striving to make wholesome decisions diligently, with one's commitment driven by Buddhist ethical values such as compassion, loving, kindness, and wisdom. With positive kamma to stabilize the external and internal environments through ethical living, practitioners can thus advance their mental cultivation.

Integrating this implication of Buddhist ethics, the ethical guideline for Buddhist counselors emphasizes both personal moral cultivation and protection of clients and the community.

## A PROPOSED ETHICAL PRINCIPLE FOR PROFESSIONAL BUDDHIST COUNSELORS

First, regardless of your country of practice and discipline, a rule of thumb for all mental health professionals is to follow the ethical guidelines of your board of licensure or registration. For example, as a licensed psychologist of the state of California in the United States, I am practicing under my license as a U.S.-registered psychologist while at the same time I am adopting the role of a Buddhist counselor. In the first role, the code of ethics of the American Psychological Association (APA) serves as my fundamental ethical framework. But in the second role, I also follow the ethical considerations of Buddhist counseling. Should there be any discrepancies between the two sets of ethical systems, I will follow the APA guidelines, as it is statutory for my licensure. In the meantime, I suggest that mental health professionals continue to learn Buddhist counseling until it becomes an official professional field.

At the present time of writing, the field of Buddhist counseling is developing the core competencies of professional Buddhist counselors and the associated code of ethics for this profession. One group of developers comes from the Centre of Buddhist Studies at The University of Hong Kong (Tien et al., 2018). This section briefly introduces the ethical principles developed thus far and their implications for mental health professionals interested in becoming Buddhist counselors.

We have coined the term *Professional Buddhist Counselors* to signify competent, ethical, and professional practitioners of Buddhist counseling. We believe that professional Buddhist counselors must embody and exhibit the highest moral and spiritual principles and practice. In turn, we use the core Buddhist Ethics and the Five Precepts as theoretical foundations for this development. Across Buddhist traditions, the Five Precepts are considered the most fundamental moral principles for Buddhists to follow (McAra, 2007). This set of ethical principles aims to inform the standards of conduct expected of all professional Buddhist counselors towards those in their care as well as in their daily interactions with others. They can be used to develop standards that specify conduct in arenas typically found during the execution of the professional activities of professional Buddhist counselors.

**Guiding Principles for Professional Buddhist Counselors:**

1 Beneficence: Do no foreseeable harm
   a Refrain from taking that which is not freely given;
   b Refrain from erotic interactions;
   c Refrain from crossing professional boundaries.

2 Interconnectedness: Recognize and respect the interconnectedness of people's lives
3 Compassion: Act for the benefit of clients
   a Only say that which is true and accurate;
   b Speak, behave, and think compassionately for clients.

4 Competency: Refrain from anything that will compromise full conscious awareness
   a Refrain from intoxicants that cloud the mind;
   b Strive to be aware of one's habits;
   c Strive to be aware of mental states that interfere with being fully present with the client.

## Beneficence: Do No Foreseeable Harm

Most of the principles are elaborations of the five precepts as well as several core Buddhist concepts. The original form of the five precepts is as follows (SN 2.14):

1 Refrain from killing.
2 Refrain from taking that which is not freely given.
3 Refrain from sexual misconduct.
4 Refrain from false speech.
5 Refrain from drinking.

The principle of Beneficence takes the fundamental precept of *refraining from killing* as its foundation and extends it to doing no foreseeable harm. Parallel to ethical guidelines for medical professionals, psychologists, and social workers, the primary guideline concerns the duty of care, which also emphasizes refraining from doing any foreseeable harm. In Buddhist counseling, this principle reminds Buddhist counselors to mindfully reflect on our intentions moment-by-moment to ensure that we abandon any ill-will or wrong motive in order to protect clients and the community. For example, should conflicts arise between a Buddhist counselor and a client, Buddhist counselors should resolve them responsibly and avoid or minimize foreseeable harm to clients.

### Refrain From Taking That Which is Not Freely Given

This section uses the original precept of *refraining from taking that which is not freely given*. Some interpretations describe this precept as refraining from stealing, but our interpretation sees this precept as going beyond stealing to include any kind of manipulation or exploitation (McAra, 2007). Therefore, this precept guides Buddhist counselors to avoid taking advantage of, exploiting, or manipulating clients. For example, an ethical Buddhist counselor should not charge an unreasonable amount of money.

### Refrain From Erotic Interactions

It is commonly understood that any professional psychotherapy and counseling should not include sex. The precept of *refraining from sexual misconduct* also echoes the importance of preventing sexual exploitation. However, we believe the ethical principle should go beyond sexual misconduct to cover all erotic interactions and inappropriate crossing of boundaries in order to protect clients further. For example, on top of refraining from any sexual behaviors, Buddhist counselors should not flirt with clients.

### Refrain From Crossing Professional Boundaries

Another prerequisite on the precept of *refraining from sexual misconduct* is to set appropriate professional boundaries. Refraining from crossing professional boundaries can protect both clients and Buddhist counselors from potential harm, maintain their objectivity and competence, and protect clients' confidentiality. For example, socializing with clients outside of work settings for non-counseling reasons, or hiring your client, constitutes the crossing of professional boundaries. However, it is also important to note that different cultures and settings have different expectations, boundaries, and values. Hence, Buddhist counselors should rely on the ethical principles as guides to judging the appropriateness of boundary crossings.

## Interconnectedness: Recognize and Respect the Interdependence of People's Lives

Interconnectedness, a key concept in Buddhism, signifies that all things are interdependent, interconnected, and mutually conditioned (Keefe, 1997). Ethical principles apply this concept to the respect and understanding of the interdependent conditions that impact a client. In particular, Buddhist counselors should strive to be aware of and respect the impact of family, community, culture, and other systematic conditions on clients. They should also be mindful of any individual and cultural differences, such as age, sex, sexual identity, ethnicity, culture, national origin, religion, disability, language, social class, and socioeconomic status. Knowing how multiple conditions give rise to a phenomenon, Buddhist counselors should take a dependently co-arising outlook to understand clients' perspectives and strive to understand clients within the impact of their causes and conditions.

## Compassion: Act For the Benefit of Clients

Another key principle is compassion, which is a core motivating factor in Buddhist counseling and guidance for making selfless and skillful clinical decisions. The ethical principle of compassion refers to the commitment of Buddhist counselors to act for the benefit of those they serve and uphold a high professional standard of compassionate care.

### Only Say That Which is True and Accurate

We have strengthened the precept to *refrain from false speech* to only saying what is true and accurate. For a compassionate Buddhist counselor, speech should also be genuine, kind, and beneficial. For example, a Buddhist counselor should not deceive a client into attending more counseling sessions for financial gain when the client is ready to end treatment.

### Speak, Behave, and Think Out of Compassion For Clients

In Buddhism, body, speech, and mind acts generate kamma, affecting both the actor and receiver. Therefore, Buddhist counselors should strive to be mindful and compassionate in behavior, speech, and thoughts towards all clients during the counseling process. For example, Buddhist counselors strive to accurately understand and accompany the client's suffering without judgment, avoidance, or rejection.

## Competency: Refrain From Anything That Will Compromise Full Consciousness

The last guiding ethical principle is competency, which is an elaboration of the precept to *refrain from drinking*. Buddhist practice aims to cultivate purity, clarity, and mental stability; hence, anything that alters consciousness will hinder cultivation. A clear and focused mind is essential to one's counseling competency. Therefore, a Buddhist counselor strives to refrain from any behavior, substances, or defilements that will compromise full consciousness.

### Refrain From Intoxicants That Cloud the Mind

Since the Buddha's time, consuming consciousness-altering substances, such as alcohol, has been deemed a violation of this precept. In contemporary society, intoxicants such as marijuana, cocaine, hallucinogens, and tobacco can disturb a Buddhist counselor's consciousness and compromise competency. Therefore, Buddhist counselors should refrain from any substances which can potentially cloud one's mind during the provision of Buddhist counseling services.

### Strive to Be Aware of One's Habits

This ethical principle signifies the commitment and devotion of Buddhist counselors to continually self-cultivate and foster awareness of how one's habits impact the counseling process. Every volition is kammic energy contributing to the formation of habitual energy.

Unskillful habits, such as aversion, greed, and delusion, can lead to the judgment and rejection of clients and the intention to satisfy one's own egoistic needs. On the other hand, skillful habits of compassion and wisdom can become instinctual responses during therapeutic encounters. For this reason, Buddhist counselors strive to become aware of their habits to ensure a competent state of consciousness and prevent negative habitual tendencies from harming clients. For example, a Buddhist counselor who has a habitual tendency of conceit strives to become aware of their arrogance and avoid using a superior position to view a client's suffering.

### Strive to Be Aware of Mental States That Interfere with Being Fully Present with the Client

This ethical principle focuses on another aspect of mind awareness expected of Buddhist counselors. Mental states generally refer to different cognitive factors arising in the moment of counseling. Some mental states, such as hatred, jealousy, sloth, torpor, and doubt, are unskillful, while others, such as confidence, mindfulness, non-attachment, and equanimity, are skillful (Karunadasa, 2010). Buddhist counselors strive to become aware of their unskillful mental states, thereby endeavoring to be fully present with a client. At the same time, Buddhist counselors should also exercise reasonable judgment and take precautions to ensure that their mind conditions and the boundaries of their competence do not lead to inadequate practices. For example, when a Buddhist counselor needs to see a client suffering from cancer, he or she may seek supervision or consultation, engage in self-care, consider rescheduling a session or even refer the client to an appropriate professional.

## Ethical Considerations for Buddhist Counselors

The set of ethical principles is at a very preliminary stage, but this chapter opens the dialogue: *What is a good set of ethical principles for professional Buddhist counselors to follow?* From my experiences training Buddhist counselors, several common questions are always asked regarding the ethics of practice, such as their roles. I hope to clarify such questions in the ensuing section.

### Buddhist Counselors Are NOT Teachers

Some students seeking training to become Buddhist counselors have a strong background in Buddhism. Whether householders or monastic members, some of these students have experiences teaching Buddhism, so they can find themselves spontaneously stepping into a teaching role during counseling. For example, some students used half of the session time telling Buddhist stories and directing clients based on Buddhist scriptures. It is important to note that Buddhist counselors are not teachers of Buddhism. In some situations it can be appropriate for Buddhist counselors to provide education on Buddhist teachings for therapeutic reasons. However, the modalities of counseling and teaching are fundamentally different. Teaching tends to provide didactics, give directions and advice, and focuses less on listening. In contrast, counseling has a primary task of listening to and connecting with clients. It also aims to facilitate clients to gain awareness and insight and contain difficult emotional suffering. Again, ethical and professional Buddhist counselors provide a high standard of care for all clients.

### Buddhist Counselors Are NOT Missionaries

Another common ethical consideration is whether Buddhist counselors should preach Buddhism. The easy answer is "No"—when in situ and in role, Buddhist counselors do not preach any religion because they are not missionaries. As with the ethical standards of other mental health professions, Buddhist counselors respect the religious and spiritual values, beliefs, and practices of all clients without the imposition of personal values and beliefs. However, there are situations when clients affiliate with Buddhism and wish to benefit from some more religious Buddhist counseling techniques or to learn more about Buddhism. In these circumstances, Buddhist counselors should assess the client's background and understanding of Buddhism, explain their own background and use of Buddhist-inspired techniques, ask for permission to use these techniques or provide necessary resources and education, and monitor the client's responses throughout the exchange. Essentially, the role of a Buddhist counselor is to provide a new treatment of choice for individuals who affiliate with or accept Buddhist teachings. However, such treatment should not include any intention to convert or preach.

### Buddhist Counselors Are Mental Health Professionals Who Uphold Universal Professional Standards

Buddhist counselors should receive similar levels of professional training as their professional peers, and the standard of competency should be comparable to masters-level professional counselors. In addition to a specialist training in Buddhist counseling, Buddhist counselors receive fundamental training in psychopathology, counseling for diverse settings, theories, and other traditional training components in counseling programs. The major differences with traditional counselors are several. First, Buddhist counselors are also spiritual care providers who attend to clients' spiritual and religious needs. In this role, Buddhist counselors are trained to use more spiritual and religious techniques, including guided meditation, chanting, and Dharma talks. Second, Buddhist counselors use Buddhism as a theoretical orientation in their treatment and specialize in at least one counseling model as based on Buddhist teachings. Third, central and unique to Buddhist counselors is the endorsement and the adoption of core Buddhist tenets and practices. For this reason, there is a strong expectation that Buddhist counselors have an ongoing practice of mind cultivation that embodies Buddhist teachings.

In addition, non-Buddhist counselors may use some Buddhist counseling techniques without any associated religious background, such as the application of mindfulness in a variety of formats. However, it is recommended that non-Buddhist counselors also understand the theoretical background of Buddhism, seek sufficient training, and develop their own mind cultivation practice in order to ensure the effectiveness and safety of the techniques.

### Buddhist Counselors Should Be Mindful of the Power and Privilege Granted to Their Status

Similar to any other mental health professional, the role and title of Buddhist counselors comes with power and privilege in the inherent dynamic with clients and the community. With great power comes great responsibility, so Buddhist counselors should strive to become aware of their potential to influence assumptions, values, beliefs, wounds, and habits related to power issues. In particular, the connotation of "Buddhist" carries power and privilege in the eyes of clients who affiliate with or have a favorable feeling towards Buddhism. Therefore, Buddhist counselors should cultivate sensitivity to these ascribed power differentials between themselves and others, ensuring they do not mislead or exploit their clients.

## CONCLUSION

Ethics is a central and pivotal concept in Buddhism. It operates at the bodily, mental, and verbal levels, resulting in kammic effects on self, others, and the world. As human beings, we all carry the seeds of suffering in our defilements and hindrances, watered by our unskillful decisions that harm ourselves and others. However, mind training in Buddhism is meant to reduce and eliminate all impurities. Buddhist ethics also removes all unwanted weeds and unwholesome seeds from the garden of a cultivated mind. To be ethical is to restrain oneself, and that restraint is for the sake of liberation.

I will share my personal experience as an example. I used to enjoy drinking with friends, especially with several close male friends. This kind of social drinking made me feel more connected with others, more sociable, and more relaxed, which was highly rewarding when I was young. After taking the Buddhist precepts, I stopped drinking, which was initially difficult because it almost cut me off from my social network. Gradually, I began to reflect on the problems and suffering that drinking caused in my body, such as stomach pain, vomiting, and diarrhea. After further reflection, interestingly, the memories of drinking became more balanced: I shifted focus from fun times with friends to the unpleasant bodily sensations and repugnant smell of alcohol during a hangover. With the restraint on drinking, I felt more liberated from all the aversive effects of drinking, and I started to find different ways to connect with friends. I saw it as a cyclical process of noting potential problems with drinking, knowing that abstinence can be helpful, choosing to experiment by stopping my alcohol intake, noting the changes of not drinking, understanding the harm and discomfort of drinking as opposed to the freedom of not drinking, and choosing to continue restraining myself. In this example, ethical living is a choice we make to enjoy a better and more joyful life.

Buddhist counselors are professionals with the privilege and power to utilize and role model the noble teachings of Buddhism, and therefore they are held to a high moral ideal to safeguard the credibility of the Buddhist teachings, the trustworthiness of this new profession, the wellbeing of clients and community, and the purity of one's mind. This closing chapter proposed an ethical framework for Buddhist counselors. I invite you to participate in the ongoing meaning-making process of such a framework to complement your own professional ethics.

## Contemplative Questions for Buddhist Counselors

The last contemplative exercise goes back to the most fundamental Buddhist practice of self-discipline.

To begin with, relax your body, breath, and mind. Adjust your sitting position to a balanced posture of relaxed uprightness. Try to let go of tension in your muscles while holding your back straight to support your body. Observe your breaths at this present moment and be curious: How is the breath? Is it slow or quick? Shallow or deep? Am I intentionally breathing, or am I just following it in and out? Take a minute to reflect.

Then let go of any volition or desire to control your breath. Just simply observe it, feel it, and be with it. This process is like appreciating the sunrise and sunset without any need to change any part of it. It is natural and beautiful as it is.

When you are ready, read the following questions slowly and notice the thoughts, comments, and answers that come up:

- "Am I doing anything to hurt myself, such as lying to myself, just to make myself happy?"
- "Am I doing anything to hurt others, such as lying to them, in order to make myself happy?"
- "Have I suffered enough as a result of my choices?"
- "If so, can I forgive myself and look at my choices with some mental distance and clarity?"
- "Are there choices that can bring more sustainable happiness?"
- "What are my choices and what makes them difficult to enact?"
- "Am I willing to restrain myself in the pursuit of a more sustainable happiness?"

Such contemplations can be extended to our session times with clients. When you have difficulties connecting or empathizing with the person in front of you, pause and consider the following:

- "If I am not compassionate to this person's suffering, what would I say or do?"
- "If I am fully compassionate to this person's suffering, what could I say or do?"
- "If I put down all of my discomfort and resistance, what is this person trying to tell me?"
- "What are the choices at this moment that can bring us more sustainable happiness?"

Now begin to relax yourself. Let go of any tension in your body, breath, and mind. Feel free to write down any thoughts and reflections. It could be a challenging process, so please take a moment to rest and to acknowledge the hard work you have done. Mind cultivation is a lifelong process and there are many challenges along the way. However, from my experience, regardless of how challenging it may be, cultivation does help me, my students, and my clients live a life with less suffering. To me, the reduction of suffering is the best reward in life and the strongest motivation for practice. Therefore, I believe an investment in mental cultivation has the best return compared to any stock, property, or financial product. Finally, I wish you success in walking the path of liberation. Thank you again for reading this book.

*May you be happy with wisdom.*
*May you be fully embraced by loving-kindness and compassion.*
*May you be free to immerse yourself in the joy and equanimity of the present moment.*
*May you be free from suffering.*

# REFERENCES

Karunadasa, Y. (2010). *The Theravada Abhidhamma: Its Inquiry Into the Nature of Conditioned Reality.* Centre for Buddhist Studies, Hong Kong University.

Keefe, A. A. (1997). Visions of Interconnectedness in Engaged Buddhism and Feminist Theology. *Buddhist-Christian Studies, 17,* 61–76.

McAra, S. (2007). *Land of Beautiful Vision: Making a Buddhist Sacred Place in New Zealand.* Honolulu: University of Hawaii Press.

SN 2.14. Dhammika Sutta: Dhammika, translated from the Pali by John D. Ireland (2013, November 30). *Access to Insight (BCBS Edition).* Retrieved from www.accesstoinsight.org/tipitaka/kn/snp/snp.2.14.irel.html

Tien, L., Lee, K. C., Wu, W. Y., & Sik, H. H. (2018, December*). Core Competencies and Educational Curriculum for Buddhist Chaplaincy: A Proposal to the Experts and Professionals in Buddhist Counselling and Chaplaincy.* Paper presented at the Buddhist Counselling - Instigating Insight into the Healing Process Symposium, The University of Hong Kong, Hong Kong, China.

Oldenberg, H. (1982). *The Vinaya Pitakam: One of the Principal Buddhist Holy Scriptures in the Pali Language* (5th ed.). London: The Pali Text Society.

# Index

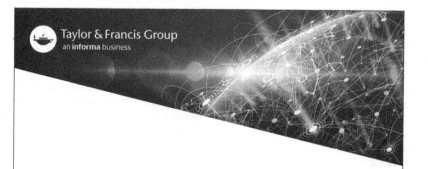